Fixing the Foundation

WORLD BANK EAST ASIA AND PACIFIC REGIONAL REPORTS

Known for their economic success and dynamism, countries in the East Asia and Pacific region must tackle an increasingly complex set of challenges to continue on a path of sustainable development. Learning from others within the region and beyond can help identify what works, what doesn't, and why, in the search for practical solutions to these challenges. This regional flagship series presents analyses of issues relevant to the region, drawing on the global knowledge and experience of the World Bank and its partners. The series aims to inform public discussion, policy formulation, and development practitioners' actions to turn challenges into opportunities.

TITLES IN THE SERIES

The Innovation Imperative for Developing East Asia

A Resurgent East Asia: Navigating a Changing World

Growing Smarter: Learning and Equitable Development in East Asia and Pacific

Riding the Wave: An East Asian Miracle for the 21st Century

Live Long and Prosper: Aging in East Asia and Pacific

East Asia Pacific at Work: Employment, Enterprise, and Well-Being

Toward Gender Equality in East Asia and the Pacific: A Companion to the World Development Report

Putting Higher Education to Work: Skills and Research for Growth in East Asia

All books in this series are available for free at
https://openknowledge.worldbank.org/handle/10986/2147.

World Bank East Asia and Pacific Regional Report

Fixing the Foundation

Teachers and Basic Education in East Asia and Pacific

Rythia Afkar
Tara Béteille
Mary E. Breeding
Toby Linden
Andrew D. Mason
Aaditya Mattoo
Tobias Pfutze
Lars M. Sondergaard
Noah Yarrow

Contents

Boxes

Figures

Tables

Foreword

Since the 1970s, countries in East Asia and Pacific have served as models for countries and economies seeking rapid economic and social development. The "East Asian Miracle" was built on a combination of policies that fostered outward-oriented, labor-intensive growth while investing in basic human capital and providing sound economic governance. This development strategy delivered rapid and sustained growth, which helped move hundreds of millions of people over successive generations out of poverty and into economic security. In addition, it enabled a succession of countries in the region to progress from low-income to middle-income status.

This model, built largely on low-cost, relatively low-skilled labor, will be insufficient for countries and economies in the region to achieve upper-middle-income and then high-income status. Shifting global value chains, declining productivity growth, and rapid technological change pose new challenges to sustaining the high growth of the past 20 years. Countries will need to focus increasingly on raising labor productivity. Raising the skills levels of workers will be a critical component of that effort.

Currently, 172 million students are in primary school in middle-income East Asia and Pacific. Making sure these children receive a high-quality education is essential to ensuring they are prepared for their futures. Quality education raises people's incomes and employability, improves their economic mobility, and enables them to escape poverty. It increases households' resilience to shocks. Quality education—and the skills it confers—are associated with higher worker and firm productivity, faster technology adoption, and greater innovation. Furthermore, a growing body of evidence shows that greater skills are associated with higher economic growth.

Although East Asian and Pacific countries and economies have made great strides in increasing access to basic education, quality varies widely. Merely attending school is insufficient. Whether children *learn* or not is fundamental. At present, in 14 of the region's 22 middle-income countries, more than half of 10-year-olds are unable to read and understand an age-appropriate reading material. Because the acquisition of advanced skills needs to be built on strong foundations, many of the region's children will never be able to develop the higher-order skills needed to propel innovative manufacturing and modern services.

Although multiple factors influence learning, including family income, parents' education, and child nutrition, once a child enters school, teachers have the largest impact. High-quality teaching will thus be essential to improving foundational learning and students' skills. However, the evidence presented in this report shows that many middle-income countries in the region continue to face significant teaching challenges. Teacher assessment tests in several countries indicate that as few as 8 percent of teachers have fully mastered the subject matter they teach, classroom observation reveals that two-thirds or more of primary school teachers employ weak teaching methods, and survey data suggest that where teacher absenteeism is high, student learning suffers.

Fortunately, a growing body of evidence is available to guide policy makers in raising teaching quality to ensure that all young children acquire strong foundational skills. Drawing upon the evidence, this report sets out a roadmap for countries, both in terms of *what* needs to be done to support teachers and *how* to do it. East Asia and Pacific remains one of the fastest growing and most dynamic regions in the world. Sustaining this dynamism and enabling today's children to enjoy better jobs and higher living standards as adults requires that they build foundational skills for lifelong learning. Following the roadmap laid out in this report will help countries in the region accelerate learning, which, in turn, will help children—and societies more broadly—to fulfill their aspirations.

Manuela V. Ferro
Vice President, East Asia and Pacific
World Bank

Acknowledgments

This report is a joint product of the Office of the Chief Economist, East Asia and Pacific Region, and the Education Global Practice, East Asia and Pacific Region, of the World Bank. The team was led by Andrew D. Mason and Lars M. Sondergaard. The core authors of the report are Rythia Afkar, Tara Béteille, Mary E. Breeding, Toby Linden, Andrew D. Mason, Aaditya Mattoo, Tobias Pfutze, Lars M. Sondergaard, and Noah Yarrow.

The report was commissioned by Victoria Kwakwa, who provided the original vision for the report, and it was prepared under the overall guidance of Manuela V. Ferro, with strategic advice from Daniel Dulitzky, Alberto Rodriguez, and Cristian Aedo. Cecile Wodon, Caroline Gerd G De Roover, and Sharon Shen provided administrative, logistical, and production support.

The report draws on the following background papers commissioned for this study, which are available on request:

- Tara Béteille: "Vibrant or Stuck?"
- Mary E. Breeding: "Teacher Professional Development in East Asia and the Pacific: Evidence vs. Practice"
- Paul Cahu and Lars M. Sondergaard: "Estimating Interim Learning Poverty for Pacific Island Countries"
- Arthur Mendes, Steven Pennings, and Federico Fiuratti: "The Long-Term Growth Effects of Improved Education Quality in Middle-Income East Asian and Pacific Countries"
- Nobuyuki Tanaka and Lars M. Sondergaard: "Analysis of Teacher Stock versus Flow in Primary Education in East Asia and the Pacific Middle-Income Countries: A Simple Model and Results from Simulation between 2020 and 2030"
- Noah Yarrow, Cody Abbey, Sharon Shen, and Kevin Alyono: "Using Education Technology to Improve K–12 Student Learning in East Asia and Pacific: Promises and Limitations"
- Noah Yarrow, Paul Cahu, Mary E. Breeding, and Rythia Afkar: "What I Really Want: Policymaker Views on Education in East Asia Pacific"
- Shuwen Zheng and Lars Sondergaard: "Private Spending on Education and Enrollment in Non-Government Schools."

The team benefited tremendously from comments provided by colleagues within and outside the World Bank and from colleagues attending several events where preliminary findings were presented and discussed. Particular thanks go to Deon Filmer, Halsey Rogers, and Mitsue Uemura for serving as peer reviewers for the report. Insightful feedback and advice were also provided during both formal and informal reviews of the report by Luis Benveniste, Ndiamé Diop, Rinku Murgai, Mamta Murthi, Jaime Saavedra, Norbert Rudiger Schady, Mariam Sherman, and Mara Warwick.

Helpful comments and inputs were provided at critical stages of the report's preparation by Izzati Ab Razak, Cody Abbey, Kevin Alyono, Paul Cahu, Yu Cao, Pinyi Chen, Daisuke Fukuzawa, Pagma Genden, Ergys Islamaj, Sachiko Kataoka, Noviandri Khairina, Dilaka Lathapipat, Duong Trung Le, Diego Luna-Bazaldua, Kevin Macdonald, Adam Merican Mohd Din, Ezequiel Molina, Shinsaku Nomura, Nutchapon Prasertsoong, Akiko Sawamoto, Nobuyuki Tanaka, Ryoko Tomita, Nguyet Thi Anh Tran, Andrew Trembley, Dung Vo, and Shuwen Zheng.

The team also appreciates the important insights on the politics of education reform provided by Samer Al-Samarrai, Edward Aspinall, Simeth Beng, Leandro Costa, Zahid Hasnain, Sachiko Kataoka, Ratna Kesuma, Jonathan London, Andre Loureiro, Yasuhiko Matsuda, Hanh Minh Bui, Fata No, Viengmala Phomsengsavanh, Andrew Ragatz, and Chindavanh Vongsaly.

Mary Fisk and Patricia Katayama provided excellent advice and guidance on the publication process. The cover and graphics were designed by Bill Pragluski. Mary Anderson edited the report.

The team also thanks others who have helped prepare this report and apologizes to any who may have been overlooked inadvertently in these acknowledgments.

About the Authors

Rythia Afkar is an economist with the World Bank's Human Capital Project. She is based in Washington, DC, and engages with national governments and international organizations to help countries build, protect, and utilize their human capital. Her work focuses on various areas, including quality of education, public finance, and gender issues. She previously worked on education operations and research with the East Asia and Pacific Unit and on poverty and social assistance with the poverty team in Indonesia. Her recent policy-oriented research focuses on improved efficiency of education expenditure in Indonesia and Papua New Guinea. She holds a doctorate in economics from the University of Bonn and received a master's degree in quantitative economics from the University of Paris 1 Panthéon-Sorbonne.

Tara Béteille is the World Bank's human development program leader for Cambodia, the Lao People's Democratic Republic, and Myanmar. She served as the global lead for the Teachers Thematic Group of the World Bank's Education Global Practice from 2017 to 2022. She has led World Bank projects in early childhood education, school education, skills, and higher education in countries in the South Asia and the East Asia and Pacific regions. She was a core team member of the *World Development Report 2018: Learning to Realize Education's Promise*. Her research interests span teacher labor markets, the politics of education reform, and higher education—topics on which she has published in journals such as *Education Finance and Policy*, *PNAS*, and *Nature Human Behavior*, as well as World Bank reports such as *Ready to Learn: Before School, In School, and Beyond School in South Asia*. Before joining the World Bank, she worked as a postdoctoral fellow at the Center for Education Policy Analysis at Stanford University, and before that, at ICICI Bank, India. She holds a doctorate in the economics of education from Stanford University, as well as a master's degree in economics from Stanford University and a master's degree in economics from the Delhi School of Economics.

Mary E. Breeding is a consultant in education at the World Bank, where she has worked on multiple types of education projects since 2010. Her primary areas of specialization are teacher policy, school accountability, and monitoring and evaluation. She has also worked to provide support on a range of policy projects in the areas of student assessment and school finance. Before joining the World Bank, she was a postdoctoral fellow at Georgetown

University (2008–10), and she held the William E. Miller Fellowship at the American Political Science Association in 2007–08. She received her doctorate in political science and public policy from American University in 2008.

Toby Linden has had a long and diverse career working in countries across the globe with the World Bank, including in South Asia, Southeast and Central Europe, and Southern and Eastern Africa. His publications include *Lifelong Learning in the Global Knowledge Economy: Challenges for Developing Countries*, with Harry Patrinos, and *Getting the Right Teachers into the Right Schools: Managing India's Teacher Workforce*, with Vimala Ramachandran and others. He also served as director of the Roma Education Fund, an international nongovernmental organization working to improve the educational outcomes of Roma (Gypsies), the poorest minority in Europe. Previously, he worked for the British Council and England's national Department for Education.

Andrew D. Mason is deputy chief economist for the World Bank's East Asia and Pacific Region. He has carried out policy research on a range of issues, including poverty, social protection, education and skills, labor, and gender equality. He is coauthor of several World Bank flagship reports, including *The Innovation Imperative for Developing East Asia; A Resurgent East Asia: Navigating a Changing World; Toward Gender Equality in East Asia and the Pacific: A Companion to the World Development Report;* and *Informality: Exit and Exclusion*, as well as the World Bank Policy Research Working Paper, "Engendering Development: Through Gender Equality in Rights, Resources, and Voice." He has also been an affiliated professor at the Georgetown Public Policy Institute (now the McCourt School of Public Policy) of Georgetown University. He holds a doctorate in applied economics from Stanford University and a master's degree in public policy from Harvard University.

Aaditya Mattoo is chief economist of the World Bank's East Asia and Pacific Region. He specializes in development, trade, and international cooperation and provides policy advice to governments. He was codirector of the *World Development Report 2020: Trading for Development in the Age of Global Value Chains*. Previously, he was the research manager, trade and integration, at the World Bank. Before joining the World Bank, he was economic counsellor at the World Trade Organization and taught economics at the University of Sussex and Churchill College, Cambridge University.

Tobias Pfutze is a former senior economist in the Office of the Chief Economist for the World Bank's East Asia and Pacific Region and associate professor of economics at Florida International University. He is an applied microeconomist with an interest in social protection policies, land tenure systems, and institutional economics. He has also held academic positions at Georgetown University, American University, and Oberlin College and worked as a consultant for the World Bank and the United Nations Development Programme. His research has been published in leading peer-reviewed journals, including the *Journal of Development Economics, Journal of Economic Behavior and Organization, Economic Development and Cultural Change*, and *World Development*. He completed his undergraduate studies at Humboldt University in Berlin and Pompeu Fabra University in Barcelona. He holds a doctorate in economics from New York University.

Lars M. Sondergaard is a lead economist in the World Bank's Education Global Practice, East Asia and Pacific Region. In different regions of the world, he has led both operational and analytical work to support improvement in educational outcomes. His policy research encompasses a range of issues, including education, poverty, growth, and fiscal policy. He is the coauthor of several World Bank publications, including *Skills, Not Just Diplomas: Managing Education for Results in Eastern Europe and Central Asia* and the Thailand Systematic Country Diagnostic, "Getting Back on Track: Reviving Growth and Securing Prosperity for All." Before joining the World Bank, he was a senior economist at the European Central Bank. He holds doctoral and master's degrees in economics from Georgetown University.

Noah Yarrow joined the World Bank in 2010 as a part of the Education Global Practice, Latin America and the Caribbean. He is based in Washington, DC, and works on system capacity, education technology, and learning-quality issues with a special focus on refugee and internally displaced persons education. He previously worked on operations and research in the East Asia and Pacific and Middle East and North Africa regions. Prior to joining the World Bank, he worked in the Russian Federation and Asia for agencies such as the Education Development Center and the International Committee of the Red Cross, in addition to teaching for several years at the primary and secondary levels. He holds master's degrees in development management from the London School of Economics and in adolescent education from Pace University.

Main Messages

Early investments in education were key to the remarkable economic development of East Asia and Pacific. Basic literacy and numeracy equipped farmers to adopt new seeds and fertilizers and usher in the Green Revolution. The resulting increase in productivity enabled workers with basic skills to move out of agriculture and into export-oriented manufacturing. This structural transformation boosted economywide productivity growth driven by investments in human capital.

However, past successes obscure educational inadequacies in today's middle-income East Asia and Pacific. Despite significant advances in school enrollment and attainment, many countries still face significant learning challenges, starting at the most basic level. In 14 of the region's 22 middle-income countries, more than half of 10-year-olds are unable to read and understand an age-appropriate text—a phenomenon known as *learning poverty*. With weak foundations, many of these children will never be able to develop the skills needed to succeed in the labor market or to help propel innovative manufacturing and modern services. This will make it harder to generate the productivity growth needed to propel East Asian and Pacific countries from middle- to high-income status.

Learning outcomes are unequal across and within middle-income East Asian and Pacific countries and economies. Learning poverty in all the region's middle-income countries is significantly higher than in high-income Japan, the Republic of Korea, and Singapore, where learning poverty rates stand at 3–4 percent. The challenges are much greater in lower-middle-income Cambodia, the Lao People's Democratic Republic, and Papua New Guinea than in upper-middle-income China, Malaysia, and Thailand. However, even in the latter group, learning outcomes are highly unequal within countries—between cities and villages and between the rich and poor. In all of East Asia and Pacific's middle-income countries and economies, basic learning deficits, exacerbated by the COVID-19 pandemic, represent a serious risk to future development.

Although many factors affect student learning—household income, parents' education levels, and child nutrition—once children enter school, teachers are the most important factor. However, data from across the region indicate that many countries still face challenges with respect to teaching quality.

- Teachers often have limited knowledge of the subject they teach. In Indonesia and Lao PDR, for example, only 8 percent of fourth-grade teachers scored 80 percent or higher on subject assessment tests for language and math, respectively.
- Many teachers also employ ineffective teaching practices. For instance, in Mongolia and the Philippines, classroom observation revealed that fewer than one in five teachers employ good- or best-practice teaching methods.
- Teacher absenteeism remains a problem in several countries. While the extent of absenteeism varies across countries, when teachers are absent, students do not learn.

The report, therefore, focuses on teachers to enhance teaching quality and improve foundational learning. Research shows that teacher-focused interventions have the largest impact on student learning outcomes. Because teachers' salaries make up the largest share of government spending on education, building a strong cadre of teachers will be critical to ensuring that countries get the most from their scarce public resources.

Building on regional and global evidence, the report lays out a three-pronged program of action:

- Attract and recruit effective teachers.
- Enhance existing teachers' capacity to teach.
- Motivate greater teacher effort.

Special emphasis is placed on improving the capabilities of existing teachers, because most teachers who will be employed in 2030 have already been recruited. One key element of raising existing teachers' capacity involves delivering more effective training to teachers that includes: (1) a focus on subject content knowledge; (2) opportunities to practice newfound knowledge with colleagues; (3) ongoing support, including follow-up coaching and mentoring; and (4) career incentives through promotion or increased salary. A second key element of raising teachers' capacity involves the provision of enhanced tools, such as structured lesson plans, targeted instruction, and educational technologies (EdTech). These tools, when well-designed and implemented, have the potential to transform teaching and learning for students.

The proposed reforms will need to be financed by a combination of more efficient public spending and additional budgetary resources. Public spending on education in most middle-income East Asian and Pacific countries and economies is well below what other countries with similar incomes spend. More public resources must go to disadvantaged and poorly performing areas to address learning inequalities within countries. Because countries and economies across the region are diverse, policy makers will need to tailor their actions to their countries' specific circumstances.

Finally, the report highlights that successful reform will require more than identifying the best technical solutions. Bridging the basic learning gap in middle-income East Asia and Pacific will take sustained commitment by all stakeholders, officials, teachers, and parents to find common ground in the interests of children and development.

Abbreviations

CAL	computer-assisted learning
CEFR	Common European Framework of Reference for Languages
CLRW	Come Let's Read and Write (Tonga)
EdTech	educational technology
ELTC	English Language Teaching Centre (Malaysia)
GDP	gross domestic product
LGTM	Long-Term Growth Model
NCT	National Capital Territory (Delhi)
NPV	net present value
PILNA	Pacific Islands Literacy & Numeracy Assessment
PISA	Programme for International Student Assessment
ProELT	Professional Upskilling for English Language Teachers (Malaysia)
RCT	randomized controlled trial
SAM	social accountability mechanism
SAS	Sa Aklat Sisikat (Philippines)
SEA-PLM	Southeast Asia Primary Learning Metrics
TFP	total factor productivity
UNESCO	United Nations Educational, Scientific and Cultural Organization

All dollar amounts are US dollars unless specified otherwise.

Overview

Introduction

Early investments in education were key to East Asia's remarkable development. Basic literacy and numeracy equipped farmers to adopt new seeds and fertilizers and to usher in the Green Revolution. The resulting increase in productivity allowed workers to move out of agriculture and to use their basic skills in export-oriented manufacturing. This structural transformation boosted economywide productivity growth.

However, past successes risk obscuring educational inadequacies in today's middle-income East Asia and Pacific. Despite significant advances in school enrollment and educational attainment, more than half of 10-year-olds in most middle-income countries cannot read and understand an age-appropriate text—a phenomenon known as *learning poverty*. Because learning is cumulative, many of these children will never develop the more advanced skills needed for innovative manufacturing and sophisticated services—the productivity-boosting economic activities that could propel countries in the region from middle- to high-income status.

Learning poverty in all the region's middle-income countries is significantly higher than that in the high-income countries: Japan, the Republic of Korea, and Singapore. However, the challenges are even greater in lower-middle-income Cambodia, the Lao People's Democratic Republic (PDR), and Papua New Guinea. In all countries, the quality of education is much weaker in rural and poorer regions than in urban and richer areas. These persistent deficits in basic learning have been significantly exacerbated by the COVID-19 (coronavirus) pandemic.

This report, therefore, focuses on foundational learning—basic literacy and numeracy—which is necessary for the development of more advanced skills. The report focuses on public schools, where most of the region's students obtain their basic education.[1] Finally, the report focuses on teachers, who are central to children's learning. Research shows that teacher-focused interventions have the largest impacts on student learning (Snilstveit et al. 2015). Moreover, given that teachers' salaries make up the largest share of government spending on education, countries that strengthen the cadre of teachers will help optimize the use of scarce public resources.

In analyzing how to strengthen foundational learning in middle-income East Asian and Pacific countries, this report examines the nature of the basic learning deficit in the region, the relationship between improved education and the region's economic prospects, and the policies that can support teachers in raising basic learning outcomes. Because the region is so diverse, the report highlights the need for tailoring policy responses to specific country circumstances.

The region's basic learning deficit

Basic learning outcomes are poor in middle-income countries

Ask a typical 10-year-old student in middle-income East Asia or the Pacific to read a simple paragraph and answer basic questions about it, and there is a good chance they will not be able to. Even before the COVID-19 pandemic, more than half of 10-year-olds in most middle-income countries could not read and understand an age-appropriate text. In eight countries (Cambodia, Kiribati, Lao PDR, Myanmar, Papua New Guinea, the Philippines, Tonga, and Tuvalu), this learning poverty rate exceeds two-thirds, and even in upper-middle-income Malaysia it is over 40 percent (figure O.1). In contrast, learning poverty in high-income Japan, Korea, and Singapore is only 3–4 percent.

Basic learning outcomes were also unequal within countries

Students from disadvantaged socioeconomic backgrounds demonstrated lower learning proficiency on average than those from more advantaged backgrounds (figure O.2).

FIGURE O.1 **In many middle-income East Asian and Pacific countries, learning poverty rates exceed the levels their incomes would predict**

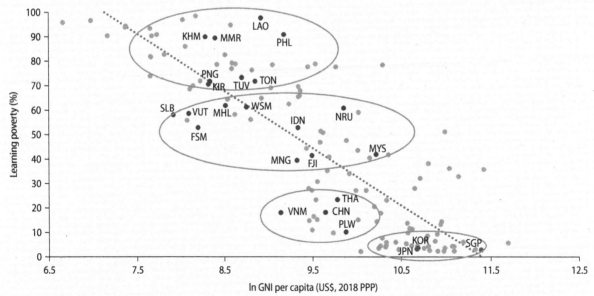

Sources: World Bank and UIS 2022; Cahu and Sondergaard 2023; World Development Indicators database.
Note: "Learning poverty" is the inability to read and understand a simple text by age 10. Middle-income countries in East Asia and Pacific are designated by ISO alpha-3 code. Those shown as brown dots are middle-income countries from the East Asia and Pacific region, whereas those shown as orange dots are from other regions. Red dots designate high-income East Asian countries. GNI = gross national income; ln = natural logarithm; PPP = purchasing power parity.

FIGURE O.2 **Poorer students in Southeast Asia have worse basic learning outcomes than wealthier students**

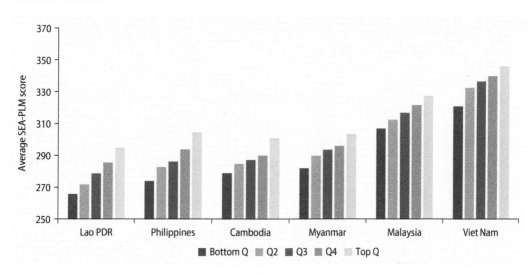

Source: World Bank estimates, using 2019 Southeast Asia Primary Learning Metrics (SEA-PLM) data (UNICEF and SEAMEO 2020).
Note: The chart shows average fifth-grade SEA-PLM assessment scores, by household socioeconomic status quintile (Q)—a nationally derived measure based on (a) highest parental occupation of either parent, (b) highest education level of either parent, and (c) family's home resources through the home resources scale (UNICEF and SEAMEO 2020, 66).

Differences in learning proficiency between students in the top and bottom quintiles could represent more than two years of schooling in the most unequal settings, by World Bank estimates. Similar inequalities are observed between major urban areas and more remote rural settings.

Students lacking foundational skills struggle to acquire advanced skills. Reading proficiency among 15-year-olds in Indonesia, Malaysia, the Philippines, and even Thailand falls well below the levels predicted by those countries' per capita incomes, while learning inequality persists between poorer and wealthier children.

COVID-19–related learning disruptions made things worse

School disruptions during the COVID-19 pandemic have exacerbated the region's preexisting learning challenges. To compensate for school closures, countries in East Asia and Pacific implemented distance learning initiatives, including offering classes online, on television, and on the radio. Many high-income countries such as Japan, Korea, and Singapore also faced challenges with these adjustments but adapted their approaches over the period of school closures (OECD 2020a [Japan]; UNESCO 2022 [Korea]; Goh, Wong, and Kwek 2023 [Singapore]). However, in low- and middle-income countries, a new global study finds that for every month schools were closed, students lost nearly one month of learning (Schady et al. 2023). Within the region, data from Cambodia and Indonesia indicate significant learning losses during the pandemic (figure O.3). Similar effects were observed in assessment data from Pacific Island countries during the period.

The pandemic also exacerbated learning inequality in the region. Wealthier households generally had greater access than poorer ones to interactive distance learning opportunities (World Bank 2021). In Indonesia, for example, fourth-grade students lost the equivalent of 11 months of learning, on average, but students from the poorest households lost significantly more (figure O.3, panel b).

FIGURE O.3   Assessment scores in Cambodia and Indonesia indicate significant COVID-19–related declines in primary grade outcomes in language and mathematics

a. Average sixth-grade assessment scores in Khmer language and mathematics in Cambodia, 2013, 2016, and 2021

b. Average learning loss of fourth-grade Indonesian students in 2023 relative to 2019, by subject and by top and bottom quintile

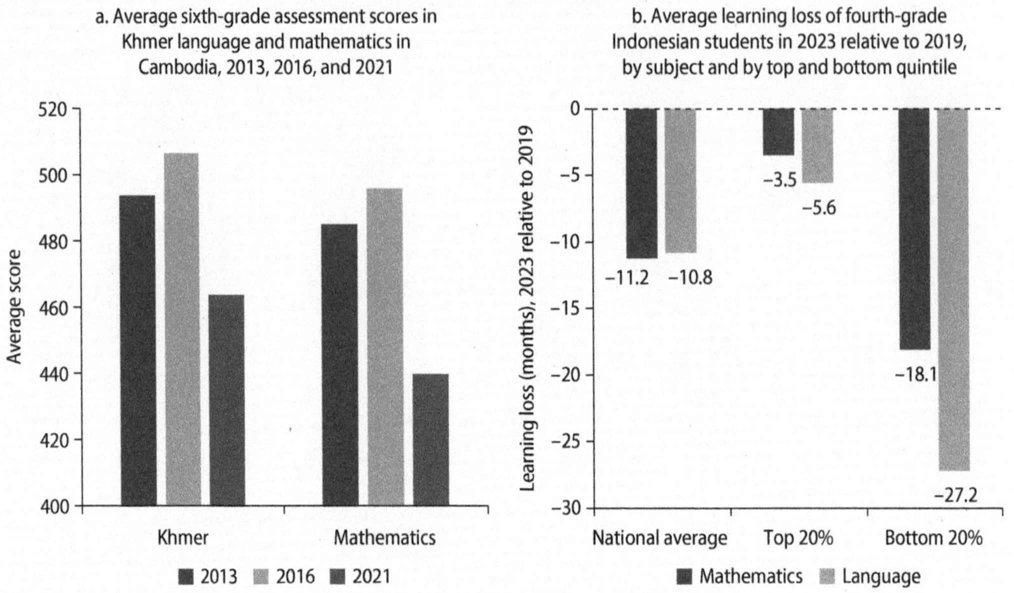

Sources: World Bank estimates, based on Cambodia's national assessment of sixth graders (panel a); World Bank 2023b (panel b).
Note: In panel b, the scores were standardized with the mean of 0 and standard deviation of 1. Based on the standardized score, students' performance was converted to the month-equivalent by using the internationally used rule of thumb; that is, an average student learning in a year is equal to about 0.3 of a standard deviation.

A new World Bank study proposes actions to remedy learning losses associated with the pandemic (Schady et al. 2023):

- Keeping schools open and restoring or increasing instructional hours
- Assessing learning and matching instruction to students' levels
- Focusing on foundational learning and streamlining the curriculum
- Tracking students at risk of dropping out
- Providing incentives for at-risk students to remain in school
- Generating political commitment for learning recovery.

However, middle-income countries in East Asia and Pacific must do more than recover COVID-19–related learning losses. This report focuses, therefore, on remedying countries' long-standing learning deficits.

Better teaching, improved learning, and higher productivity

Good teachers are essential to student learning

This report is motivated by the links from teaching to learning and from improved learning to higher labor productivity and growth. A child's family background remains the most important predictor of learning outcomes, including parents' income and education levels, as well as a child's nutrition, health, and cognitive and socioemotional development in the early years of life. However, once children get to school, no single factor is as critical as the quality of their teachers (Béteille and Evans 2021; Bruns and Luque 2015).

Research shows that going from a low-performing teacher to a high-performing one increases student learning dramatically. In Viet Nam, differences in teaching quality mean that, over a three-year period, an average second-grade student can end up in either the top third or the bottom third of the class, depending on whether they benefit from a high- or low-quality teacher during that time (figure O.4, panel a).[2] Across middle-income Southeast Asia, better teaching practices are consistently associated with better student learning outcomes (figure O.4, panel b).

Greater learning boosts productivity and growth

Education confers a broad range of economic benefits on low- and middle-income societies (World Bank 2018b). It increases people's incomes and employability, improves economic mobility, and enables families to escape poverty (figure O.5). It increases individuals' and families' resilience to shocks. In economies with large informal sectors, education is associated with greater access to full-time, formal sector jobs.

The skills students obtain are associated with greater productivity, technology adoption, and innovation. During the Green Revolution in Asia, farmers with basic education made more efficient allocation decisions in the face of technological changes (Foster and Rosenzweig 1996).[3]

FIGURE O.4   **Assessment data show that teacher quality is central to student learning**

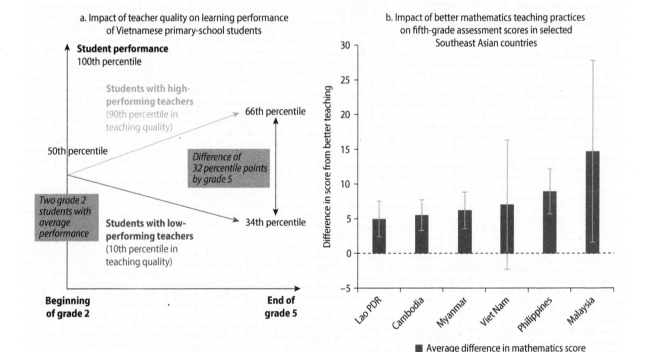

Sources: World Bank estimates based on Carneiro et al. 2022 (panel a); 2019 Southeast Asia Primary Learning Metrics (SEA-PLM) data (panel b).
Note: Panel a compares the effects on two "average" (50th percentile) second-grade students of having either low-performance or high-performance teachers from second grade through fifth grade. If a student had 90th percentile teachers rather than 10th percentile ones, the student would be in the top third of the class, rather than the bottom third, by the time the student finished fifth grade. Panel b shows the estimated effects of "better teaching practices," on fifth-grade students' mathematics proficiency. Practices that correlate positively with mathematics scores are reflected in student questionnaire responses such as "I know what my teacher expects me to do"; "My teacher is easy to understand"; "I am interested in what my teacher says"; "My teacher gives me interesting things to do"; and "My teacher encourages me to do extra mathematics exercises in class." The 2019 SEA-PLM data cover only the six countries shown.

Greater education and skills also raise *firms'* productivity and enable innovation. In manufacturing firms across China, increases in employee education resulted in greater total factor productivity (TFP) growth, technology adoption, and research and development (R&D) investment among firms operating in more human capital-intensive industries (Che and Zhang 2017) as shown in figure O.6. Similar results are seen among firms in Organisation for Economic Co-operation and Development (OECD) countries (Criscuolo et al. 2021).

FIGURE O.5   **Education is consistently associated with higher earnings**

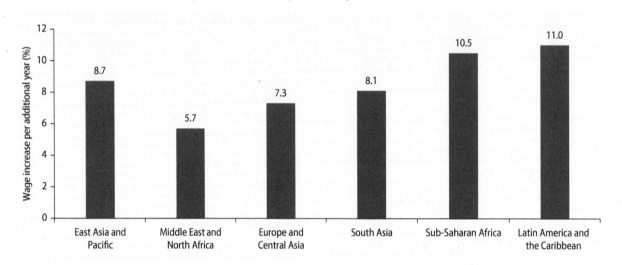

Source: Psacharopoulos and Patrinos 2018.
Note: The figure shows the average percentage increase in wages associated with each additional year (beyond 0) of schooling in low- and middle-income countries, by region. Regional country groups are defined by World Bank classifications.

FIGURE O.6   **Education increases firm productivity, technology adoption, and innovation**

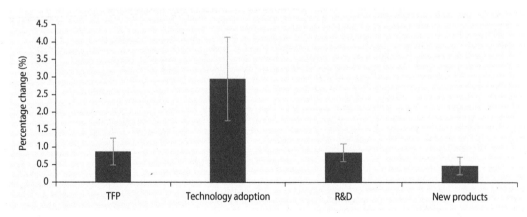

Source: Adapted from Che and Zhang 2017.
Note: The figure shows the average increases (in percent) resulting from a 1 percentage point increase in the share of college graduates employed in Chinese manufacturing firms—the impact of a policy-induced surge in China's college-educated workforce that took effect starting in 2003. The analysis uses a difference-in-difference approach and, in general, the measured impacts are compared before and after 2003. TFP refers to total factor productivity; "technology adoption" to the value of firm imports of high-technology capital goods; R&D to firm-level research and development spending; and "new products" to the value of new products introduced by the firm. Error bars show "robust standard errors" clustered at the firm level. All the results shown are significant at the 1 percent level.

FIGURE O.7 Learning and associated skills development, not simply years of schooling, contributes to higher GDP growth

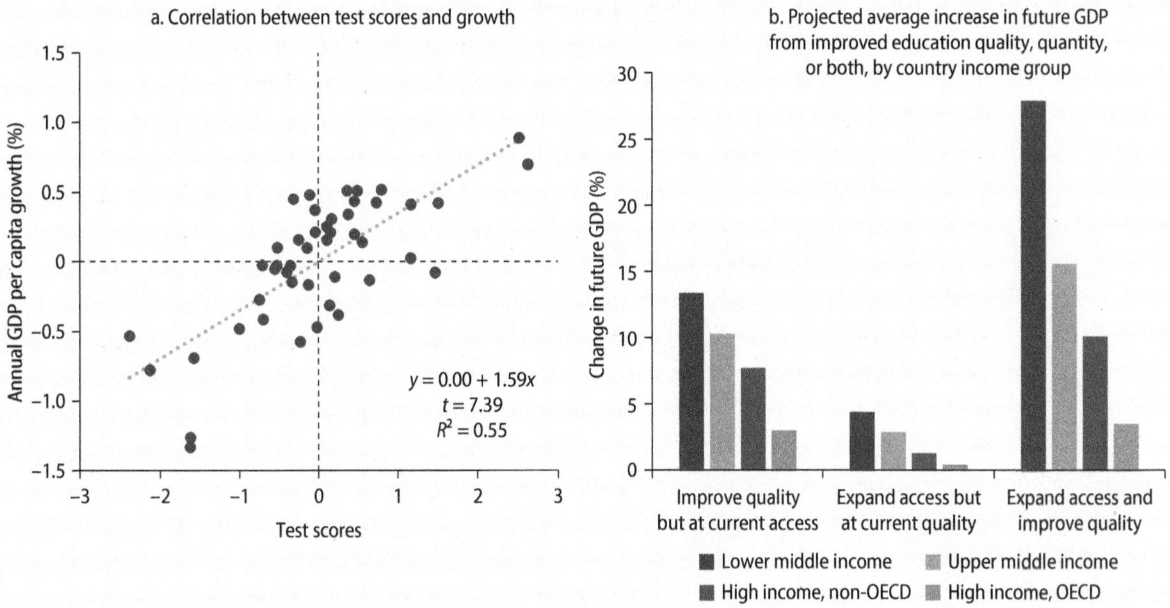

a. Correlation between test scores and growth

$$y = 0.00 + 1.59x$$
$$t = 7.39$$
$$R^2 = 0.55$$

b. Projected average increase in future GDP from improved education quality, quantity, or both, by country income group

Legend: Lower middle income; Upper middle income; High income, non-OECD; High income, OECD

Sources: World Bank 2018b, 46 (panel a); Hanushek and Woessman 2021 (panel b).
Note: Panel a shows annual average per capita growth in GDP, 1970–2015, and test scores conditional on initial GDP per capita and years of schooling completed. It includes a global sample of countries, albeit a subset based on availability of the relevant data. Panel b shows the projected average economic gains (percentage increase in future GDP) in middle- and high-income countries from improving the workforce's cognitive skills, by country income group (World Bank classifications). Improvement in education "quality" is measured by rising test scores, such as in the Programme for International Student Assessment (PISA) or the Trends in International Mathematics and Science Study (TIMSS). Expansion of "access" refers to ensuring school access for all children through the lower secondary levels. Raising cognitive skills of the workforce can be achieved by raising education quality and by giving children more years of schooling. OECD = Organisation for Economic Co-operation and Development. GDP = gross domestic product.

Education—and the skills it confers—also contributes to higher growth (Barrow and Keeney 2001; Cohen and Soto 2007; Glewwe, Maïga, and Zheng 2014; Hanushek and Woessman 2015; Krueger and Lindahl 2001; Mankiw, Romer, and Weil 1992). In particular, cross-country analysis reveals a robust relationship between the cognitive skills conferred by education and economic growth (figure O.7, panel a). Moreover, given recent increases in years of schooling attained, analysis suggests that improving education quality will be particularly important to boosting countries' growth performance in middle-income countries (figure O7, panel b).

Poor teaching impedes basic learning in much of the region

Many of the region's middle-income countries still face serious challenges in achieving high teaching quality, such as the following:

• Education systems are not attracting or selecting those who would be the best teachers.
• Teaching capacity—teachers' knowledge and teaching practices—is often weak.
• Teacher behavior often does not support student learning.

These three challenges are examined in turn.

Education systems do not attract or select the best candidates

The teaching profession does not attract the best academic performers. Teachers' salaries are relatively low in many countries, and poor working conditions (especially in poor and remote areas) along with weak career progression mechanisms limit the attractiveness of the teaching profession. Moreover, admission into preservice education programs and recruitment into teaching jobs often lack selectivity. Even where countries have formal criteria for teacher selection, those criteria are often not followed, with political factors playing a role in recruitment.

Many teachers have limited knowledge of their subjects and how to teach them

Far too many teachers in middle-income East Asia and Pacific have not mastered the content they are expected to teach, as these examples show:

- *In Lao PDR,* only 8 percent of fourth-grade teachers scored 80 percent or higher on an assessment of fourth-grade mathematics content knowledge (figure O.8, panel a).
- *In Indonesia,* only 8 percent of fourth-grade teachers who were tested received an 80 percent or higher on an assessment of their Indonesian language skills (Yarrow et al. 2020) (figure O.8, panel b).
- *In Malaysia,* only 53 percent of English language teachers tested in 2020 were judged to be sufficiently proficient in English to teach (Malaysia MOE 2020).

Many teachers in the region also do not employ effective teaching practices. Only 7 percent or less of teachers in Mongolia, the Philippines, Viet Nam, and the poorer provinces

FIGURE O.8   **Most Lao PDR mathematics teachers and Indonesian language teachers have not mastered the curriculum they teach**

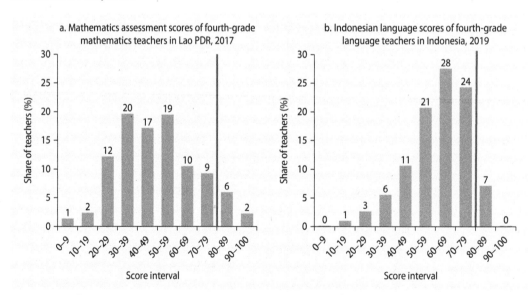

Sources: World Bank 2017 (panel a); Yarrow et al. 2020 (panel b).
Note: Percentages represent the share of teachers achieving scores within each score interval. The red line marks the expected "minimum proficiency score," defined as a score of 80 percent or better on the exam. For Indonesia, the results are from a nationally representative sample of schools of the Ministry of Religious Affairs and a smaller sample of schools of the Ministry of Education, Culture, Research, and Technology (MoECRT). The survey was conducted in 2019 and used the same survey instrument (Service Delivery Indicators) used in Lao PDR. Shares do not always total 100 due to rounding.

FIGURE O.9   **Many of the region's teachers use ineffective teaching practices**

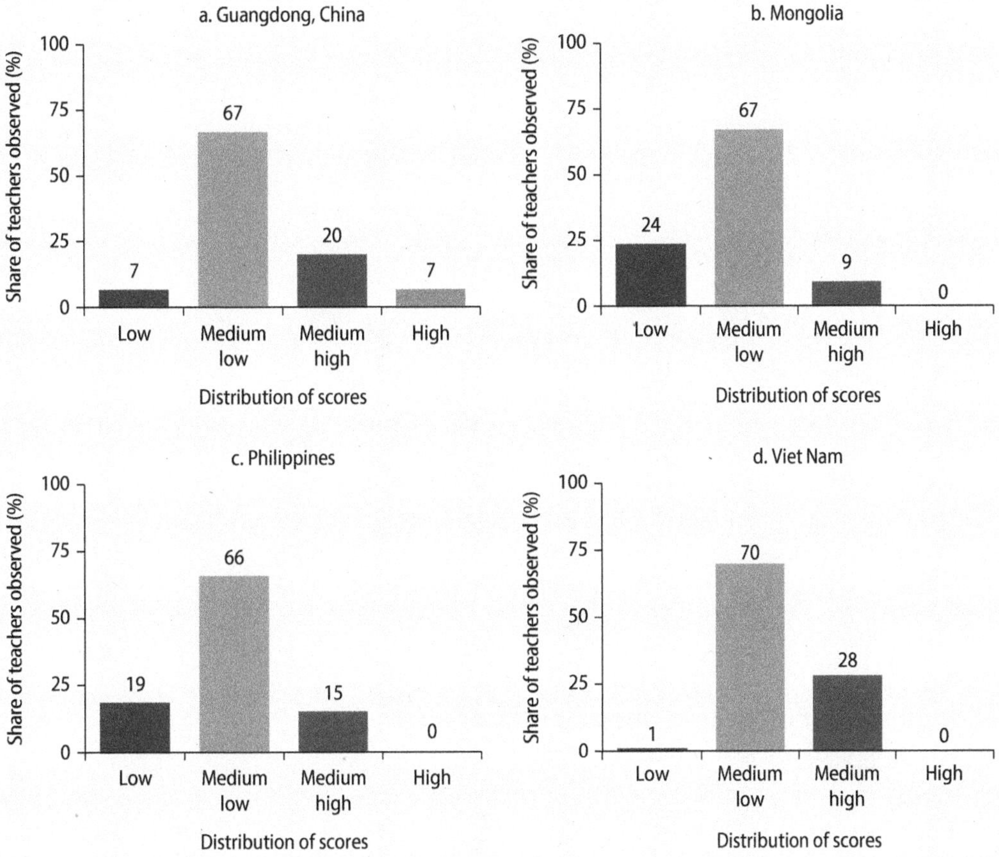

a. Guangdong, China

b. Mongolia

c. Philippines

d. Viet Nam

Sources: Coflan et al. 2018 (China); Lai 2019 (Mongolia); Molina et al. 2018 (Philippines); Carneiro et al. 2022 (Viet Nam); additional World Bank calculations of Mongolia and Philippines data to ensure comparability (details available upon request).
Note: The figures show data collected from classroom observations. For Guangdong, China, the figure is based on a classroom observations tool called the *Classroom Assessment Scoring System (CLASS)*, whereas the figures for the other countries are based on a classroom observational tool called *Teach*. The figures reflecting the *Teach* tool (panels b, c, and d) show, for each country, the average of teachers' global scores (that is, teachers' composite scores from the different indices of the tool). This score, based on classroom observation, captures teachers' capacity to create a classroom culture conducive to learning, to challenge and engage students, and to foster students' socioemotional skills to be successful learners. (Shares do not always total 100 due to rounding.) For more details, see the World Bank education brief, "Teach Primary: Helping Countries Track and Improve Teaching Quality," August 30, 2022, https://www.worldbank.org/en/topic/education/brief/teach-helping-countries-track-and-improve-teaching-quality. Panel b, showing results for Mongolia, differs slightly from what appeared in World Bank (2019) because an effort was made to harmonize the *Teach* data across the countries for which we have such data.

in Guangdong, China, demonstrate highly effective practices, while more than two-thirds use ineffective or weak practices (figure O.9). Weak teaching practices translate into poorer learning outcomes.

As with foundational learning outcomes, there is inequality in the quality of teachers' teaching practices. In Cambodia, Lao PDR, Myanmar, and the Philippines, mathematics teaching practices in socioeconomically disadvantaged schools are significantly worse than in the best-off schools (figure O.10). Disparities in teaching quality across socioeconomic categories are more muted in Malaysia and Viet Nam, where average student learning outcomes are also much better.

FIGURE O.10   **In most Southeast Asian countries, students from the poorest households are not being taught by the most effective teachers**

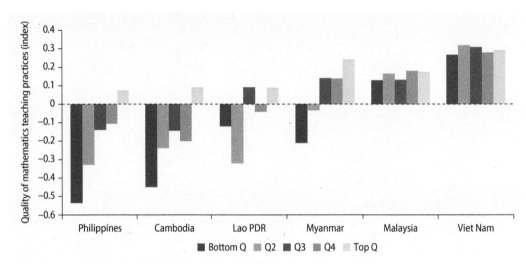

Source: World Bank estimates, based on 2019 Southeast Asia Primary Learning Metrics (SEA-PLM) data (UNICEF and SEAMEO 2020).
Note: The figure shows the quality of mathematics teaching practices (index), by household socioeconomic status quintile (Q)—a nationally derived measure based on (a) highest parental occupation of either parent, (b) highest education level of either parent, and (c) family's home resources through the home resources scale (UNICEF and SEAMEO 2020, 66). The average value of the teaching practices index is normalized to zero; schools reporting poorer-than-average teaching practices are thus shown to have negative values in the figure.

Teacher behavior often does not support learning

Teacher absences as well as poor classroom management adversely affect student learning. For example, around 14 percent of students surveyed in Cambodia, Lao PDR, Malaysia, Myanmar, the Philippines, and Viet Nam report, on average, that their teachers are often absent. Across 15 Pacific Island countries, 36 percent of students attend a school whose principal reports that instruction was hindered by teacher absenteeism (EQAP 2022). In contrast, data from Japan, Korea, and Shanghai, China, show teacher absence rates of 1 percent or less, and data from Singapore show only 3 percent absenteeism (OECD 2020b).

Moreover, the class time dedicated to foundational learning is often low. For example, less than one-third of fifth-graders in Lao PDR, Malaysia, Myanmar, and the Philippines have daily mathematics and language lessons.[4]

Most teachers will remain in place for the near future

Improving the capacity and behavior of existing teachers will be critical to improving learning outcomes because, in every East Asian and Pacific country, most of the teachers expected to be employed in 2030 have already been recruited (figure O.11). In China, Indonesia, Malaysia, the Marshall Islands, the Federated States of Micronesia, Mongolia, the Philippines, and Tonga, three-quarters or more of teachers expected to be employed in 2030 are already in place (Tanaka and Sondergaard 2023).

Even in countries that will need to increase the number of teachers, the large stock of existing teachers will make up at least half of the teaching workforce at the start of the next decade. For example, although Cambodia may need to recruit as many as 22,000 new teachers in the decade to 2030, more than 30,000 current teachers are still expected to be teaching at that time.

FIGURE O.11 . **Most of those expected to be teaching in East Asia and Pacific by 2030 have already been recruited**

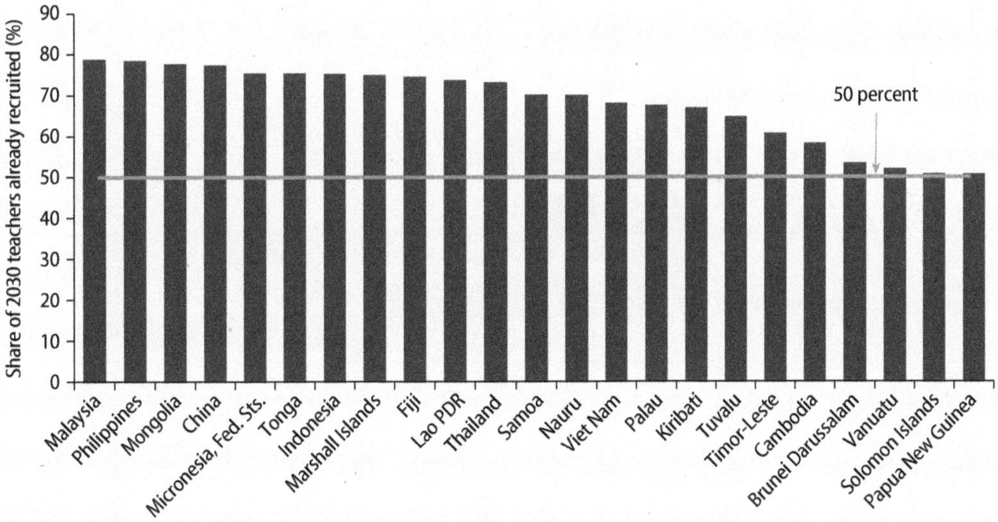

Source: Tanaka and Sondergaard 2023.
Note: The figure shows the percentage of primary-school teachers projected to be teaching in 2030 who had already joined the teaching workforce by 2020. Simulations use the United Nations' *World Population Prospects 2022* (medium scenario) for children of primary age (UN DESA 2022) and the following assumptions: (a) countries will reach a net enrollment rate of 100 percent at least by 2030; (b) countries will lower pupil-teacher ratios to 25 to 1 (or maintain current levels if below that ratio) by 2030; and (c) teacher attrition rates are the average country-reported attrition rates for the past five years (if reported in the UNESCO Institute for Statistics database), or if countries are not reporting attrition rates, we use the average attrition rate over the past five years of the countries who do report.

Teachers' professional development is often ineffective

Evidence on teacher professional development from high-income countries shows that concrete, classroom-based programs make the most difference to teachers and raise student learning (Darling-Hammond et al. 2009; Walter and Briggs 2012). However, new survey data collected for this report indicate that many East Asian and Pacific countries' in-service training programs lack the four elements of effective teacher training programs—which this report also calls the "four C's": (a) a focus on *content* knowledge, (b) opportunities to practice what is learned with *colleagues*, (c) *continued* support through follow-up visits focused on training content, and (d) *career* incentives through promotion or increased salary (figure O.12).

Strengthening teaching for improved learning

Strengthening the quality and effectiveness of teaching in the region will require action on three fronts (figure O.13):

- Attracting and selecting more effective teachers
- Enhancing teachers' capacity to teach (that is, strengthening their subject knowledge and pedagogical skills as well as improving the tools they use)
- Encouraging greater teacher effort.

An important element of all three of these areas involves improving the information base upon which policy choices are made and implemented.

FIGURE O.12   **Teacher training programs in nine middle-income East Asian and Pacific countries do not generally employ practices linked to improved student learning**

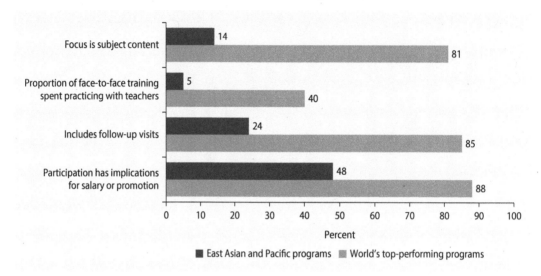

Sources: Popova et al. 2022 (for top performers worldwide); World Bank calculations, based on 2022 In-Service Teacher Training Survey Instrument (ITTSI) data for 65 programs in nine middle-income East Asian and Pacific countries.

Note: Percentages represent the proportion of programs containing a given feature, except for "practicing with teachers," where the percentage is the proportion of time training courses devote to this activity. The nine East Asian and Pacific countries are Cambodia, Fiji, Lao PDR, Mongolia, the Philippines, Thailand, Timor-Leste, Tonga, and Viet Nam. Orange bars designate "top performers" from a global study of training programs in 14 countries (Popova et al. 2022). Brown bars designate percentages of only the 65 training programs in the nine East Asian and Pacific countries. Detailed data were collected on large-scale teacher professional development programs conducted in countries between January 2018 and June 2022 to observe the landscape of in-service teacher training both before and during the COVID-19 pandemic.

FIGURE O.13   **Policy to strengthen teaching for public basic education has several entry points**

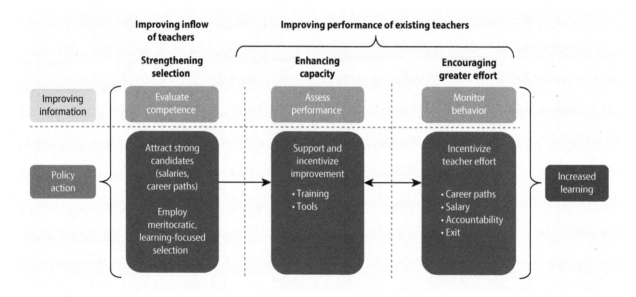

High-performing education systems make teaching attractive and selective

High-performing education systems in East Asia and Pacific have been effective in making teaching both attractive and selective, through a combination of mechanisms:

- In *Shanghai, China,* for example, teaching is a highly attractive career, driven by several factors, including competitive pay, attractive working conditions, manageable pupil-to-teacher ratios, and clear career progression structures. The Teacher Law stipulates that teachers' average salary should be equal to or higher than the national average salary of civil servants.
- In *Korea,* the education system uses rigorous, merit-based screening processes. Only the top 10 percent of high school graduates are admitted to the country's teacher education programs, and only 1 in 20 candidates passes the arduous exams to become a teacher (Ferreras, Kessel, and Kim 2015).
- In *Singapore,* a demanding training regime is accompanied by professional incentives for admitted candidates (World Bank 2018a). Before becoming a teacher, candidates must undergo preparatory training that includes both compulsory contract teaching and formal study to earn the proper qualifications. Admitted candidates are paid throughout their training period, and teachers receive attractive salary packages.

The right training and tools can enhance teaching capacity

Teaching capacity can be strengthened through training to enhance teachers' knowledge and skills and through tools that have been shown to be effective in improving student learning.

Training content and methods

To be effective, training must be guided by data and evidence for multiple reasons: First, regular assessment of teachers' knowledge and pedagogical skills generates data to focus training on identified needs. Second, the design of effective training programs should be informed by what works. As noted earlier, high-impact teacher training programs include the four C's: (a) a focus on *content* knowledge, (b) opportunities to practice what is learned with *colleagues,* (c) *continued* support through follow-up visits focused on training content, and (d) *career* incentives through promotion or increased salary.

Research shows that such training can be effective in improving student learning. For instance, the Tonga "Come Let's Read and Write" (CLRW) program provided training focused on content, instructional materials, and coaching on a new method to teach reading. The program improved average reading scores by 0.19 standard deviations after one year and 0.33 standard deviations after two years of intervention (figure O.14, panel a), increasing the proportion of second-grade students who could read from 18 percent to 29 percent (Macdonald et al. 2018). The CLRW program also provided follow-up in the form of regular coaching focused on subject content.

Even the relatively short Sa Aklat Sisikat (SAS) program in the Philippines—whose main activity was a read-a-thon over 31 days—improved students' reading skills by 0.13 standard deviations (Abeberese, Kumler, and Linden 2014), as shown in figure O.14, panel b. However, some of the gains were lost after three months, highlighting the importance of follow-up teacher support to ensure that the full benefits of teacher training are maintained.

Effective teacher training programs have positive financial returns, with benefits far outweighing costs. Programs in East Asia and Pacific have found benefit-cost ratios ranging from 7.5 to 1 to 12.3 to 1. For the Tonga CLRW program, for example, the present value of per pupil program costs is $116, as compared with the $1,425 present value of the per pupil benefits

FIGURE O.14   **Rigorous impact evaluations of in-service teacher training programs in East Asia and Pacific show that well-designed, well-implemented training can lead to better learning outcomes**

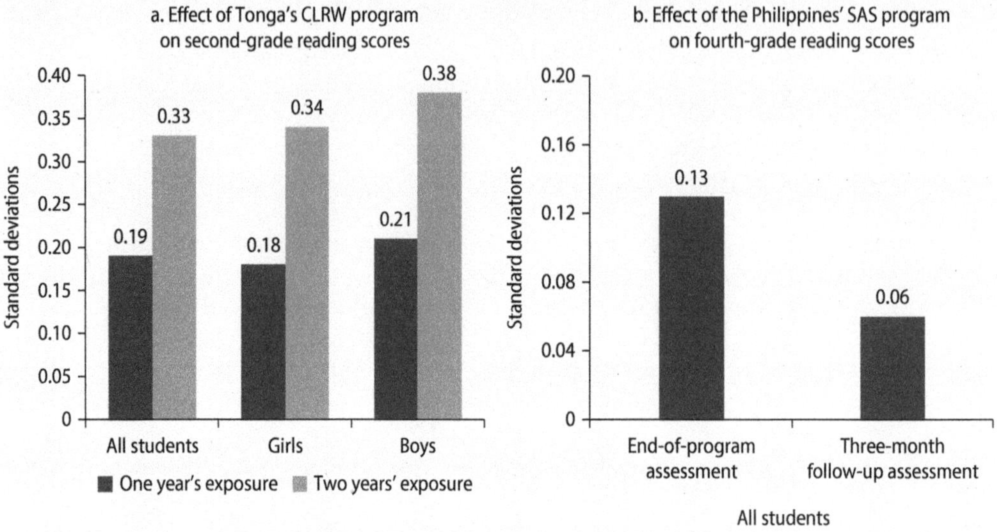

Sources: Macdonald et al. 2018 (panel a); Abeberese, Kumler, and Linden 2014 (panel b).

Note: Panel a shows the improvement (in standard deviations) in reading scores from the Tonga Early Grade Reading Assessment (TEGRA) of second-grade students at one and two years after their teachers received training through the Come Let's Read and Write (CLRW) program. The estimated effect size for all students lies outside the range estimates for girls and boys. This is likely due to the fact that the gender-specific effects were estimated separately from the all-student effects. Panel b shows the improvement (in standard deviations) in reading scores from a bespoke reading skills assessment, based in part on a national reading examination created and administered annually by the Philippine Department of Education after teachers received training through the Sa Aklat Sisikat (SAS) (loosely, "Books Make You Cool") program and led fourth-grade students in a 31-day read-a-thon. The follow-up assessment was conducted three months later.

from higher future earnings projected from increased cognitive skills obtained through the program (figure O.15).[5] In the case of the Philippines SAS program, the corresponding figures are costs of $85 per student, set against $640 in benefits. These positive returns are consistent with evidence from beyond East Asia and Pacific (see, for example, Evans and Yuan 2019).

One key feature of effective training programs is follow-up, through visits to teachers once they return to their schools, focused on the content of the training. Coaching and mentoring support teachers, either one-on-one or through teacher groups, to address the challenges they face in applying the lessons from training to their classrooms. No rigorous evaluations of coaching and mentoring have been carried out in East Asian or Pacific countries, but evidence from other middle-income countries highlights coaching's contribution to improved learning. In Peru, for example, a program of monthly coaching visits to teachers was found to raise reading comprehension by 0.25 standard deviations and mathematics performance by 0.38 standard deviations (Castro, Glewwe, and Montero 2019).

Effective tools to support teachers

Teachers can be supported to be more effective with several different tools, such as (a) structured lesson plans, (b) targeted instruction, (c) educational technologies, and (d) the dual teacher model.

Structured lesson plans are especially useful where teachers lack pedagogical skills or subject knowledge, because these plans lead the teacher, and thus the student, through a series of activities designed by the best teachers. These plans can be highly scripted lessons that teachers follow carefully, reading from a prepared script. Teachers with higher capacity can

FIGURE O.15   **Effective teacher training programs in East Asia and Pacific yield positive rates of return on investment**

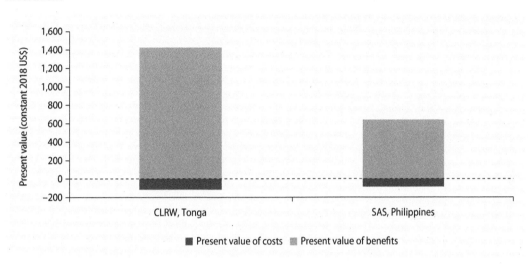

Sources: Macdonald et al. 2018 (for Tonga's CLRW program); World Bank estimates (for the Philippines' SAS program).
Note: Figure shows the estimated present value of costs and benefits per student (in US dollars) of two countries' teacher training interventions. Benefits are estimated as the effects on future earnings per student from increases in either cognitive skills or educational attainment. CLRW = Come Let's Read and Write; SAS = Sa Aklat Sisikat (loosely, "Books Make You Cool").

use them more flexibly like guides. These lesson plans—along with training to use them—lead to significant learning gains, equivalent to an additional half year or more of learning, raising student language scores by 0.23 standard deviations and mathematics scores by 0.14 standard deviations on average (Snilstveit et al. 2015). In the region, the Papua New Guinea's Reading Booster Program had particularly large effects on student reading skills for grade 3 students, ranging from 0.6 to 0.7 standard deviations (Macdonald and Vu 2018). In Cambodia, structured lesson plans had large positive impacts for grade 1–3 students in language, of 0.5 standard deviations (Snilstveit et al. 2015).

Targeted instruction—an approach also known as teaching at the right level—helps teachers address the major challenge that, in any given classroom, children have achieved different levels of learning. Targeted instruction involves grouping students in school by learning levels, rather than by age or grade, and engaging them in activities appropriate to their achievement levels, often in small groups. Targeted instruction can be highly effective. For example, in the Indian state of Uttar Pradesh, there was a 25 percentage point increase in the likelihood of being able to read a story (Banerjee et al. 2017). Targeted instruction can also be highly cost-effective, delivering as much as three years of learning per $100 spent (Angrist et al. 2020).

Educational technologies (EdTech) also show promise for improving teaching. Computer-assisted learning (CAL) has proven effective both in the region's middle-income countries (figure O.16) and high-income countries (Hattie 2009). *CAL* refers to interventions in which students engage in self-directed learning with the assistance of a computer software program. CAL software packages aim to improve student learning in a specific subject area through drills and exercises that give students opportunities to practice material learned in class and by providing immediate feedback. The evidence suggests that CAL is most effective in improving learning outcomes when it is used to complement classroom learning and not as a substitute for instruction by a teacher. EdTech also appears to hold some promise in

FIGURE O.16 **Computer-assisted learning programs have helped improve student learning in selected East Asian economies**

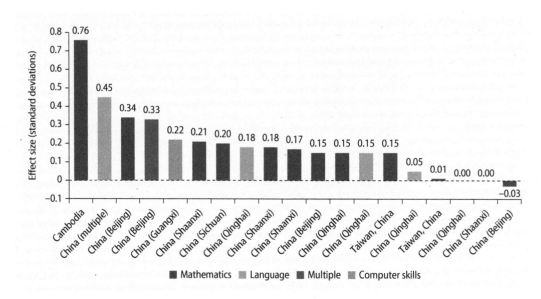

Source: Adapted from Yarrow et al., forthcoming.
Note: The figure shows the impact (in standard deviations) of computer-assisted learning programs on student performance, by subject area. Parentheses indicate Chinese provinces.

the implementation of structured lesson plans, as lessons can be loaded onto a website or on tablets for offline use.

The dual teacher model extends the reach of the best teachers by enabling them to provide content and model elements of effective pedagogy through either prerecorded or livestreamed sessions. This approach, in which expert teachers provide content through either prerecorded or livestreamed sessions, has had significant positive impacts on learning in several rural contexts where high-quality teachers are in short supply, including in China, Ghana, India, Mexico, and Pakistan (Bcg et al., 2019; Borghesan and Vasey, forthcoming; Johnston and Christopher 2017; Li et al., 2023; Naik et al. 2020).

Impacts have been found in multiple subject areas across a range of grade levels. In the East Asia and Pacific region, a study of seventh to ninth graders in China found improvements in student learning of 0.23 standard deviations in language and 0.18 standard deviations in mathematics (Bianchi, Lu, and Song 2022). It is important to note that these remote instruction interventions took place in classrooms during the regular school day and involved a teacher's classroom presence with the students in addition to the remote teacher.

Incentives can motivate greater teacher effort

Teachers need to be present in the classroom and use their knowledge and the tools to help students learn. In principle, several types of incentives could motivate teachers to perform effectively, including professional advancement, financial incentives, accountability mechanisms, and measures to deal with chronic underperformance. However, there is limited evidence on what works in practice.

Evidence on performance pay, a financial incentive policy used in some countries, is mixed, although one study on promotion incentive among primary- and middle-school teachers in

China found positive results (Karachiwalla and Park 2017). Overall, global evidence suggests that where there is an impact, it tends to be small. Moreover, survey evidence suggests there is little support for it in the region's high-income countries.

Accountability mechanisms, such as school-based management (SBM), can affect teacher effort. SBM can induce change at the school level by increasing parental involvement and changing teacher behavior (for example, reducing absenteeism), and at the pupil level, by lowering repetition and dropouts. In Viet Nam, where teacher absenteeism is significantly lower than elsewhere in the region, teachers take part in regular internal and external evaluations that hold them accountable for teaching quality. Teachers may be dismissed for misconduct, child abuse, absenteeism, or consistently poor performance.

This report focuses largely on improving the performance of existing teachers. Some teachers may be unable or unwilling to improve their performance to acceptable levels, despite support to improve. Exiting these teachers, especially those with the status of civil servants, takes considerable time and political commitment. However, where it is feasible to identify persistent weak performers, inducing exit would strengthen incentives for other teachers to improve their performance—by demonstrating that the system sets standards for capacity and behavior, assesses performance against those standards, and acts when they are not met.

Public education spending, used efficiently, can improve both learning and equity

Countries in middle-income East Asia and Pacific can improve teaching and student learning by implementing the types of interventions discussed earlier. However, effectively implementing these interventions will require resources. In most countries in the region, this will require both additional public spending and more efficient spending of existing budget allocations. Addressing learning inequalities within countries will also require that policy makers make sure that sufficient public resources are directed toward disadvantaged and poorly performing areas.

Public spending for education in most middle-income East Asian countries is well below what would be expected given their level of development (figure O.17). In contrast, Pacific Island countries commonly spend more than the middle-income country average of 4.7 percent of gross domestic product (GDP) because the cost of delivering education services is high owing to substantial geographic dispersion and diseconomies of scale. Private (household) spending is less, on average, in East Asia and Pacific than in other middle-income regions, and much of households' spending is focused on secondary and tertiary education, not on building basic skills. Moreover, private spending on education tends to be concentrated among the wealthiest 40 percent of households, making it a poor substitute for public spending. Indeed, public spending on education plays an important role in redressing inequality, with greater public spending associated with higher intergenerational mobility (van der Wiede et al. 2021).

Existing levels of public resources will also need to be better spent. For every middle-income country in the region except Viet Nam, there is a peer at a similar level of development that has achieved lower levels of learning poverty—often at lower levels of public spending. A striking comparison between income peers involves Malaysia and Kazakhstan. Kazakhstan has achieved a learning poverty rate of 2 percent as compared with Malaysia's rate of 42 percent while spending roughly two-thirds as much as Malaysia as a share of GDP.

Within the region, Viet Nam's performance on basic learning stands out. The country spends about 4.2 percent of GDP on education and has achieved a learning poverty rate of 18 percent. Consistent with the evidence presented in this report, one school-level variable has a particularly large explanatory effect on Viet Nam's superior performance: the pedagogical skills of primary-school mathematics teachers (Glewwe et al. 2021).

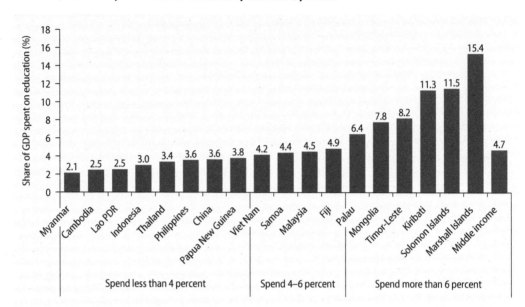

Sources: UIS 2022 except for Papua New Guinea and Timor-Leste, whose data are from the World Bank's BOOST databases for each respective country (https://www.worldbank.org/en/programs/boost-portal/country-data).
Note: The figure shows average public spending on education, as a share of GDP, in only middle-income countries for which a full set of 2016–19 data are available from UIS (2022). For this reason, the following countries are excluded: the Federated States of Micronesia, Papua New Guinea, Tonga, and Vanuatu. The "Middle income" bar at far right represents the average of middle-income countries globally. GDP = gross domestic product.

In short, although many countries in the region need to spend more on education, simply allocating additional resources to do more of the same is unlikely to improve learning outcomes. However, increasing the efficiency of education spending will be both technically and politically challenging. The technical challenge is that the underlying causes of inefficient spending vary across countries and are difficult to diagnose without better data and in-depth country-level analysis. The political challenge is that divergent political interests within countries often impede meaningful education reforms. The need to tailor reforms to specific country circumstances—through better data and diagnosis—and to navigate the political economy of reform are now discussed in turn.

Reforms must be tailored to country and within-country circumstances

Reforms will need to reflect different circumstances across and within countries. In general, countries with high levels of learning poverty (such as Cambodia, Lao PDR, Myanmar, and the Philippines) will need to focus on fostering systemic improvements and supporting all teachers, whereas countries with more moderate levels of learning poverty (such as China, Palau, Thailand, and Viet Nam) can take more targeted approaches, focusing on specific challenges such as remedial support for lagging school districts. The Pacific Island countries face additional challenges—small size, significant population dispersion, and linguistic diversity—that make education reform particularly costly and logistically difficult to implement (World Bank 2023c).

Even the limited available data can help policy makers identify priorities for reform. For example, countries like Cambodia, Papua New Guinea, and Vanuatu, which expect substantial growth in their teacher workforces, will need to place a greater emphasis on strengthening teacher selection as compared with countries like Fiji, Malaysia, and the Philippines, which project stable or negative growth in the size of the teaching corps (see annex O.1). Where the data indicate that teacher capacity is particularly low (as in the Solomon Islands, Timor-Leste, and Vanuatu), more intense training and coaching as well as greater use of tools like highly scripted lessons and the dual-teacher model will be needed to provide adequate support to teachers. In addition, countries such as Cambodia, Kiribati, and Myanmar, where learning poverty is high and public spending on education is low, must direct additional public resources to education to support reform initiatives.[6]

All middle-income countries in the region, regardless of their levels of learning poverty, will need to address differences within their countries in teaching quality and learning outcomes across socioeconomic groups and across different parts of the country. Even in Viet Nam, among the best-performing middle-income countries in the region, learning outcomes are substantially lower among children from the poorest households than among their better-off peers (as shown earlier in figure O.2).

Among other challenges, countries commonly struggle to recruit, deploy, and retain high-quality teachers in poor and remote areas. In Papua New Guinea, for example, the Western Province, which has a large proportion of difficult-to-reach schools, has teacher vacancy rates that are twice as high as in the Southern Highlands, where schools are generally accessible: 34 percent versus 17 percent. Similarly, in Bangkok, nearly 20 percent of teachers have at least a bachelor's degree, relative to less than 10 percent in Mae Hong Son, a remote, mountainous region in northern Thailand.[7]

Reducing basic learning inequalities within countries will require additional resources to ensure a more equitable allocation of well-trained, effective teachers to disadvantaged schools. In addition to better designed and implemented professional development programs, special measures will also be needed to support teachers in lagging areas, including more intensive use of highly scripted lessons, enhanced coaching and mentoring, and increased use of dual teacher models.

However, the data needed to diagnose problems and support evidence-based, targeted policy making within countries remains scarce in much of the region. In some countries, like Malaysia and Viet Nam, relatively sophisticated databases contain up-to-date information about each teacher and his or her current and past employment, qualifications, and training received. In other countries, including the Pacific Island countries, even basic information on teachers is missing. In Papua New Guinea, for example, the most recent digitized teacher data are from 2018.

Virtually no middle-income country in the region collects data on teachers' content knowledge and teaching practices. Few countries collect regular information on teachers' presence in the classroom at times when they should be teaching.

The political economy of reform

Implementing effective reforms at scale—to bring about the transformation of the education systems in the region—will require policy makers to understand the depth of their countries' learning challenges and to navigate the political winds associated with undertaking major reforms.

Policy makers often do not recognize the magnitude of the problem

Surveys of government officials around the world suggest they are not always aware of the magnitude of their countries' foundational learning deficits. A recent survey of more than 1,000 senior policy makers in 40 low- and middle-income countries around the world found that they systematically underestimate the magnitude of their countries' learning deficits (figure O.18, panel a). In five of the seven countries surveyed in the region—Indonesia, Lao PDR, Mongolia, the Philippines, and Viet Nam—policy makers' estimates of 10-year-olds' literacy levels exceeded measured levels by substantial margins (figure O.18, panel b). Surveys also found that senior officials often prioritize socialization and nation-building goals for education above foundational learning.

Political interests play a key role in teacher hiring and promotions

Divergent incentives along the education service delivery chain also impede effective reform, even when sound technical solutions have been identified (World Bank 2018b). Although resistance from teacher unions does not appear to impede reform in East Asia and Pacific, politics continues to play an important role in the selection and promotion of teachers in many countries (Béteille, 2022). Across middle-income East Asia and Pacific, politicians and bureaucrats use their ability to create jobs, their access to information on job availability, and their role in the selection of teachers to establish systems of patronage, with the objective of securing teachers' loyalty (Béteille 2022; Hickey and Hossain 2019; Rosser and Fahmi 2018). In return, teachers receive transfers of their choice or jobs, even though unqualified, and are protected from the consequences associated with absenteeism, weak effort, or lack of accountability. Evidence indicates that patronage hires, having circumvented meritocratic selection procedures, tend to be of lower quality (Béteille and Evans 2021; Pierskalla and Sacks 2020).

In four of five countries for which there are data (Lao PDR, Mongolia, the Philippines, and Viet Nam), more than half of the senior officials surveyed indicated that the politically

FIGURE O.18   Policy makers do not (or choose not to) recognize the magnitude of their countries' learning deficits

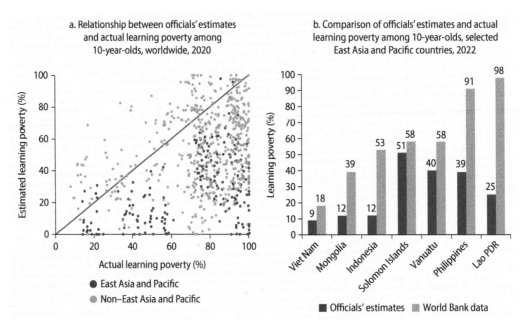

Sources: World Bank calculations, based on Crawfurd et al. 2021 and 2022 Center for Global Development—World Bank survey (panel a); and Yarrow et al. 2023 (panel b).
Note: Learning poverty refers to the percentage of 10-year-olds in school who cannot read and understand a short, age-appropriate text. Panel a: The survey of more than 1,000 senior government education officials in 40 low- and middle-income countries, including two Pacific Island countries, asked respondents to estimate the share of 10-year-old children in their countries who can read. The remaining percentage is the learning poverty rate. The study compared these estimates with the actual shares of children who can read, based on formal assessments of students' reading skills. Panel b: The survey reported policy makers' perceptions and compared them with literacy levels in seven East Asian and Pacific countries: Indonesia, Lao PDR, Mongolia, the Philippines, the Solomon Islands, Vanuatu, and Viet Nam. Vanuatu and Solomon Islands LP rates are interim estimates/not World Bank official data (from Cahu and Sondergaard).

connected candidate had at least an equal if not better chance of being selected than the candidate with good test scores (figure O.19, panel a). Only in Indonesia did most officials (65 percent) say the candidate with good test scores was most likely to be hired. An earlier study on Indonesia found that the Ministry of Education and Culture (MoE&C) was more likely than most other government ministries to circumvent formal processes in giving promotions, with political reasons listed as most important (figure O.19, panel b). The more recent survey results suggest there is hope: Indonesia's new teacher policy reforms focusing on meritocracy and performance appear to be bearing fruit.

Navigating political interests to enact reform is possible

Despite these political challenges, several middle-income countries—in developing East Asia and beyond—have managed to enact quality-enhancing reforms. For example, Brazil (Sobral municipality), Ecuador, India (Karnataka and Delhi), and Indonesia were able to implement difficult reforms because of the efforts of reform-minded politicians and administrators as well as many willing, committed teachers. Reforms included making teacher selection and deployment more meritocratic (Ecuador, Indonesia, Karnataka, and Sobral), undertaking regular performance evaluation and enabling dismissal of teachers when improvements in performance were not forthcoming (Ecuador and Sobral), and improving teaching practices in the classroom (Delhi).

FIGURE O.19 **Informal mechanisms play an important role in teacher selection and promotions, making performance-based reform difficult in East Asia and Pacific**

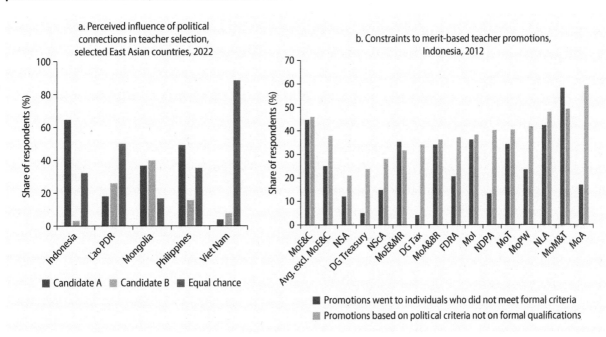

Sources: World Bank calculations, 2022 Center for Global Development—World Bank survey. More detailed information about the survey can be found in Yarrow et al. 2023 (panel a) and Keefer 2012 (panel b).

Note: Panel a: In the survey, senior government officials were asked, regarding teacher candidates in the capital city of their countries, "Who is most likely to get the job? Candidate A has good test scores but is not well connected politically. Candidate B does not have good test scores but is well connected politically." Panel b: The figure shows data from the 2012 Indonesia Survey of Public Servants (Keefer 2012), which surveyed 3,903 public servants from three employee ranks across 15 government institutions about the effects of the Bureaucratic Reform allowances on the performance, efficiency, and morale of public servants in Indonesia. Each percentage (bar) shown represents responses from that same agency or ministry. DG Treasury = Directorate General Treasury, Ministry of Finance; DG Tax = Directorate General Tax, Ministry of Finance; FDRA = Food and Drug Regulatory Agency; MoA = Ministry of Agriculture; MoA&BR = Ministry of Administrative and Bureaucratic Reform; MoE&C = Ministry of Education and Culture; MoE&MR = Ministry of Energy and Mineral Resources; MoI = Ministry of Industry; MoM&T = Ministry of Manpower and Transmigration; MoPW = Ministry of Public Works; MoT = Ministry of Transportation; NDPA = National Development Planning Agency; NLA = National Land Agency; NSA = National Statistics Agency; NScA = National Science Agency.

These politicians and bureaucrats addressed key political economy challenges by focusing on the following:

- *Effective outreach and communication* ensured that information on specific challenges, whether low learning levels or unfilled teacher vacancies in schools, is widely available; presented in a manner that motivates action; and focused on key stakeholders such as teachers, parents, and the general public. These actions brought teachers on board (Indonesia, Karnataka, and Sobral), engaged parents (Ecuador and Delhi), and built public support for quality-enhancing reforms.
- *Building strong coalitions and teams* can spur reforms and help sustain them. Coalitions were built among district politicians, administrators, and teachers (Indonesia) and between teachers and parents (Delhi and Ecuador). Reform efforts in Delhi, Ecuador, Karnataka, and Sobral also benefited from strong technical teams, working with committed, reform-minded officials for nearly a decade. This resulted in high-quality inputs to the reforms as well as continuity of reform implementation.
- *Buying out vested interests* may be necessary to weaken opposition to reforms. In Indonesia, teachers opposed to the redeployment policy could opt out of recertification if they were prepared to forgo the salary supplement. In Ecuador, when teachers and school directors opposed the new meritocracy-related policies, the government offered an attractive early retirement package, stemming opposition early. In Sobral, salary increases, incentives, and professional recognition muted opposition.
- *Adaptive implementation* helped ensure that reforms were politically sustainable because phased rollout provided an opportunity to remedy initial design or implementation flaws, to demonstrate benefits, to build ownership, and to avoid early large-scale confrontation with different interest groups.

The way forward

Successful reforms require sustained and aligned efforts across a range of stakeholders: heads of government, ministries of education, ministries of finance, teachers, and parents. Heads of government provide vision and political leadership, which will be needed across successive government administrations. Ministries of education must develop credible agendas for reform. Ministries of finance will have to allocate sufficient resources to enable implementation of the reform agenda and get stakeholders on board. Teachers will need new tools and enhanced support and be ready to step up to the challenge. Parents and caregivers will need to be engaged in, and advocates for, improved learning.

In the aftermath of the COVID-19 pandemic, garnering the resources to support successful reform will be a challenge in many countries. To convince officials from the region's finance ministries that additional resources will be used productively, education ministries must develop credible, evidence-based programs of reform. They will also need to improve data and information to underpin the design, implementation, and evaluation of reform initiatives. Better and more accessible information will also be critical to empowering parents to support teachers—and to hold them to account—in the quest for improved foundational learning for their children.

Such mutually reinforcing, and long-term, relationships between key stakeholders—between ministries of education and finance, between parents and teachers, and between heads of government and the general public—will be critical in countries' efforts to bridge the basic learning gap in middle-income East Asia and Pacific. Those efforts would set the stage for higher productivity and growth and more prosperous societies in the years to come. Progress takes time under the best of circumstances, so action must begin now.

Annex O.1 Countries in East Asia and Pacific confront different policy challenges based on their circumstances

Country	Country context GDP per capita 2021 (US$)[a]	Learning deficit Learning poverty rate (%)[b]	Fiscal resources spent Government expenditure on education (% GDP)[c]	Government expenditure on education (% total spending)[d]	Teacher capacity Share of qualified teachers in primary education (%)[e]	Teacher behavior Teachers are often absent (%)	Data availability Participation in international assessments[f]	Quality of EMIS (score 1–6)[g]	Selection vs. capacity (flow vs. stock) Teacher persistence to 2030 (%)	Projected change in teacher positions by 2030 (%)
Palau	13,251	10	6.8	15.7			1		68	0.12
China	11,188	18	3.5	11.2	95.7		1		77	−0.32
Malaysia	10,827	42	4.2	17.7	98.9	4.9	2	4.5	79	0.01
Thailand	6,270	23	3	13.7	100		0	4.5	73	−0.19
Fiji	4,708	41	5.1	16.8			1	4	74	0.02
Tonga	4,630	72	8	11.9	92.5		1	2	75	−0.05
Mongolia	4,121	39	4.9	16.5	93.7		0		78	0.07
Tuvalu	4,019	73			100		1	2.5	65	0.16
Samoa	3,972	61	4.7	15.6			1	2.5	70	0.07
Indonesia	3,856	53	2.8	17.3	87.5		0	3.5	75	−0.05
Philippines	3,413	91	3.2	17.5	99.8	14	2	3.5	79	0.11
Marshall Islands	3,397	62	15.8	24.8			1	3	75	−0.1
Viet Nam	3,373	18	4.1	14		1.4	2	4.5	68	−0.03
Micronesia	2,720	53	9.7	18.1	90.8		1	3	76	0.01
Papua New Guinea	2,655	72	3.6	21.1			1	1	51	0.42
Vanuatu	2,613	58	1.8	5.6	71.8		1	3	52	0.38
Lao PDR	2,582	98	2.3	14	90.2	18.3	2	3	74	0.08
Solomon Islands	2,081	58	11.1	30.1	79.6		1	2.5	51	0.33
Timor-Leste	1,626		8.1	10.9	76.5		1	3	61	0.22
Kiribati	1,474	71	12.4	12.4	99.7		1	2.5	67	0.11
Cambodia	1,400	90	2.2	11.8	100	23.7	2	3	58	0.26
Myanmar	1,292	89	2.1	10.6	91.3	20.2	2	1		

(1) Constant 2015 US$; 2021 or latest; (2) % of GDP; 2019 or latest pre-pandemic; (3) % of total expenditure; 2019 or latest available; (4) 2019 or latest pre-pandemic; (5) Participation in int'l assessments of primary students in past three years? (2 = yes and data are available; 1 = yes, data are not publicly available; 0 = no). (6) (1 = poor quality; 6 = high quality).

Source: Compilation from World Bank databases; teacher absence data from UNICEF 2020.

Note: Red cells indicate countries in the bottom tercile; yellow cells, the middle tercile; and green cells, the top tercile. Gray cells indicate missing data. In the two rightmost columns, the darker the orange, (a) the lower the country's persistence of current teacher stock or (b) the larger the projected increase in future teaching positions. GDP = gross domestic product.

a. GDP per capita is in constant 2015 US$, using 2021 or latest data.

b. Learning poverty is the percentage of children who cannot read and understand a simple, age-appropriate text by age 10.

c. Government expenditure on education, as a percentage of GDP, uses 2019 or the latest prepandemic data.

d. Expenditure on education, as a percentage of total government expenditure, uses 2019 or the latest prepandemic data.

e. The percentage of qualified teachers in primary education—a proxy for existing teacher capacity—uses 2019 or latest available data.

f. Participation in international assessments of primary students measures participation in any of the past three years (2019–21). 2 = yes, data are publicly available; 1 = yes, data are not publicly available; 0 = no.

g. Quality of education management information systems (EMIS) ranges from 1 (poor quality) to 6 (high quality).

Notes

1. Approximately 90 percent of the region's primary students were enrolled in public schools in 2019 (UIS 2022). In high-income Japan, Korea, and Singapore, more than 95 percent attend public schools. In the region's middle-income countries, the focus of this report, the figure ranges from 99 percent in Viet Nam to 75 percent in the Solomon Islands.
2. In India, the estimated impact of having a high-performing versus low-performing teacher is even larger: the difference between an average student ending up in the top or the bottom 12 percent of the class (World Bank estimates).
3. The *Green Revolution,* also known as the *Third Agricultural Revolution,* refers to the introduction of new high-yielding seed varieties in the mid-1960s, which contributed to significantly higher agricultural productivity, especially when combined with modern chemical fertilizers, pesticides, and controlled irrigation. Productivity using Green Revolution technologies differed in important ways depending on farmers' ability to make appropriate use of these new agricultural inputs and technologies.
4. The findings on low class time devoted to learning are from World Bank estimates, based on Southeast Asia Primary Learning Metrics (SEA-PLM) data (UNICEF and SEAMEO 2020).
5. The benefits may be even larger if increased cognitive skills of students also translate into students completing more years of schooling. In the case of Tonga, when making this additional assumption, the estimated benefits would increase by $560. The present value of future earnings is derived from Mincerian earnings functions, which model individuals' future earnings. In the case of Tonga, the relationship between cognitive skills and earnings is estimated using the Tonga Household Income and Expenditure Survey (Abeberese, Kumler, and Linden 2014; Evans and Yuan 2019; Macdonald and Vu 2018; Montenegro and Patrinos 2014).
6. As discussed in more detail in World Bank 2023a, the military coup in Myanmar in February 2021 has severely disrupted the education sector in Myanmar. As the report documents, the disruptions in the education sector caused by the pandemic were compounded by the military coup as many officials in the Ministry of Education (MoE) and a large number of public school teachers throughout the country joined the civil disobedience movement (CDM) to protest against the military takeover.
7. Data on teachers' education levels are from World Bank calculations using 2011 Office of the Basic Education Commission (OBEC) data (World Bank 2015).

References

Abeberese, A. B., T. J. Kumler, and L. L. Linden. 2014. "Improving Reading Skills by Encouraging Children to Read in School: A Randomized Evaluation of the Sa Aklat Sisikat Reading Program in the Philippines." *Journal of Human Resources* 49 (3): 611–33.

Angrist, N., D. K. Evans, D. Filmer, R. Glennerster, F. H. Rogers, and S. Sabarwal. 2020. "How to Improve Education Outcomes Most Efficiently? A Comparison of 150 Interventions Using the New Learning-Adjusted Years of Schooling Metric." Policy Research Working Paper 9450, World Bank, Washington, DC.

Banerjee, A., R. Banerji, J. Berry, E. Duflo, H. Kannan, S. Mukerji, M. Shotland, and M. Walton. 2017. "From Proof of Concept to Scalable Policies: Challenges and Solutions, with an Application." *Journal of Economic Perspectives* 31 (4): 73–102. https://doi.org/10.1257/jep.31.4.73.

Barrow, R., and P. Keeney. 2001. "Lifelong Learning and Personal Fulfillment." In *International Handbook on Lifelong Learning,* edited by D. A. Chapman. London: Kluwer.

Beg, S. A., A. M. Lucas, W. Halim, and U. Saif. 2019. "Beyond the Basics: Improving Post-Primary Content Delivery through Classroom Technology." Working Paper 25704, National Bureau of Economic Resarch, Cambridge, MA.

Béteille, T. 2022. "Vibrant or Stuck?" Background paper for this report, World Bank, Washington, DC.

Béteille, T., and D. K. Evans. 2021. "Successful Teachers, Successful Students: Recruiting and Supporting Society's Most Crucial Profession." Report No. 164810, World Bank, Washington, DC.

Bianchi, N., Y. Lu, and H. Song. 2022. "The Effect of Computer-Assisted Learning on Students' Long-Term Development." *Journal of Development* 158: 102919.

Borghesan, E., and G. Vasey. Forthcoming. "The Marginal Returns to Distance Education: Evidence from Mexico's Telesecundarias." Accepted for publication in *American Economic Journal: Applied Economics*. https://gabriellevasey.github.io/MarginalReturns_BorghesanVasey.pdf.

Bruns, B., and J. Luque. 2015. *Great Teachers: How to Raise Student Learning in Latin America and the Caribbean.* Washington, DC: World Bank.

Cahu, P., and L. M. Sondergaard. 2023. "Estimating Interim Learning Poverty for Pacific Island Countries." World Bank, Washington, DC.

Carneiro, P., P. Glewwe, A. Guha, and S. Krutikova. 2022. "Unpacking the Black Box of School Quality." Unpublished manuscript. https://drive.google.com/file/d/1MQDGSL5nan1v7Mry29XgJ6T5P7NQZ bIf/view?pli=1.

Castro, J. F., P. Glewwe, and R. Montero. 2019. "Work with What You've Got: Improving Teachers' Pedagogical Skills at Scale in Rural Peru." Working Paper No. 158, Peruvian Economic Association, Lima.

Che, Y., and L. Zhang. 2017. "Human Capital, Technology Adoption and Firm Performance: Impacts of China's Higher Education Expansion in the Late 1990s." *Economic Journal* 128 (614): 2282–2320.

Coflan, A., A. Ragatz, A. Hasan, and Y. Pan. 2018. "Understanding Effective Teaching Practices in Chinese Classrooms: Evidence from a Pilot Study of Primary and Junior Secondary Schools in Guangdong, China." Policy Research Working Paper 8396, World Bank, Washington, DC.

Cohen, D., and M. Soto. 2007. "Growth and Human Capital: Good Data, Good Results." *Journal of Economic Growth* 12 (1): 51–76.

Crawfurd, L., S. Hares, A. Minardi, and J. Sandefur. 2021. "Understanding Education Policy Preferences: Survey Experiments with Policymakers in 35 Developing Countries." Working Paper 596, Center for Global Development, Washington, DC.

Criscuolo, C., P. Gal, T. Leidecker, F. Losma, and G. Nicoletti. 2021. "The Role of Telework for Productivity During and Post-COVID-19: Results from an OECD Survey Among Managers and Workers." Organisation for Economic Co-operation and Development (OECD) Productivity Working Papers No. 31, OECD Publishing, Paris.

Darling-Hammond, L., R. C. Wei, A. Andree, N. Richardson, and S. Orphanos. 2009. "Professional Learning in the Learning Profession: A Status Report on Teacher Development in the United States and Abroad." Report, National Staff Development Council, Washington, DC.

EQAP (Education Quality & Assessment Programme). 2022. *Pacific Islands Literacy and Numeracy Assessment 2021 Regional Report.* Suva, Fiji: Pacific Community. https://pilna.eqap.spc.int/2021/regional.

Evans, D. K., and F. Yuan. 2019. "Economic Returns to Interventions that Increase Learning." Policy Research Working Paper. World Bank, Washington, DC.

Ferreras, A., C. Kessel, and M.-H. Kim. 2015. *Mathematics Curriculum, Teacher Professionalism, and Supporting Policies in Korea and the United States: Summary of a Workshop.* Washington, DC: National Academies Press.

Foster, A., and M. R. Rosenzweig. 1996. "Technical Change and Human-Capital Returns and Investments: Evidence from the Green Revolution." *American Economic Review* 86 (4): 931–53.

Glewwe, P., E. Maïga, and Z. Zheng. 2014. "The Contribution of Education to Economic Growth: A Review of the Evidence, with Special Attention and an Application to Sub-Saharan Africa." *World Development* 59: 379–93.

Glewwe, P., Z. James, J. Lee, C. Rolleston, and K. Vu. 2021. "What Explains Vietnam's Exceptional Performance in Education Relative to Other Countries? Analysis of the Young Lives Data from Ethiopia, Peru, India and Vietnam." RISE Working Paper 21/078, Research on Improving Systems of Education (RISE), Oxford, UK.

Goh, H. H., H. M. Wong, and D. Kwek. 2023. "Home-Based Learning during School Closure in Singapore: Perceptions from the Language Classrooms." *Educational Research for Policy and Practice.* Published ahead of print, January 29, 2023. https://doi.org/10.1007/s10671-023-09329-4.

Hanushek, E. A., and L. Woessmann. 2015. "The Economic Impact of Educational Quality." In *Handbook of International Development and Education,* edited by P. Dixon, S. Humble, and C. Counihan, 6–19). Cheltenham, UK: Edward Elgar Publishing.

Hanushek, E. A., and L. Woessmann. 2021. "Education and Economic Growth." In *Oxford Research Encyclopedia of Economics and Finance.* Online collection, Oxford University Press. https://doi .org/10.1093/acrefore/9780190625979.013.651.

Hattie, J. A. 2009. *Visible Learning: A Synthesis of Over 800 Meta-Analyses Relating to Achievement.* Oxford, UK: Routledge.

Hickey, S., and N. Hossain, eds. 2019. *The Politics of Education in Developing Countries: From Schooling to Learning.* Oxford, UK: Oxford University Press.

Johnston, J., and K. Christopher. 2017. "Effectiveness of Interactive Satellite-Transmitted Instruction: Experimental Evidence from Ghanaian Primary Schools." CEPA Working Paper No. 17-08, Stanford Center for Education Policy Analysis, Stanford, CA.

Karachiwalla, N., and A. Park. 2017. "Promotion Incentives in the Public Sector: Evidence from Chinese Schools." *Journal of Public Economics* 146: 109–28.

Keefer, P. 2012. "Survey of Public Servants, Indonesia 2012." Survey data, World Bank Microdata Library, https://microdata.worldbank.org/index.php/catalog/5226.

Krueger, A. B., and M. Lindahl. 2001. "Education for Growth: Why and for Whom?" *Journal of Economic Literature* 39 (4): 1101–36.

Lai, K. 2019. "Teacher Practices in Mongolia: Results from the *Teach* Classroom Observation Study." Unpublished manuscript, World Bank, Washington, DC.

Li, H., Z. Liu, F. Yang, and L. Yu. 2023. "The Impact of Computer-Assisted Instruction on Student Performance: Evidence from the Dual-Teacher Program." SSRN Electronic Journal. https://doi.org/10.2139/ssrn.4360827.

Macdonald, K., S. Brinkman, W. Jarvie, M. Machuca-Sierra, K. McDonall, S. Messaoud-Galusi, S. Tapueluelu, and B. T. Vu. 2018. "Intervening at Home and Then at School: A Randomized Evaluation of Two Approaches to Improve Early Educational Outcomes in Tonga." Policy Research Paper 8682, World Bank, Washington, DC.

Macdonald, K., and B. T. Vu. 2018. "A Randomized Evaluation of a Low-Cost and Highly Scripted Teaching Method to Improve Basic Early Grade Reading Skills in Papua New Guinea." Policy Research Working Paper 8427, World Bank, Washington, DC.

Malaysia MOE (Ministry of Education). 2020. "Annual Report 2020: Malaysia Education Blueprint (2013–2025)." Report, MOE, Putrajaya, Malaysia.

Mankiw, N. G., D. Romer, and D. N. Weil. 1992. "A Contribution to the Empirics of Economic Growth." *Quarterly Journal of Economics* 107 (2): 407–37.

Molina, E., S. F. Fatima, T. Iva, and T. Wilichowski. 2018. "Teacher Practices in Mindanao: Result of the *Teach* Classroom Observation Study." Report No. 134535, World Bank, Washington, DC.

Montenegro, C. E., and H. A. Patrinos. 2014. "Comparable Estimates of Returns to Schooling Around the World." Policy Research Working Paper No. 7020, World Bank, Washington, DC.

Naik, G., C. Chitre, M. Bhalla, and J. Rajan. 2020. "Impact of Use of Technology on Student Learning Outcomes: Evidence from a Large-Scale Experiment in India." *World Development* 127: 104736.

OECD (Organisation for Economic Co-operation and Development). 2020a. "School Education during COVID-19: Were Teachers and Students Ready?" Japan country note, OECD, Paris. https://www.oecd.org/education/Japan-coronavirus-education-country-note.pdf.

OECD (Organisation for Economic Co-operation and Development). 2020b. *TALIS 2018 Results (Volume II): Teachers and School Leaders as Valued Professionals,* Annex C., table II.2.60, "Teachers' Absenteeism, by School Characteristics: Results Based on Responses of Lower Secondary Principals." Version 2. Last updated March 11, 2020. Paris: TALIS, OECD Publishing. https://doi.org/10.1787/1d0bc92a-en.

Pierskalla, J. H., and A. Sacks. 2020. "Personnel Politics: Elections, Clientelistic Competition and Teacher Hiring in Indonesia." *British Journal of Political Science* 50 (40): 1283–1305.

Popova, A., D. Evans, M. E. Breeding, and V. Arancibia. 2022. "Teacher Professional Development Around the World: The Gap between Evidence and Practice." *The World Bank Research Observer* 37 (1): 107–36.

Psacharopoulos, G., and H. A. Patrinos. 2018. "Returns to Investment in Education: A Decennial Review of the Global Literature." Policy Research Working Paper 8402, World Bank, Washington, DC.

Rosser, A., and M. Fahmi. 2018. "The Political Economy of Teacher Management Reform in Indonesia." *International Journal of Educational Development* 61: 72–81.

Schady, N., A. Holla, S. Sabarwal, J. Silva, and A. Y. Chang. 2023. *Collapse and Recovery: How the COVID-19 Pandemic Eroded Human Capital and What to Do about It.* Washington, DC: World Bank.

Snilstveit, B., J. Stevenson, D. Phillips, M. Vojtkova, E. Gallagher, T. Schmidt, H. Jobse, M. Geelen, M. G. Pastorello, and J. Eyers. 2015. "Interventions for Improving Learning Outcomes and Access to Education in Low- and Middle-Income Countries: A Systematic Review." Systematic Review 24, International Initiative for Impact Evaluation (3ie), London.

Tanaka, N., and L. Sondergaard. 2023. "Analysis of Teacher Stock versus Flow in Primary Education in East Asia and the Pacific Middle-Income Countries: A Simple Model and Results from Simulation between 2020 and 2030." Policy Research Working Paper 10479, World Bank, Washington, DC.

UIS (United Nations Educational, Scientific and Cultural Organization [UNESCO] Institute for Statistics). 2022. SDG 4 Data Explorer (browser). http://sdg4-data.uis.unesco.org/.

UN DESA (United Nations Department of Economic and Social Affairs). 2022. *World Population Prospects 2022: Summary of Results*. New York: United Nations.

UNESCO (United Nations Educational, Scientific and Cultural Organization). 2022. "National Distance Learning Programmes in Response to the COVID-19 Education Disruption: Case Study of the Republic of Korea." Case study, UNESCO, Paris.

UNICEF (United Nations Children's Fund). 2020. "Country Results," South-East Asia Primary Learning Metrics (SEA-PLM) 2019 dataset, SEA-PLM Secretariat, Bangkok. https://www.seaplm.org/index .php?option=com_content&view=article&id=56&Itemid=441.

UNICEF and SEAMEO (United Nations Children's Fund and Southeast Asian Ministers of Education Organization). 2020. *SEA-PLM 2019 Main Regional Report: Children's Learning in 6 Southeast Asian Countries*. Bangkok: UNICEF and SEAMEO.

van der Weide, R., C. Lakner, D. G. Mahler, A. Narayan, and R. Ramasubbaiah. 2021. "Intergenerational Mobility around the World." Policy Research Working Paper 9707, World Bank, Washington, DC.

Walter, C., and J. Briggs. 2012. "What Professional Development Makes the Most Difference to Teachers?" Report, University of Oxford Department of Education, Oxford University Press.

World Bank. 2015. "Thailand: Wanted: A Quality Education for All." Report No. AUS13333, World Bank, Bangkok.

World Bank. 2017. "SABER Service Delivery 2017, Measuring Education Service Delivery." Survey LAO _2017_SABER-SD_v01_M, Microdata Library, World Bank, Washington, DC.

World Bank. 2018a. "Growing Smarter: Learning and Equitable Development in East Asia and Pacific." Report No. 126675, World Bank, Washington, DC. https://doi.org/10.1596/978-1-4648-1261-3.

World Bank. 2018b. *World Development Report 2018: Learning to Realize Education's Promise*. Washington, DC: World Bank.

World Bank. 2019. "Teacher Practices in Mongolia: Results of the Teach Classroom Observation Study." Unpublished. World Bank, Washington, DC.

World Bank. 2021. *Long COVID: Supporting Analysis*. Report published in conjunction with *Long COVID: East Asia and Pacific Economic Update (October)*. Washington, DC: World Bank. https://openknowledge .worldbank.org/server/api/core/bitstreams/36c5ea96-c5c1-5d72-a7d2-a80bc7218b11/content.

World Bank. 2023a. "Education in Myanmar: Where Are We now?" World Bank, Washington, DC. https:// thedocs.worldbank.org/en/doc/716418bac40878ce262f57dfbd4eca05-0070012023/original/State-of -Education-in-Myanmar-July-2023.pdf.

World Bank. 2023b. "The Invisible Toll of COVID-19 on Learning." Indonesia Economic Prospects, June 23 edition, World Bank, Washington, DC.

World Bank. 2023c. "Raising Pasifika: Strengthening Government Finances to Enhance Human Capital in the Pacific. A Public Expenditure Review of Nine Pacific Island Countries." World Bank, Washington, DC.

World Bank and UIS (UNESCO Institute for Statistics). 2022. "Learning Poverty Global Database: Historical Data and Sub-Components." https://datacatalog.worldbank.org/search/dataset/0038947.

Yarrow, N., C. Abbey, S. Shen, and K. Alyono. Forthcoming. "Using Education Technology to Improve K–12 Student Learning in East Asia and Pacific: Promises and Limitations." Report, World Bank, Washington, DC.

Yarrow, N., R. Afkar, E. Masood, and B. Gauthier. 2020. "Measuring the Quality of MoRA's Education Services." Report, World Bank, Jakarta, Indonesia.

Yarrow, N., P. Cahu, M. E. Breeding, and R. Afkar. 2023. "What I Really Want: Policymaker Views on Education in East Asia and Pacific." Report, World Bank, Washington, DC.

The Learning Deficit in Middle-Income East Asia and Pacific | 1

"Learning poverty" rates in the region

Ask a typical 10-year-old student from a middle-income country in East Asia and Pacific to read a simple paragraph and answer basic questions from it, and there is a good chance they will not be able to. Even before the COVID-19 pandemic, more than half of 10-year-olds in most middle-income East Asia and Pacific countries could not read and understand an age-appropriate text. In eight countries (Cambodia, Kiribati, the Lao People's Democratic Republic (PDR), Myanmar, Papua New Guinea, the Philippines, Tonga, and Tuvalu) this "learning poverty" rate exceeded two-thirds (figure 1.1, panels a and b).[1] Even in Malaysia, a country poised to reach high-income status in the next several years, over 40 percent of 10-year-olds could not read and understand an age-appropriate text.

Globally, a country's per capita income is a strong predictor of the learning poverty rate. However, many East Asian and Pacific countries—especially the lower-middle income countries—have higher learning poverty rates than their per capita income levels would predict (figure 1.2). Several Southeast Asian and Pacific Island countries "underperform" in this regard by large margins. Even the region's best-performing middle-income countries have learning poverty rates considerably above those of East Asia's high-performing, high-income countries; Japan, the Republic of Korea, and Singapore have learning poverty of only 3–4 percent (figure 1.2).

Inequality of learning outcomes within countries

Data from the 2019 Southeast Asia Primary Learning Metrics (SEA-PLM)—an international student assessment covering Cambodia, Lao PDR, Malaysia, Myanmar, the Philippines, and Viet Nam—shows that in all six countries, students from disadvantaged socioeconomic backgrounds demonstrated lower learning proficiency on average than those from more advantaged backgrounds (figure 1.3). Based on international benchmarks, differences in learning proficiency between students in the top and bottom socioeconomic quintiles could represent more than two years of schooling in the most unequal settings.[2] Similar

FIGURE 1.1 **Many 10-year-old children lacked basic reading proficiency before the COVID-19 pandemic**

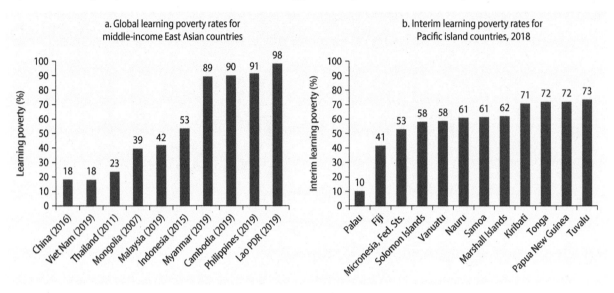

a. Global learning poverty rates for middle-income East Asian countries

b. Interim learning poverty rates for Pacific island countries, 2018

Sources: World Bank and UIS 2022 (panel a); estimates as described in Cahu and Sondergaard 2023 (panel b).
Note: Panel a: "Learning poverty" rates are the percentages of 10-year-olds who cannot read and understand a short, age-appropriate text. "Global" learning poverty rates, as opposed to "interim" rates, refer to official student assessment data reported for each country to the UNESCO Institute for Statistics (UIS). Panel b: Because no official learning poverty estimates had yet been provided to the UIS for middle-income Pacific island countries, "interim" estimates were generated from data from the Pacific Islands Literacy and Numeracy Assessment, with details described in Cahu and Sondergaard (2023). Details of these estimates, including the data used, can be found in Cahu and Sondergaard (2023).

FIGURE 1.2 **In many middle-income East Asian and Pacific countries, learning poverty rates exceed the levels their incomes would predict**

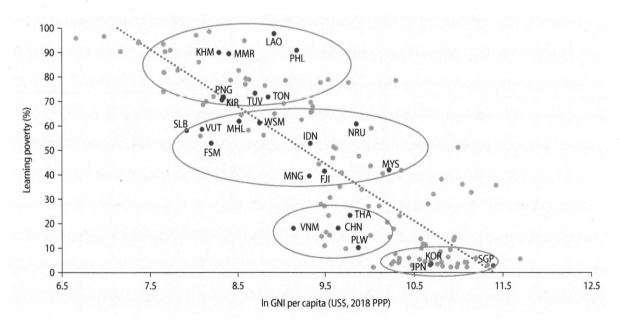

Sources: World Bank and UIS 2022; Cahu and Sondergaard 2023; World Development Indicators database.
Note: "Learning poverty" is the inability to read and understand a simple text by age 10. The countries' latest reported learning poverty rates are from varying years. Middle-income countries in East Asia and Pacific are designated by ISO alpha-3 code. Those shown as brown dots are middle-income countries from the East Asia and Pacific region, whereas those shown as orange dots are from other regions. Red dots designate high-income East Asian countries. GNI = gross national income; ln = natural logarithm; PPP = purchasing power parity.

FIGURE 1.3   Poorer students in Southeast Asia have worse basic learning outcomes than wealthier students

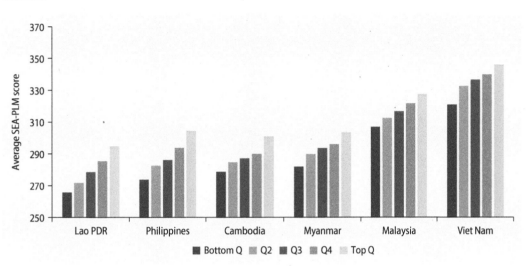

Source: World Bank estimates, using 2019 Southeast Asia Primary Learning Metrics (SEA-PLM) data.
Note: The chart shows average fifth-grade SEA-PLM assessment scores, by household socioeconomic status quintile (Q)—a nationally derived measure based on (a) highest parental occupation of either parent, (b) highest education level of either parent, and (c) family's home resources through the home resources scale (UNICEF and SEAMEO 2020, 66).

inequalities in learning outcomes are also observed between major urban areas and more remote rural settings in these countries.

Weak foundations for future learning

Weak foundational skills lead to poor outcomes later in education. Among those countries that participate in the Programme for International Student Assessment (PISA) tests of 15-year-olds in school in reading, mathematics, and science, several of the region's large middle-income economies (including Indonesia, Malaysia, the Philippines, and Thailand) all perform well below expectations given their per capita gross domestic product levels (figure 1.4, panel a). The exceptions are Viet Nam and four wealthy urban centers in China; however, both sets of results must be interpreted with caution—in the case of China, because other research indicates that human capital development is significantly worse in rural parts of the country (Rozelle and Hell 2020; World Bank 2019), and in the case of Viet Nam, because full international comparability of the 2018 PISA results could not be assured (OECD 2019).

Within countries, learning inequalities between poorer and wealthier students persist as children grow; in fact, they widen over time. Growing learning inequalities across socioeconomic groups reflect two separate but related phenomena: First, children from the poorest households are less likely to enroll and stay in school than those from wealthier households. Second, even when poorer students do enroll, their learning outcomes are significantly worse than those of their richer peers (figure 1.4, panel b). Again, the PISA results for China reflect the participation of only four wealthy urban centers and thus underestimate national inequality in learning outcomes across socioeconomic groups.[3]

FIGURE 1.4   **Several East Asia and Pacific countries underperform in basic learning outcomes among adolescents, with substantial inequalities across socioeconomic groups within countries**

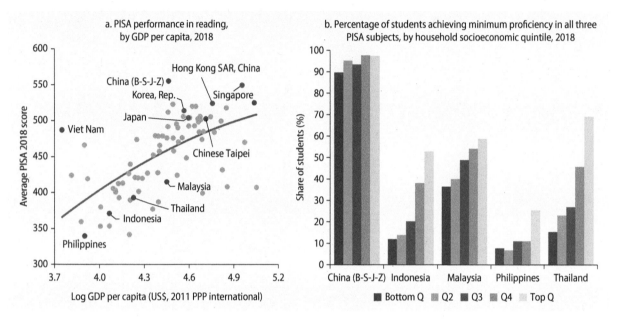

Sources: Cirera et al. 2021; World Bank estimates using OECD 2022.
Note: The Programme for International Student Assessment (PISA) measures 15-year-olds' knowledge and skills in reading, mathematics, and science. In 2018, PISA was administered in 79 participating countries and economies. "China (B-S-J-Z)" reflects test scores from Beijing, Shanghai, Jiangsu, and Zhejiang provinces only; they are not nationally representative. Panel a: Brown dots indicate middle-income East Asia and Pacific countries, and orange dots, other countries. Red dots designate high-income East Asian economies. There is theoretically no minimum or maximum PISA score; rather, the results are scaled to fit approximately normal distributions. In Organisation for Economic Co-operation and Development (OECD) countries, for example, the mean across countries is around 500 score points and standard deviations around 100 score points. Less than 2 percent of students across OECD countries reach scores above 700 points, and at most a handful of students in the PISA sample for any country reach scores above 800 points. Panel b: "Minimum proficiency" is defined as achievement of at least Level 2 scores on a 1–6 scale. Household socioeconomic status quintile (Q) is a nationally derived measure based on (a) highest parental occupation of either parent, (b) highest education level of either parent, and (c) family's home resources through the home resources scale (UNICEF and SEAMEO 2020, 66). GDP = gross domestic product; PPP = purchasing power parity.

The high cost of pandemic-related learning disruptions

Evidence from middle-income countries around the world indicates that school disruptions due to the COVID-19 pandemic have had high costs in terms of student learning losses. Although the extent of learning loss has differed across countries, a new global study finds that, for every month schools were closed, students averaged nearly one month of learning loss (Schady et al. 2023). Several country-specific studies also found the following pandemic-related results:

- *In Bangladesh,* 18 months of school closures resulted in a loss of 0.5–0.9 learning-adjusted years of schooling for the average student (Rahman and Sharma 2021).
- *In rural Chhattisgarh, India,* COVID-19–related school disruptions doubled the proportion of students in grades 2–4 who could not even recognize letters or basic numbers, comparing 2021 results with those of 2018 (ASER Centre 2022).
- *In South Africa,* second-grade students lost 57–70 percent of learning over one year relative to a prepandemic cohort, whereas fourth-grade students lost 56–60 percent (Ardington, Wills, and Kotze 2021).
- *On Mexico's Yucatán peninsula,* student test scores declined by 0.34–0.45 standard deviations in reading and 0.62–0.82 in mathematics (Hevia et al. 2022).
- *In the state of São Paulo, Brazil,* quarterly standardized test scores declined by an average of 0.32 standard deviations in 2020 compared with 2019 (Lichand and Doria 2022).[4]

To compensate for school closures, most countries in East Asia and Pacific implemented distance learning initiatives, which included offering classes online, on television, and on the radio. Many high-income countries such as Japan, Korea, and Singapore faced challenges with these adjustments and adapted their approaches over the period of school closures (OECD 2020; UNESCO 2022; and Goh, Wong, and Kwek 2023). However, efforts to substitute distance learning for face-to-face instruction appear to have had limited impact in offsetting disruptions in low- and middle-income countries.

Data indicate significant learning losses in East Asia and Pacific

Although direct evidence on learning loss from low- and middle-income East Asian and Pacific countries is scarce, new analyses indicate that pandemic-related learning losses have been substantial.

Student assessment data show declines

In Cambodia, for example, national sixth-grade learning assessment data in mathematics and Khmer language for 2013, 2016, and 2021 are available, enabling the report authors to assess COVID-19–related learning loss. Assessment scores rose slightly between 2013 and 2016, but they dropped substantially in both mathematics and Khmer between 2016 and 2021 (figure 1.5, panel a). The decline was larger for mathematics than for Khmer. For Khmer, student scores declined by 42.8 points on average—equivalent to an 8.4 percent (or 0.42 standard deviations) decrease relative to 2016. The average score for mathematics fell by 56 points, equivalent to an 11.3 percent (or 0.54 standard deviations) decline.

FIGURE 1.5 **Assessment scores in Cambodia and Indonesia indicate significant COVID-19–related declines in primary grade outcomes in language and mathematics**

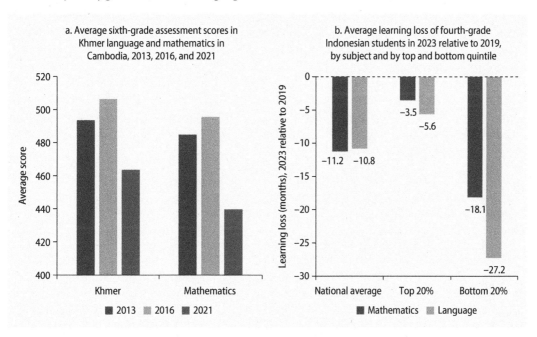

Sources: World Bank estimates, based on Cambodia's national assessment of sixth graders (panel a); World Bank 2023 (panel b).
Note: In panel b, the scores were standardized with the mean of 0 and standard deviation of 1. Based on the standardized score, students' performance was converted to the month-equivalent by using the internationally used rule of thumb; that is, an average student learning in a year is equal to about 0.3 of a standard deviation.

Similarly, in Indonesia, a new study finds that fourth-grade students in 2023 had lost the equivalent of 11.2 months in mathematics skills and 10.8 months in language skills compared with fourth-grade students in 2019 (World Bank 2023). The study also finds that students from the poorest households lost the most (figure 1.5, panel b).

Students' academic performance also declined in the Pacific islands, according to the 2021 Pacific Islands Literacy & Numeracy Assessment (PILNA) (EQAP 2021).[5] Average performance in numeracy, reading, and writing had been rising or stable among year 4 and year 6 students since PILNA's inception in 2012. Between 2018 and 2021, however, numeracy and reading scores declined. Average numeracy scores declined more than reading scores for both year 4 and year 6 students. The decline in year 4 numeracy scores was particularly striking: having increased from 486 in 2012 to 504 in 2018, average scores declined to 479 in 2021— that is, entirely wiping out the gain over the previous six years.

Although COVID-19 outbreaks did cause schooling disruptions in several Pacific island countries, isolating the impacts of the pandemic is difficult given the occurrence of several natural disasters in the Pacific during the period, including tsunamis, cyclones, and floods. Nevertheless, the observed declines in numeracy and reading underscore the importance of acting to address the consequences of these multiple shocks and, more generally, the frequent disruptions to schooling due to natural disasters in the subregion.

The pandemic's effect on attendance and dropout rates was more muted

Available data from the region suggests that the effect of the pandemic on school attendance and dropouts has been mixed. Beyond short-term learning losses, policy makers have been concerned that the pandemic increased school dropouts—an increase that, if not remedied, could amplify learning losses over time. However, evidence from the region suggests that the pandemic's impact on attendance and dropouts has been relatively muted, with some exceptions. This outcome is consistent with emerging evidence from other low- and middle-income regions (Schady et al. 2023).

Analysis of household survey or administrative data from Cambodia, Indonesia, Lao PDR, and Thailand indicates, for example, that enrollment or attendance levels have been stable, with no evidence of structural breaks between the prepandemic and pandemic periods. Not all countries in the region had stable enrollments, however. In the Philippines, Department of Education data indicate a 5.8 percent decline in enrollment in K–12 education between the 2019–20 and 2020–21 school years. These declines are in line with high-frequency phone survey data showing that by spring 2022, nearly 27 percent of households with school-age children reported that at least one child had dropped out of school (World Bank 2022a).

School closures widened the preexisting learning inequality gaps

The pandemic also exacerbated learning inequality in the region. For those children who remained engaged in educational activities during school closures, learning became more challenging during the pandemic, especially for the poor. Countries in East Asia and Pacific, like those around the world, employed a wide variety of distance learning modalities while schools were closed to in-person learning (World Bank 2021).

However, access to and use of these modalities, especially those relying on information technology, were uneven. Richer households had much greater access than poor ones to interactive learning opportunities, even though overall access levels were often low (figure 1.6). In some countries, such as Lao PDR and Myanmar, participation in interactive distance learning activities was extremely low—below 10 percent—among all segments of the student population. Across countries, even among students in richer households, participation was substantially below their educational participation before the pandemic, which had been close to universal.

FIGURE 1.6   **Poorer households had less access to interactive distance learning opportunities than wealthier households during the COVID-19 pandemic**

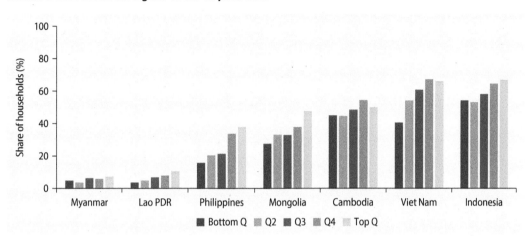

Source: World Bank 2021.
Note: The figure shows the share of households that had school-enrolled children before the COVID-19 pandemic who engaged in interactive distance learning, by country and household welfare quintile (Q) as calculated for each country using the methodology in Kim et al. (2021).

After schools closed, households and countries tried to compensate

Households tended to spend more on education, especially on tutoring and technology
To compensate for school closures, many households increased spending on education during the pandemic—on tutoring, improved internet connections, and to a lesser extent on computer equipment (figure 1.7). The highest share of households incurring additional expenditures (60 percent) was in Malaysia. The lowest was in Myanmar, where a little over 20 percent increased education-related spending during the pandemic, although this might reflect the broader economic and political situation.

The two most important categories of spending were tutoring (most important in Lao PDR and Myanmar) and improved internet connections (most important in Indonesia, Cambodia, and Malaysia). Except in Indonesia and Myanmar, expenditure on improved computer equipment (including tablets, cell phones, and the like) was also substantial.

Countries' public education spending tended to decrease
In contrast, the region's public education spending response to the pandemic was weak, with budgetary allocations declining—in constant price terms—in many countries. Globally, roughly 2.9 percent of countries' total COVID-19–related stimulus packages were dedicated to education (UNESCO 2021). The share was much lower in Asian and Pacific countries (0.41 percent), which was even lower than the shares observed in Latin America and the Caribbean (0.64 percent), Africa (0.82 percent), and the Arab States (1.25 percent).[6]

In fact, analysis of country-specific data from the region indicates that 9 of the 19 countries for which data are available decreased their public budgetary allocations (in constant prices) on education in 2020–21 relative to 2017–19 (figure 1.8). Some of the shifts were dramatic—with Samoa and Vanuatu increasing the government's allocations by nearly 30 percent (and Kiribati by even more); while Fiji, Lao PDR, Myanmar, and Tuvalu decreased budgetary allocations by 10 percent or more.[7] Combined with the data on increased household spending on education, the evidence suggests that the pandemic may have induced a shift in the financial burden of schooling from governments to households, at least in the short term.

FIGURE 1.7   **Many households reported increasing their spending on education because of COVID-19–related school closures, most notably on tutoring and improved internet connections**

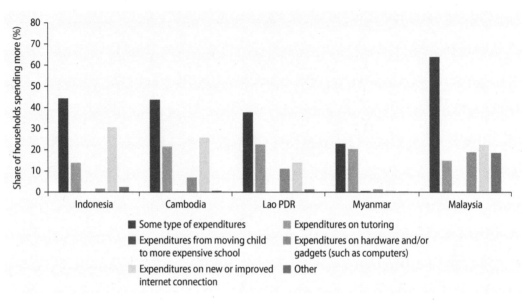

Source: World Bank estimates, based on World Bank 2022.
Note: The figure shows the share of households undertaking additional spending, by country and type of expenditure, based on responses to this question: Did you incur additional expenses out of your own pocket for your child's education because of the school closures during the pandemic? If so, on what? (a) Yes, on tutoring; (b) Yes, by moving my child to a more expensive school; (c) Yes, on hardware and/or gadgets (e.g., laptop, computer, tablet); (d) Yes, on a new or improved internet connection; (e) Yes, other, specify; (f) No; (g) Don't know.

FIGURE 1.8   **During the COVID-19 pandemic, public education sector budgets declined in half of East Asian and Pacific countries**

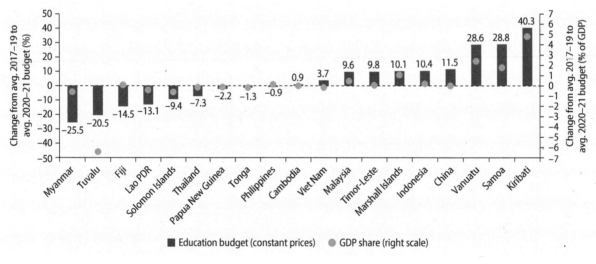

Source: World Bank estimates based on government budget documents.
Note: The figure shows changes in countries' education sector budget allocations between 2017–19 (before the COVID-19 pandemic) and 2020–21 (during the pandemic). Data are missing for some years for Lao PDR, Malaysia, Myanmar, and the Solomon Islands. GDP = gross domestic product.

After schools reopened, countries took remedial measures

Once schools reopened for face-to-face learning, many countries in the region initiated measures to address the pandemic-related learning disruptions. Measures have focused on several policy areas identified as important to learning recovery:[8]

- Assessing the learning situation
- Prioritizing teaching of the fundamentals
- Increasing the efficiency of instruction
- Ensuring children return to school
- Supporting student and teacher well-being.

Most of these five policy areas encompass multiple, often complementary, measures. Three-quarters of the surveyed East Asian and Pacific countries reported undertaking measures to adjust their curricula to focus on the fundamentals (figure 1.9). Half reported undertaking learning assessments and implementing measures to help students return to school—for example, through automatic reenrollment, community mobilization campaigns, and cash transfer programs to help prevent disadvantaged students from dropping out. However, a much smaller share of countries reported undertaking measures to increase the efficiency of instruction, including through teacher training or implementation of accelerated programs. The focus and intensity of countries' responses have also varied substantially across the region (figure 1.10).

FIGURE 1.9 **Countries in East Asia and Pacific took various measures in 2022 to address the education impacts of COVID-19 once schools reopened**

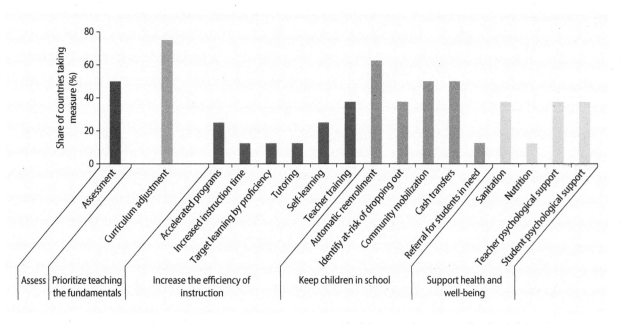

Source: World Bank calculations, based on 4th Survey on National Education Responses to COVID-19 School Closures 2022 (UIS, UNICEF, World Bank, and OECD 2022).
Note: The figure summarizes data collected from eight middle-income countries in East Asia and Pacific: Cambodia, China, Indonesia, Mongolia, Myanmar, the Philippines, Thailand, and the Solomon Islands. Data on the COVID-19 pandemic's impacts on schooling and country responses were also collected for Tuvalu and Vanuatu; however, the figure excludes those two countries because they reported schools being completely or partially closed for less than a total of 15 days between March 2020 and March 2022, and neither country reported taking any specific actions focused on learning recovery.

FIGURE 1.10   **The focus and intensity of countries' COVID-19 response measures have varied substantially across the East Asia and Pacific region**

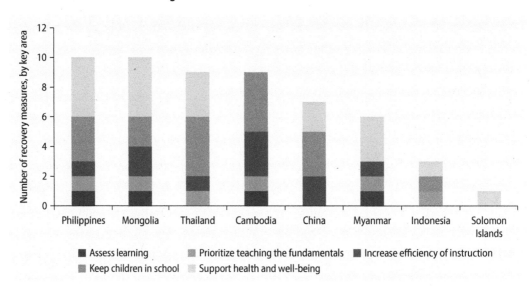

Source: World Bank calculations, based on 4th Survey on National Education Responses to COVID-19 School Closures 2022 (UIS, UNICEF, World Bank, and OECD 2022).
Note: The figure summarizes data collected from eight middle-income countries in East Asia and Pacific: Cambodia, China, Indonesia, Mongolia, Myanmar, the Philippines, Thailand, and the Solomon Islands. Data on COVID-19 pandemic's impacts on schooling and country responses were also collected for Tuvalu and Vanuatu; however, the figure excludes those two countries because they reported schools being completely or partially closed for less than a total of 15 days between March 2020 and March 2022, and neither country reported taking any specific actions focused on learning recovery.

Bold action will be needed to ensure that pandemic-related learning disruptions do not lead to permanent losses in human capital and, with it, lost economic opportunities for individuals, families, and countries' economies. In the absence of decisive action, students might never fully rebuild their human capital, thus bearing lifelong costs of the pandemic. A recent global study estimates that, absent corrective actions, COVID-19–induced learning losses could cost the current generation of students in low and middle-income countries as much as $17 trillion in lifetime earnings, or the equivalent of 14 percent of today's global GDP (World Bank, UNESCO, and UNICEF 2021).

However, if policy makers take bold action in line with the growing international consensus, it is possible for students to recover lost learning and even to go beyond the prepandemic status quo (Schady et al. 2023). Indeed, reforms that strengthen teaching and that better target instruction to students' levels are both essential to addressing short-term learning losses (box 1.1) and critical to strengthening long-term learning outcomes. And better learning outcomes will be critical to propelling the future development of countries across the East Asia and Pacific region.

BOX 1.1   **Six essential actions toward recovering learning losses from the COVID-19 pandemic**

A recent World Bank report highlights six sets of actions that will be essential to countries' efforts to ensure that COVID-19–related learning losses do not result in permanent losses of human capital (Schady et al. 2023).

To address learning losses

- *Keeping schools open and restoring or increasing instructional hours.* More time in school critical to enabling students to make up lost learning.
- *Assessing learning and matching instruction to students' levels.* Measuring learning losses is crucial to understanding the extent of those losses and enabling teachers to develop learning plans that are well adapted to students' needs. Evidence indicates that programs that adapt instruction to students' levels are effective in promoting learning (Banerjee et al. 2017; Duflo, Kiessel, and Lucas 2020). Indeed, initiatives that focus on "teaching at the right level" in Botswana and India are showing promising results in recouping learning losses (Pratham 2022; Schady et al. 2023).
- *Focusing on foundations and streamlining the curriculum.* In many countries, school curricula focus on a broad range of subjects, trading off breadth for depth. Streamlining curricula, with a focus on foundational knowledge, can thus help accelerate learning recovery. Such an approach has been taken in South Africa as part of the government's Curriculum Recovery Plan (Giannini, Jenkins, and Saavedra 2022).

To minimize dropouts

- *Tracking students at risk of dropping out.* Identifying and keeping track of at-risk students is important to ensuring that schools can intervene early to prevent COVID-19–related losses from becoming permanent. Several middle-income countries in Latin America (including Brazil, Chile, and Peru) have developed early warning systems that use information on attendance, performance, and other factors to predict a student's risk of dropping out (UIS, UNICEF, World Bank, and OECD 2022).
- *Providing incentives for at-risk students to remain in school.* Scholarships and fee waivers can be effective in reducing dropouts, as was found in Indonesia during the Asian financial crisis (Cameron 2009). Cash and in-kind transfers (such as school feeding programs) have also been effective in promoting school attendance.

To enable effective action

- *Generating political commitment for the recovery of learning.* Implementing a program to recover lost learning is not only a technical undertaking but also a political one. It will require leadership at the highest levels of government as well as political alignment across countries' educational services delivery chain. This includes building support for concerted action among teachers and parents.

Notes

1. "Learning poverty," a concept and indicator developed by the World Bank and the United Nations Educational, Scientific and Cultural Organization (UNESCO) Institute for Statistics, is defined as the inability to read and understand a simple, age-appropriate text by age 10. No official learning poverty estimates exist for middle-income Pacific island countries. To address this knowledge gap, and in support of better learning diagnostics, the authors have generated interim estimates of learning poverty in the Pacific islands. Details of the estimates, including the data used, can be found in Cahu and Sondergaard (2023).

2. The differences in learning proficiency are from World Bank estimates, using 2019 SEA-PLM data. "Quintile" in this chapter refers to household socioeconomic status quintile—a nationally derived measure based on (a) highest parental occupation of either parent, (b) highest education level of either parent, and (c) family's home resources through the home resources scale (UNICEF and SEAMEO 2020, 66).
3. There are gender inequalities too, with boys far behind girls in virtually all outcome measures and in all countries (UNICEF and SEAMEO 2020; EQAP 2021).
4. The same study also found that the reopening of schools in some São Paulo municipalities in the fourth quarter of 2020 resulted in an increase of test scores by 20 percent compared with municipalities where schools remained closed (Lichand and Doria 2022).
5. PILNA assesses the numeracy, reading, and writing capabilities of year 4 and year 6 students in 15 Pacific island economies: the Cook Islands, Fiji, Kiribati, the Marshall Islands, the Federated States of Micronesia, Nauru, Niue, Palau, Papua New Guinea, Samoa, the Solomon Islands, Tokelau, Tonga, Tuvalu, and Vanuatu. Only Pacific-wide PILNA 2021 results were available as of the time of writing; no country-specific results had yet been released. For more information, see the PILNA website: https://pilna.eqap.spc.int/.
6. In the UNESCO data, "Asia and the Pacific" also includes countries in the World Bank's "South Asia" region. UNESCO's "Arab States" region includes the following 19 States Parties to the Convention Concerning the Protection of the World Cultural and Natural Heritage: Algeria, Bahrain, the Arab Republic of Egypt, Iraq, Jordan, Kuwait, Lebanon, Libya, Mauritania, Morocco, Oman, Qatar, Saudi Arabia, Sudan, the Syrian Arab Republic, Tunisia, the United Arab Emirates, West Bank and Gaza, and the Republic of Yemen ("Arab States," UNESCO World Heritage Convention website: https://whc.unesco.org/en/arabstates/.
7. As discussed in World Bank 2022b: Myanmar Budget Brief (November 2022), following the military coup, budgetary allocations to education has continued to shrink in Myanmar. In FY2022, education accounted for just 5.6 percent of the total government spending, the lowest since FY2012.
8. A recent report coauthored by UNESCO, UNICEF, the OECD, and the World Bank introduces the RAPID framework and discusses related policy measures in detail. For more information, see World Bank, Bill & Melinda Gates Foundation, FCDO, UNESCO, UNICEF, and USAID (2022).

References

Ardington, C., G. Wills, and J. Kotze. 2021. "COVID-19 Learning Losses: Early Grade Reading in South Africa." *International Journal of Educational Development* 86 (5): 102480.

ASER Centre. 2022. "Annual Status of Education Report Chhattisgarh (Rural) 2021." Report, Annual Status of Education Report (ASER) Centre, New Delhi.

Banerjee, A., R. Banerji, J. Berry, E. Duflo, H. Kannan, S. Mukerji, Marc Shotland, and M. Walton. 2017. "From Proof of Concept to Scalable Policies: Challenges and Solutions, with an Application." *Journal of Economic Perspectives* 31 (4): 73–102. https://doi.org/10.1257/jep.31.4.73.

Cahu, P., and L. M. Sondergaard. 2023. "Estimating Interim Learning Poverty for Pacific Island Countries." World Bank, Washington, DC.

Cameron, L. 2009. "Can a Public Scholarship Program Successfully Reduce School Dropouts in a Time of Economic Crisis? Evidence from Indonesia." *Economics of Education Review* 28 (3): 308–17.

Cirera, X., A. D. Mason, F. de Nicola, S. Kuriakose, D. S. Mare, and T. T. Tran. 2021. *The Innovative Imperative for Developing East Asia.* World Bank East Asia and Pacific Regional Report. Washington, DC: World Bank.

Duflo, A., J. Kiessel, and A. Lucas. 2020. "Experimental Evidence on Alternative Policies to Increase Learning at Scale." Working Paper 27298, National Bureau of Economic Research, Cambridge, MA.

EQAP (Education Quality & Assessment Programme). 2021. *Pacific Islands Literacy & Numeracy Assessment 2021 Regional Report.* Suva, Fiji: Pacific Community. https://pilna.eqap.spc.int/2021/regional.

Giannini, S., R. Jenkins, and J. Saavedra. 2022. "100 Weeks into the Pandemic: The Importance of Keeping Schools Open and Investing in Learning Recovery Programs." *Education for Global Development* (blog), January 24. https://blogs.worldbank.org/education/100-weeks-pandemic-importance-keeping -schools-open-and-investing-learning-recovery.

Goh, H. H., H. M. Wong, and D. Kwek. 2023. "Home-Based Learning during School Closure in Singapore: Perceptions from the Language Classrooms." *Educational Research for Policy and Practice*. Published ahead of print, January 29, 2023. https://doi.org/10.1007/s10671-023-09329-4.

Hevia, F. J., S. Vergara-Lope, A. Velásquez-Durán, and D. Calderón. 2022. "Estimation of the Fundamental Learning Loss and Learning Poverty Related to the COVID-19 Pandemic in Mexico." *International Journal of Educational Development* 88 (1):102515.

Kim, L. Y., M. A. Lugo, A. D. Mason, and I. Uochi. 2021. "Inequality under COVID-19: Taking Stock of High-Frequency Data for East Asia and the Pacific." Policy Research Working Paper 9859, World Bank, Washington, DC.

Lichand, G., and C. A. Doria. 2022. "The Lasting Impacts of Remote Learning in the Absence of Remedial Policies: Evidence from Brazil." Paper, Department of Economics, University of Zurich. Retrieved from Fundação Getulio Vargas Library System: https://sistema.bibliotecas.fgv.br.

OECD (Organisation for Economic Co-operation and Development). 2019. "Programme for International Student Assessment (PISA) Results from PISA 2018: Vietnam." Country note, OECD, Paris. https:// www.oecd.org/pisa/publications/PISA2018_CN_VNM.pdf.

OECD (Organisation for Economic Co-operation and Development). 2020. "School Education during COVID-19: Were Teachers and Students Ready?" Japan country note, OECD, Paris. https://www.oecd .org/education/Japan-coronavirus-education-country-note.pdf.

OECD (Organisation for Economic Co-operation and Development). 2022. PISA 2018 Database, OECD, Paris. https://www.oecd.org/pisa/data/2018database.

Pratham. 2022. "Teaching at the Right Level." Article, Pratham, New Delhi. https://www.pratham.org /about/teaching-at-the-right-level.

Rahman, T., and U. Sharma. 2021. "A Simulation of COVID-19 School Closure Impact on Student Learning in Bangladesh." Note (Report No. 155962), World Bank, Washington, DC.

Rozelle, S., and N. Hell. 2020. *Invisible China: How the Urban-Rural Divide Threatens China's Rise.* Chicago: University of Chicago Press.

Schady, N., A. Holla, S. Sabarwal, J. Silva, and A. Y. Chang. 2023. *Collapse and Recovery: How the COVID-19 Pandemic Eroded Human Capital and What to Do about It.* Washington, DC: World Bank.

UIS, UNICEF, World Bank, and OECD (UNESCO Institute for Statistics, United Nations Children's Fund, World Bank, and Organisation for Economic Co-operation and Development). 2022. "From Learning Recovery to Education Transformation: Insights and Reflections from the 4th Survey on National Education Responses to COVID-19 School Closures." Survey report, UIS, Montreal; UNICEF, New York; World Bank, Washington, DC; OECD, Paris.

UNESCO (United Nations Educational, Scientific and Cultural Organization). 2021. "Uneven Global Education Stimulus Risks Widening Learning Disparities." Document, Section of Education Policy, UNESCO, Paris.

UNESCO (United Nations Educational, Scientific and Cultural Organization). 2022. "National Distance Learning Programmes in Response to the COVID-19 Education Disruption: Case Study of the Republic of Korea." Education 2030 case study, UNESCO, Paris.

UNICEF and SEAMEO (United Nations Children's Fund and Southeast Asian Ministers of Education Organization). 2020. *SEA-PLM 2019 Main Regional Report: Children's Learning in 6 Southeast Asian Countries.* Bangkok: UNICEF and SEAMEO. https://www.seaplm.org/PUBLICATIONS/regional%20 results/SEA-PLM%202019%20Main%20Regional%20Report.pdf.

World Bank. 2019. "Ending Learning Poverty: What Will It Take?" Report, World Bank, Washington, DC.

World Bank. 2021. *Long COVID: Supporting Analysis.* Report published in conjunction with *Long COVID: East Asia and Pacific Economic Update (October).* Washington, DC: World Bank. https://openknowledge.worldbank.org/server/api/core/bitstreams/36c5ea96-c5c1-5d72-a7d2 -a80bc7218b11/content.

World Bank. 2022a. "High-Frequency Phone Surveys." Microdata Library collection, World Bank, Washington, DC. https://microdata.worldbank.org/index.php/catalog/hfps/?page=1&ps=15 &repo=hfps.

World Bank. 2022b. "Myanmar Budget Brief." World Bank, Washington, DC. https://documents1.worldbank
.org/curated/en/099335012232233060/pdf/P17910601de02e0880b23b076d6f795c50d.pdf.

World Bank. 2023. "The Invisible Toll of COVID-19 on Learning." Indonesia Economic Prospects, June 23
edition, World Bank, Washington, DC.

World Bank, Bill & Melinda Gates Foundation, FCDO, UNESCO, UNICEF, and USAID (UK Foreign,
Commonwealth and Development Office; United Nations Educational, Scientific and Cultural
Organization; United Nations Children's Fund; and United States Agency for International
Development). 2022. "Guide for Learning Recovery and Acceleration: Using the RAPID Framework
to Address COVID-19 Learning Losses and Build Forward Better." Policy guidance document,
World Bank, Washington, DC.

World Bank and UIS (UNESCO Institute for Statistics). 2022. "Learning Poverty Global Database:
Historical Data and Sub-Components." https://datacatalog.worldbank.org/search/dataset/0038947.

World Bank, UNESCO, and UNICEF (United Nations Educational, Scientific and Cultural Organization
and United Nations Children's Fund). 2021. The State of the Global Education Crisis: A Path to
Recovery. Washington, DC: World Bank, UNESCO, and UNICEF.

Better Teaching, Improved Learning, and Higher Productivity | 2

Importance of good teachers to student learning

This report is motivated by the links from more effective teaching to improved student learning and from improved student learning to higher labor productivity and economic growth. Teachers play a central role in children's learning. Strong basic skills contribute directly to increased labor productivity but also provide a critical foundation for the development of more advanced skills. Such advanced skills enable firms to adopt new technologies and to innovate, which help further propel productivity growth.

Multiple household and school-level factors affect student learning. The most important predictor of learning outcomes remains a child's family background, including the parents' income and education levels as well as a child's nutrition, health, cognitive, and socioemotional development in the early years of life. Research over the past decade indicates, however, that once a child starts school, no single factor is as critical as the quality of their teachers (Béteille and Evans 2021; Bruns and Luque 2015).

Evidence from a range of countries, and grade levels, shows that going from a low-performing teacher to a high-performing one increases student learning dramatically. The effect has been measured—from more than 0.2 standard deviations in Viet Nam to more than 0.9 standard deviations in India, the equivalent of multiple years of schooling (Carneiro et al. 2021; Evans and Yuan 2018). In Viet Nam, differences in teaching quality mean that an average second-grade student can end up in either the top third or the bottom third of the class by the end of fifth grade, depending on whether they have benefited from high-quality or low-quality teachers during those school years (figure 2.1, panel a). Data from India indicate that the impact of high-performing versus low-performing teachers could be even larger: an average student could either end up in the top or the bottom 12 percent of the class depending on teaching quality.[1]

Assessment data from middle-income countries in Southeast Asia reinforce the message regarding the importance of teachers. Better teaching practices are consistently associated with better student learning outcomes in mathematics (controlling for student and school characteristics), according to these data from the Southeast Asia Primary Learning Metrics (SEA-PLM) (figure 2.1, panel b).

FIGURE 2.1   **Assessment data show that teacher quality is central to student learning**

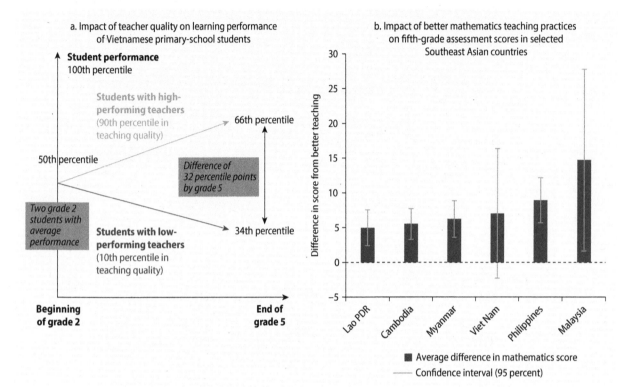

Sources: World Bank estimates based on Carneiro et al. 2022 (panel a) and 2019 Southeast Asia Primary Learning Metrics (SEA-PLM) data (panel b).
Note: Panel a compares the effects on two "average" (50th percentile) second-grade students of having either low-performance or high-performance teachers from second grade through fifth grade. If a student had 90th percentile teachers rather than 10th percentile ones, the student would be in the top third of the class, rather than the bottom third, by the time the student finished fifth grade. Panel b shows the estimated effects of "better teaching practices" on fifth-grade students' mathematics proficiency. Practices that correlate positively with mathematics scores are reflected in student questionnaire responses such as "I know what my teacher expects me to do"; "My teacher is easy to understand"; "I am interested in what my teacher says"; "My teacher gives me interesting things to do"; and "My teacher encourages me to do extra mathematics exercises in class." The 2019 SEA-PLM data cover only the six countries shown.

Productivity and growth gains from greater learning

A significant body of research shows that education confers a broad range of economic benefits on low- and middle-income economies (World Bank 2018). By raising human capital, education increases people's incomes and employability, improves economic mobility, and enables families to escape poverty (figure 2.2). It increases individuals' and families' resilience to shocks. In economies with large informal sectors, education is associated with greater access to full-time jobs in the formal sector.

Higher learning and skills boost firm-level productivity, technology, and innovation

The skills students obtain thanks to good teachers are associated with greater productivity, technology adoption, and innovation. Analysis of agricultural productivity during the Green Revolution in Asia underscored the importance of basic education in enabling farmers to make more efficient allocation decisions in the face of technological change (Foster and Rosenzweig 1996).[2]

FIGURE 2.2 **Education is consistently associated with higher earnings**

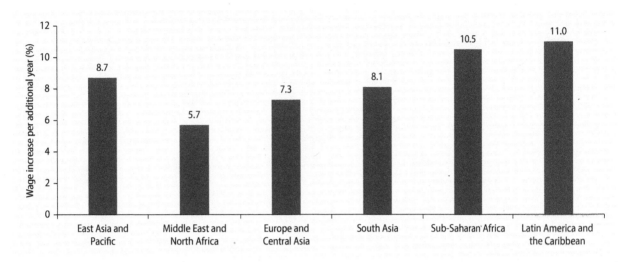

Source: Psacharopoulos and Patrinos 2018.
Note: The figure shows the average percentage increase in wages associated with each additional year (beyond 0) of schooling in low- and middle-income countries, by region. Regional country groups are defined by World Bank classifications.

Higher levels of education and skills also raise firm productivity, increasing technology adoption and enabling innovation in manufacturing. One study of manufacturing firms in urban China estimated, for example, that an additional year of school raised workers' marginal product by 30.1 percent (Fleisher et al. 2011). A separate study of manufacturing firms across China found that increases in employee education—following an exogenous, policy-induced increase in schooling—resulted in greater total factor productivity (TFP) growth, technology adoption, and research and development (R&D) investment in firms operating in more human capital-intensive industries (Che and Zhang 2017), as shown in figure 2.3. Similarly, a study of firms in 10 Organisation for Economic Co-operation and Development (OECD) countries found that greater cognitive skills among workers and managers raised firm productivity, particularly among enterprises operating some distance from the productivity frontier (Criscuolo et al. 2021).

Improving education will help drive country-level productivity growth

Improving educational outcomes—learning and skills—will be critical to improving countries' economic performance given the array of challenges now facing the region, including slowing productivity growth. Despite a history of strong growth performance before the COVID-19 pandemic, countries in middle-income East Asia and Pacific currently still face important productivity challenges. As in countries elsewhere around the world, productivity growth has slowed in East Asian and Pacific countries over the past decade. Indeed, the region has experienced the second steepest slowdown in labor productivity growth of all emerging markets and developing economies since the 2008–09 global financial crisis (World Bank 2020).

A decomposition of productivity growth in the region shows that the slowdown largely reflects weaker TFP growth (figure 2.4). Uncertainty in the global trade environment, rapid technological advances, the COVID-19 shock, and most recently, the Russian Federation's invasion of Ukraine all raise questions about whether the region's labor-intensive, outward-oriented growth model will be sufficient to propel it through COVID-19 pandemic recovery to robust and sustained growth. Indeed, recent World Bank analysis suggests that middle-income

FIGURE 2.3   **Education increases firm productivity, technology adoption, and innovation**

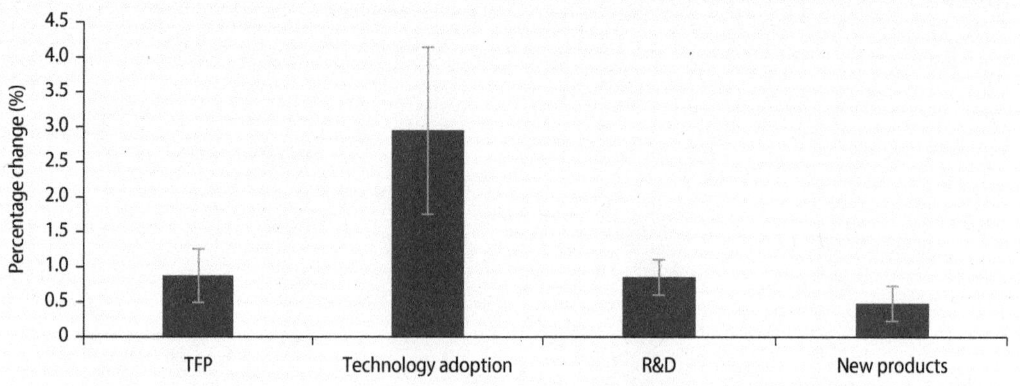

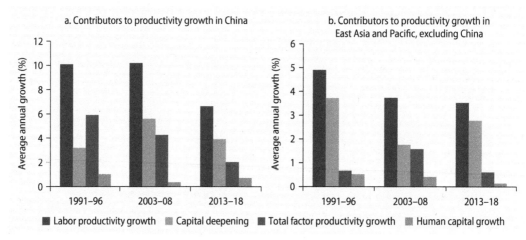

Source: Adapted from Che and Zhang 2017.
Note: The figure shows the average increases (in percent) resulting from a 1 percentage point increase in the share of college graduates employed in Chinese manufacturing firms—the impact of a policy-induced surge in China's college-educated workforce that took effect starting in 2003. The analysis uses a difference-in-difference approach and, in general, the measured impacts are compared before and after 2003. TFP refers to total factor productivity; "technology adoption" to the value of firm imports of high-technology capital goods; R&D to firm-level research and development spending; and "new products" to the value of new products introduced by the firm. Error bars show "robust standard errors" clustered at the firm level. All the results shown are significant at the 1 percent level.

FIGURE 2.4   **Labor productivity and TFP growth were declining in the region prior to the COVID-19 pandemic**

a. Contributors to productivity growth in China

b. Contributors to productivity growth in East Asia and Pacific, excluding China

■ Labor productivity growth   ■ Capital deepening   ■ Total factor productivity growth   ■ Human capital growth

Sources: Cirera et al. 2021, using data from the Conference Board; Asian Productivity Organization (APO) Database 2019, version 2 (https://www.apo-tokyo .org/wedo/productivity-measurement/); Penn World Table (PWT) version 9.1 data; van der Eng 2009; World Bank calculations.
Note: Labor productivity is measured as GDP per worker. PWT data were used as the baseline. When PWT (version 9.1) data were not available, the APO Database 2019 (version 2) was used. Conference Board data were used for 2018. Panel b shows weighted averages calculated using GDP weights at 2010 prices. Countries included are Cambodia, Indonesia, Lao PDR, Malaysia, Mongolia, Myanmar, the Philippines, Thailand, and Viet Nam. For Indonesia, capital stock was calculated by World Bank staff, extending data from van der Eng (2009). TFP = total factor productivity.

East Asian and Pacific countries will need more productivity- and innovation-led engines of growth in the future (Cirera et al. 2021; World Bank 2023).

Education, reflected in increased skills, is associated with faster growth

Education—and the skills it confers—also contributes to higher gross domestic product (GDP) growth. Although data and methodological challenges have made it difficult to analyze the links between education and growth, the collection of evidence makes a convincing case that higher levels of education are associated with faster growth.[3] An analysis of state-level data from the United States finds, for example, that exogenous increases in educational investments positively affected growth, with the effects varying depending on the type of education and a state's distance from the technological frontier (Aghion et al. 2009).

Cross-country analysis reveals a robust relationship between economic growth and the cognitive skills conferred by education (measured by test scores)—indeed, a substantially stronger relationship than between growth and years of schooling (figure 2.5; see also Hanushek and Woessmann 2015). Such analyses highlight that the key channel through which education raises growth is through its impacts on learning and skills development.[4]

Raising education quality—and thus learning outcomes—will thus be critical to reaping the productivity and growth benefits of education in middle-income East Asia and Pacific. Hanushek and Woessmann (2021) find that strengthening basic skills in middle- and high-income economies would have a substantially larger effect on GDP growth than would achieving universal access to education in those economies—although increasing both skills and access would have the largest effects (figure 2.6).

Simulations, using the World Bank's Long-Term Growth Model (LTGM), produce similar findings for middle-income East Asian and Pacific countries (Mendes, Pennings, and Fiuratti 2022). Although the effects of raising education quality on growth in any given year are modest, they are persistent, so the cumulative effects are substantial in the long run. By 2050, GDP levels could be an estimated 7 percent higher, on average, and as much as 16 percent higher in the case of the Philippines.[5] The LTGM also highlights that it will become increasingly difficult for countries to compensate for the low quality of education with higher investment in physical capital, given that the higher investment rates required tend to reduce the marginal productivity of capital over time.

FIGURE 2.5 **Learning and associated skills development, not simply years of schooling, contributes to higher economic growth**

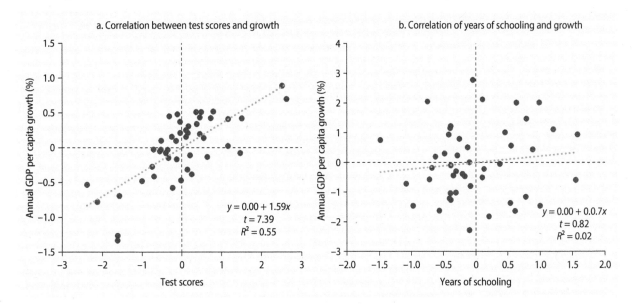

Source: World Bank 2018, 46.
Note: The scatterplots show, by country, annual average per capita growth in GDP, 1970–2015, and average test scores conditional on initial GDP per capita and years of schooling completed. They show a global sample of countries, albeit a subset based on availability of the relevant data. GDP = gross domestic product.

FIGURE 2.6   **Increasing education quality, and thus basic skills, is particularly important for GDP growth**

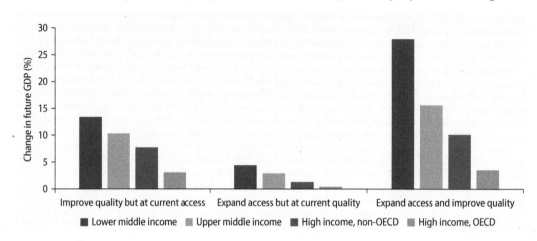

Source: Hanushek and Woessman 2021.
Note: The figure shows the projected average economic gains (percentage increase in future GDP) in middle- and high-income countries from improving the workforce's cognitive skills, by country income group (World Bank classifications). Improvement in education "quality" is measured by rising test scores, such as in the Programme for International Student Assessment (PISA) or the Trends in International Mathematics and Science Study (TIMSS). Expansion of "access" refers to ensuring school access for all children through the lower secondary levels. Raising cognitive skills of the workforce can be achieved by raising education quality and by giving children more years of schooling. OECD = Organisation for Economic Co-operation and Development.

Summary

Strengthening basic skills is a necessary foundation for building more advanced skills. While much of the evidence on education, productivity, and growth focuses on higher levels of education, developing a strong foundation of basic skills remains a priority in countries with high learning poverty and poor adolescent learning outcomes. Building labor forces with more advanced skills will be increasingly important as technology continues to advance. Nevertheless, strengthening basic skills can yield important productivity gains in the meantime. As the research on the Green Revolution highlights, even basic education contributes to people's ability to adopt and benefit from technology. Building a strong basic skills foundation is hence of immediate economic importance in middle-income East Asia and Pacific, where the diffusion of existing technologies lags. For example, in Viet Nam, where most firms use basic production techniques, even modest increases in the adoption and use of existing technologies raise firms' labor productivity (Cirera et al. 2021).

Without securing foundational skills through basic education, countries' investments in other parts of the education sector are undermined. Students who have not acquired foundational skills, who cannot read fluently, will be unable to acquire more advanced skills at the secondary school level. Investments in secondary education will therefore be less efficient—either because secondary schools must perform remediation for what students should have learned in primary school or because students' rate of acquiring new skills will be much less than expected by the countries' curricula.

Notes

1. World Bank estimates. See Sanders and Rivers (1996) for related analysis for the United States, which shows a 53-percentile gap over three years between students taught by high-performing and those taught by low-performing teachers.
2. The Green Revolution, also known as the Third Agricultural Revolution, refers to the introduction of new high-yielding seed varieties in the mid-1960s, which contributed to significantly higher agricultural

productivity, especially when combined with modern chemical fertilizers, pesticides, and controlled irrigation. Productivity using Green Revolution technologies differed in important ways depending on farmers' ability to make appropriate use of these new agricultural inputs and technologies.

3. See Barrow and Keeney (2001); Cohen and Soto (2007); Glewwe, Maïga, and Zheng (2014); Hanushek and Woessman (2015); Krueger and Lindahl (2001); and Mankiw, Romer, and Weil (1992).

4. Hanushek and Woessmann (2015) examine a number of "threats" to identifying a causal relationship between skills and growth that are discussed in the literature, including possible confounding factors (omitted variables) and potential reverse causality. Their results are robust to a number of tests and alternative empirical specifications.

5. For details on the long-term effects on GDP growth, see appendix A.

References

Aghion, P., L. Boustan, C. Hoxby, and J. Vandenbussche. 2009. "The Causal Impact of Education on Economic Growth: Evidence from US." Working paper, Harvard University, Cambridge, MA.

Barrow, R., and P. Keeney. 2001. "Lifelong Learning and Personal Fulfillment." In *International Handbook on Lifelong Learning,* edited by D. A. Chapman. London: Kluwer.

Béteille, T., and D. K. Evans. 2021. "Successful Teachers, Successful Students: Recruiting and Supporting Society's Most Crucial Profession." Report No. 164810, World Bank, Washington, DC.

Bruns, B., and J. Luque. 2015. *Great Teachers: How to Raise Student Learning in Latin America and the Caribbean.* Washington, DC: World Bank.

Carneiro, P., P. Glewwe, A. Guha, and S. Krutikova. 2021. "What Determines Teacher Quality in a High-Performing Education System? Value-Added Estimates for Primary Schools in Vietnam." Unpublished manuscript. https://csef.it/wp-content/uploads/Anusha-Guha.pdf.

Carneiro, P., P. Glewwe, A. Guha, and S. Krutikova. 2022. "Unpacking the Black Box of School Quality." Unpublished manuscript. https://drive.google.com/file/d/1MQDGSL5nan1v7Mry29XgJ6T5P7NQZbIf/view?pli=1.

Che, Y., and L. Zhang. 2017. "Human Capital, Technology Adoption and Firm Performance: Impacts of China's Higher Education Expansion in the Late 1990s." *The Economic Journal* 128 (614): 2282–2320.

Cirera, X., A. D. Mason, F. de Nicola, S. Kuriakose, D. S. Mare, and T. T. Tran. 2021. *The Innovation Imperative for Developing East Asia.* World Bank East Asia and Pacific Regional Report. Washington, DC: World Bank.

Cohen, D., and M. Soto. 2007. "Growth and Human Capital: Good Data, Good Results." *Journal of Economic Growth* 12 (1): 51–76.

Criscuolo, C., P. Gal, T. Leidecker, F. Losma, and G. Nicoletti. 2021. "The Role of Telework for Productivity during and post-Covid-19: Results from an OECD Survey Among Managers and Workers." Organisation for Economic Co-operation and Development (OECD) Productivity Working Papers No. 31, OECD Publishing, Paris.

Evans, D. K., and F. Yuan. 2018. "The Working Conditions of Teachers in Low- and Middle-Income Countries." Background paper for *World Development Report 2018: Learning to Realize Education's Promise.* Washington, DC: World Bank.

Fleisher, B. M., Y. Hu, H. Li, and S. Kim. 2011. "Economic Transition, Higher Education and Worker Productivity in China." *Journal of Development Economics* 94 (1): 86–94.

Foster, A., and M. R. Rosenzweig. 1996. "Technical Change and Human-Capital Returns and Investments: Evidence from the Green Revolution." *American Economic Review* 86 (4): 931–53.

Glewwe, P., E. Maïga, and H. Zheng. 2014. "The Contribution of Education to Economic Growth: A Review of the Evidence, with Special Attention and an Application to Sub-Saharan Africa." *World Development* 59: 379–93.

Hanushek, E. A., and L. Woessmann. 2015. "The Economic Impact of Educational Quality." In *Handbook of International Development and Education,* edited by P. Dixon, S. Humble, and C. Counihan, 6–19). Cheltenham, UK: Edward Elgar Publishing.

Hanushek, E. A., and L. Woessmann. 2021. "Education and Economic Growth." In *Oxford Research Encyclopedia of Economics and Finance.* Online collection, Oxford University Press. https://doi.org/10.1093/acrefore/9780190625979.013.651.

Krueger, A. B., and M. Lindahl. 2001. "Education for Growth: Why and for Whom?" *Journal of Economic Literature* 39 (4): 1101–36.

Mankiw, N. G., D. Romer, and D. N. Weil. 1992. "A Contribution to the Empirics of Economic Growth." *Quarterly Journal of Economics* 107 (2): 407–37.

Mendes, A., S. Pennings, and F. Fiuratti. 2022. "The Long-Term Growth Effects of Improved Education Quality in Middle-Income East Asia and Pacific Countries." Background note, World Bank, Washington, DC.

Psacharopoulos, G., and H. A. Patrinos. 2018. "Returns to Investment in Education: A Decennial Review of the Global Literature." Policy Research Working Paper 8402, World Bank, Washington, DC.

Sanders, W. L., and J. C. Rivers. 1996. "Cumulative and Residual Effects of Teachers on Future Student Academic Achievement." Research Progress Report, University of Tennessee Value-Added Research and Assessment Center, Knoxville, TN.

van der Eng, Pierre. 2009. "Capital Formation and Capital Stock in Indonesia, 1950–2008." *Bulletin of Indonesian Economic Studies* 45 (3): 345–71. https://doi.org/10.1080/00074910903301662.

World Bank. 2018. *World Development Report 2018: Learning to Realize Education's Promise.* Washington, DC: World Bank.

World Bank. 2020. *Global Economic Prospects: Slow Growth, Policy Changes, January 2020.* Washington, DC: World Bank.

World Bank. 2023. *Reviving Growth.* East Asia and Pacific Economic Update (April). Washington, DC: World Bank.

Teachers, Teaching, and the Region's Learning Deficit | 3

Introduction

Given the central role that teachers play in determining learning outcomes, having a strong corps of effective teachers is critical. Yet the evidence indicates that teachers in middle-income East Asia and Pacific—and the systems that are expected to support them—face numerous challenges. Developing a cadre of competent and motivated teachers depends on a variety of factors, including (a) *teacher selection* and recruitment; (b) *teachers' capacity* (the knowledge and ability to engage students effectively); and (c) *teachers' effort* (figure 3.1). To better understand the challenges that countries in this region face, this chapter focuses on these three sets of challenges (box 3.1).

As discussed further in chapter 4, most of the current teacher workforce is expected still to be teaching in 2030, making up more than half of current teachers in all middle-income East Asian and Pacific countries—70 percent or more in over half the countries (Tanaka and Sondergaard 2023). As a result, the ensuing discussion gives special emphasis to strengthening the teaching capacity of the region's current stock of teachers.

Why education systems fail to attract and select the best candidates

Teacher candidate quality reflects the profession's low attractiveness

Available data indicate that the teaching profession does not attract the best-performing students. Globally, and across East Asia, youth who plan to enter teaching are not among the highest academic performers. This is evident from comparing the 2015 Programme for International Student Assessment (PISA) test scores of students who report wanting to become engineers with those who report wanting to become teachers. In nearly every country where PISA is implemented, including in middle-income East Asia, aspiring engineers achieve higher average test scores than aspiring teachers (figure 3.2). While it may not be surprising that those who are better at mathematics would aspire to engineering rather than other occupations, reading scores show similar patterns across nearly all countries.

FIGURE 3.1   **Three primary factors pose challenges to teaching in East Asian and Pacific public schools**

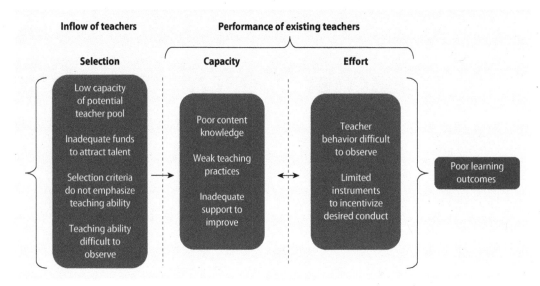

BOX 3.1   **The challenges of teacher selection, capacity, and effort: A conceptual framework**

Teachers are at the center of improved student learning. To identify sources of weaknesses in teacher performance, and hence appropriate remedial action, it is helpful to distinguish between

- The inflow of teachers (*selection*) and
- The performance of existing teachers, which may depend on
  - Teachers' content knowledge and pedagogy (*capacity*), and
  - Teachers' *effort*.

Challenges to teacher recruitment

Recruitment depends on the pool of candidates, the attractiveness of the profession, the objectives of the recruiter, and whether a candidate's ability to perform well (capacity) and effort can be observed. Poor candidates might be recruited for four different reasons:

- *A significant share of the pool of potential teachers has observably low capacity.* If the average capacity of the candidate pool is low, the overall capacity of recruited teachers will likely be as well.
- *The government lacks or will not allocate the funds necessary to build a strong teaching pool.* Budget problems may not allow for attracting better qualified individuals into the profession.
- *Teaching ability may not be the primary attribute sought by recruiters.* This may occur either because the government may have priorities for the education sector other than learning and human capital development (for example, national building) or because recruitment may be driven by personal or political considerations. These situations are discussed in greater detail in chapter 7, "The Political Economy of Education Reform."

box continues next page

BOX 3.1   The challenges of teacher selection, capacity, and effort: A conceptual framework *(Continued)*

- *Teaching ability can only be poorly observed by the recruiter.* In these circumstances, the recruiter would not be able to identify the most suitable candidates. Even worse, there could be a problem of *adverse selection* if the employer is only willing to pay a wage based on the average ability of recruits. At this wage, high-ability individuals would leave the candidate pool, lowering the average ability and hence the wage employers are prepared to pay in the future. In this scenario, only low-ability individuals with few other options may be willing to become teachers at a prevailing low wage.

Factors in weak teacher performance

Once recruited, teachers' performance may be weak either because they have low capacity to teach or because their behavior impedes their effectiveness. It may be difficult to infer individual teacher capacity or effort simply from the performance of that teacher's students because student performance also depends on unobservable characteristics, such as student readiness and aptitude; moreover, student performance is the cumulative result of *all* of that student's teachers to that point.

As further discussed throughout this chapter, challenges related to teacher selection, capacity, and effort adversely affect student learning across middle-income East Asia and Pacific. Because job turnover rates among teachers are low in the region, improving the performance of existing teachers will be particularly important to improving student learning in the short-to-medium term.

FIGURE 3.2   **Aspiring teachers generally score lower on PISA tests than aspiring engineers**

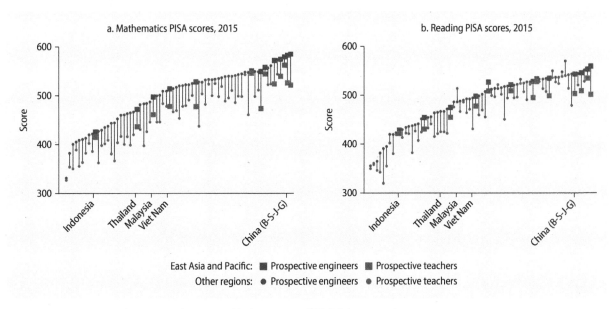

Source: World Bank estimates, based on Programme for International Student Assessment (PISA) 2015 data.
Note: The figure shows average PISA 2015 scores for participating countries and economies, by subject and self-identified prospective occupation. The x-axis shows labels for only the five middle-income East Asian countries or regions participating. "China (B-S-J-G)" reflects test scores from Beijing, Shanghai, Jiangsu, and Guangdong provinces only; they are not nationally representative.

Profession's attractiveness suffers from low salaries, poor conditions

Low salary expectations for teachers help explain the disparity in quality between teacher candidates and those for other professions. High-performing school systems in East Asia and elsewhere pay their teachers well (Dolton and Marcenaro-Gutierrez 2011; OECD 2021). This is not the case, however, in many middle-income East Asian countries, where teachers' salaries are relatively low, reducing the pool of those interested in entering the teaching profession. In Indonesia, Mongolia, the Philippines, Thailand, and Viet Nam, average salaries for teaching professionals tend to be lower than in other professions (controlling for individuals' characteristics including age, sex, marital status, education, and whether they are employed in the public or private sector) (figure 3.3).

In Indonesia, the data on average salaries conceal important differences between teachers who are civil servants and those who are not. The national government pays the former through a transfer to the district administration, directly out of national budget allocations. The remaining teachers, who make up more than 50 percent of all teachers, are hired through various mechanisms established when there were restrictions on hiring civil servant teachers (in 2011 and after). These teachers are paid either from district or school funds and on lower (often much lower) salaries and with none of the pension or other benefits of civil servant teachers (World Bank 2020). The expectation of low salaries reduces the attractiveness of the teaching profession.

Additional factors that limit the attractiveness of the teaching profession include poor working conditions, especially in poor and remote parts of the country. Data for six Southeast Asian countries indicate that between one-third and one-half of students attend schools that lack adequate infrastructure (including toilets) and basic instructional materials (UNICEF and SEAMEO 2020).

Moreover, many countries in the region lack career progression structures for teachers. Promotion is based on years of experience. Even where career frameworks exist, they have proved hard to implement.

FIGURE 3.3   **Salaries are often lower for teachers than other professionals in middle-income East Asian countries**

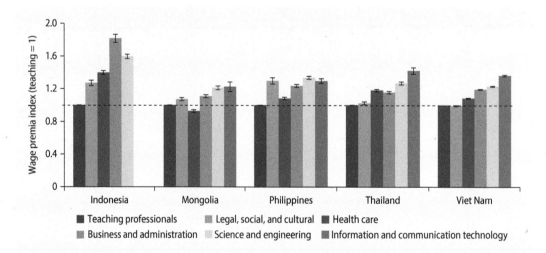

Sources: World Bank estimates, using 2015 Labor Force Survey Data for Indonesia and 2019 Labor Force Surveys for Mongolia, the Philippines, Thailand, and Viet Nam (ILO 2019).
Note: The figure shows the conditional wage premia for various professional occupations relative to teaching professionals, controlling for individual characteristics (index, teaching = 1). The error bars represent 90 percent confidence intervals.

Poor selection processes also hinder teacher quality

Beyond the attractiveness of the profession, admission into preservice education programs and recruitment into teaching positions often lack selectivity. This was the case in Cambodia in the early 2010s, where admissions requirements to enter teacher training centers (TTCs) were low. Back then, most fields in Cambodia required at least a D ("satisfactory") on the grade 12 leaving exam to apply to their courses and take the entrance exam. A high number of TTC applicants—as much as 40 percent in some programs—scored E ("limited achievement") (Tandon and Fukao 2015).[1] The Philippines similarly lacks institutional standards for selecting students for preservice teacher education, with teacher preservice institutes following an open-ended admissions policy. The Lao People's Democratic Republic also allows open enrollment into teacher preservice institutes for all high school graduates.

Although many countries in the region have formal criteria for teacher recruitment (post-training), these criteria are not followed systematically. Indeed, teacher hiring in several of the region's countries still gives high discretion to local elected officials and administrators and is a function of candidates' political connections rather than their capacity or motivation to teach (Béteille 2022).

Moreover, teacher recruitment processes have at times been relaxed to enable large-scale hiring as countries sought to achieve universal access to basic education, consistent with global commitments. In Timor-Leste, for example, a massive push in the early 2010s to reach universal primary school enrollment led to large-scale and rapid hiring of teachers, including some teachers with incomplete secondary education (World Bank 2019). In Myanmar, in the 2014/15 school year, when the government eliminated school fees and started to provide free textbooks, enrollments reportedly rose by 300,000—from 8.2 million to 8.5 million students. Because teacher training colleges could not produce graduates fast enough to accommodate the larger student numbers, the Ministry of Education allowed states and regions to recruit graduates from other disciplines, often with lower levels of education (World Bank 2015). These teachers were likely still in place, prior to the onset of the COVID and the military coup in Myanmar.[2]

The challenge of weak teacher capacity

Many teachers have limited knowledge of their subjects

Far too many teachers in middle-income East Asia and Pacific have not mastered the content they are expected to teach, as these examples show:

- *In Lao PDR,* only 8 percent of fourth-grade teachers scored 80 percent or higher on an assessment of their fourth-grade mathematics content knowledge, reflecting generally poor mastery of content (World Bank 2018) (figure 3.4, panel a).
- *In Indonesia,* similarly, only 8 percent of fourth-grade teachers who were tested got an 80 percent score or higher on an assessment of their Indonesian language skills (figure 3.4, panel b), and only one in three teachers (about 32 percent) scored 80 percent or more in mathematics (Yarrow et al. 2020).[3]
- *In Cambodia,* primary-school mathematics teachers in 2012 could answer only about half of grade 6 and grade 9 items correctly (Tandon and Fukao 2015). Since that time, the government has taken steps to improve teachers' content knowledge, including through its Teacher Upgrading Program, started in 2017. As a result, the 2012 data may not fully reflect the current situation. However, no updated data on teachers' subject content knowledge was available at the time of writing.[4]
- *In Malaysia,* when tested in 2020, only 53 percent of English language teachers were judged to be sufficiently proficient in English to teach (Malaysia MOE 2020).[5]

FIGURE 3.4   **Most Lao PDR mathematics teachers and Indonesian language teachers have not mastered the curriculum they teach**

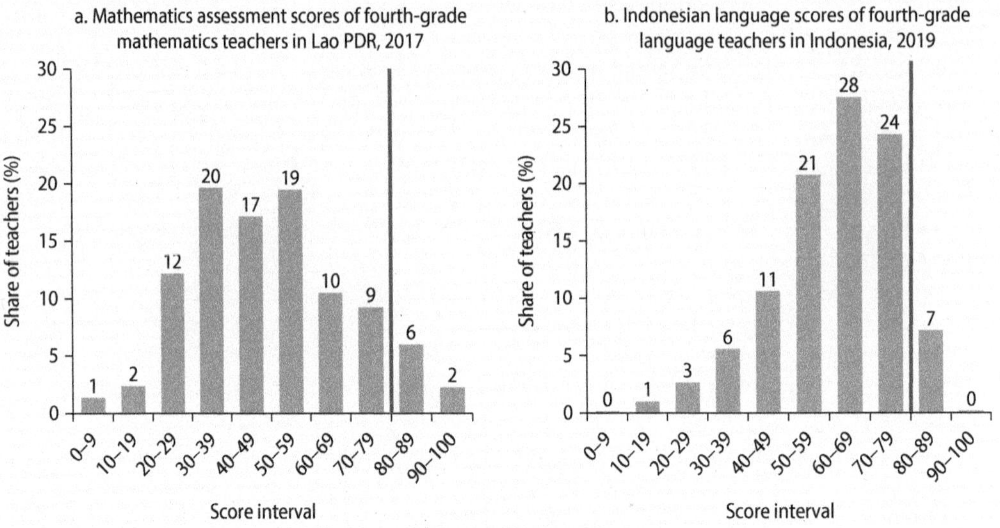

a. Mathematics assessment scores of fourth-grade mathematics teachers in Lao PDR, 2017

b. Indonesian language scores of fourth-grade language teachers in Indonesia, 2019

Sources: World Bank 2018 (panel a); Yarrow et al. 2020 (panel b).
Note: Percentages represent the share of teachers achieving scores within each score interval. The red vertical line indicates the 80 percent benchmark, which the Service Delivery Indicators program uses in cross-country comparisons to represent the minimum knowledge expected of the teacher. For Indonesia, the results are from a nationally representative sample of schools of the Ministry of Religious Affairs and a smaller sample of schools of the Ministry of Education, Culture, Research, and Technology (MoECRT), which at the time of the survey, was the Ministry of Education and Culture. The survey was collected in 2019 and used the same survey instrument (Service Delivery Indicators) used in Lao PDR. Shares do not total 100 because of rounding.

- *In the Philippines,* the average elementary or high school teacher in 2015 could answer fewer than half of the questions on subject content tests correctly, except for English where scores were slightly better (World Bank 2016).
- *In Papua New Guinea,* 25 percent of elementary teachers tested in April 2018 failed to get a passing score on an assessment of second-grade mathematics subject knowledge content (Namit 2018).

Teaching practices must improve for effective learning

Many teachers in the region also do not employ effective teaching practices. The evidence from classroom observations of teachers in the region indicates a need for improvements in pedagogy, content, and classroom practice. Only seven percent or less of teachers demonstrate highly effective practices, and two-thirds or more use ineffective or weak practices in Mongolia, the Philippines, Viet Nam, and poorer areas in Guangdong, China (Carneiro et al. 2022; Coflan et al. 2018; Lai 2019; Molina et al. 2018).

The assessment scores presented in figure 3.5 capture teachers' capacity to create a classroom culture conducive to learning, to challenging and engaging students, and to fostering students' socioemotional skills to be successful learners. As discussed in chapter 2, weak teaching practices translate into poorer learning outcomes.

Teaching practices also reinforce socioeconomic inequality

As with students' learning outcomes, there is inequality in the quality of teachers' teaching practices. In Cambodia, Lao PDR, Myanmar, and the Philippines, mathematics teaching

FIGURE 3.5   **Many of the region's teachers use ineffective teaching practices**

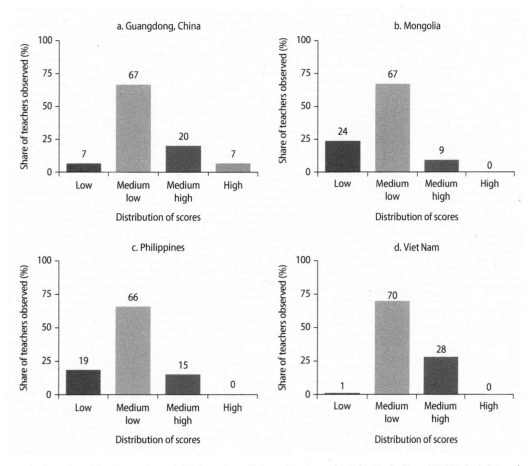

Sources: Coflan et al. 2018 (China); Lai 2019 (Mongolia); Molina et al. 2018 (Philippines); Carneiro et al. 2022 (Viet Nam); additional World Bank calculations of Mongolia and Philippines data to ensure comparability (details available upon request).
Note: The figures show data collected from classroom observations. For Guangdong, China, the figure is based on a classroom observations tool called the Classroom Assessment Scoring System (CLASS), whereas, the figures for the other countries are based on a classroom observational tool called *Teach*. The figures reflecting the *Teach* tool (panels b, c, and d) show, for each country, the average of teachers' global scores (that is, teachers' composite scores from the different indices of the tool). This score, based on classroom observation, captures teachers' capacity to create a classroom culture conducive to learning, to challenge and engage students, and to foster students' socioemotional skills to be successful learners. The results presented for Mongolia differ slightly from what appeared in World Bank (2019b) because an effort was made to harmonize the Teach data across the countries for which such data exist. (Shares do not always total 100 due to rounding.) For more details, see the World Bank education brief, "Teach Primary: Helping Countries Track and Improve Teaching Quality," August 30, 2022, https://www.worldbank.org/en/topic/education/brief/teach-helping-countries-track-and-improve-teaching-quality.

practices in socioeconomically disadvantaged schools (schools in the bottom two quintiles in terms of the average socioeconomic status of households with children) are significantly worse than in the best-off schools (figure 3.6). Notably, these are also the countries with the region's highest learning poverty rates.[6] Disparities in teaching quality across socioeconomic categories are more muted in Malaysia and Viet Nam, where average student learning outcomes are also much better.

Teachers' professional development often ineffective

Global evidence highlights the importance of training and ongoing professional development to strengthening teachers' capabilities and raising students' learning outcomes (Popova et al. 2022).

FIGURE 3.6   **In most countries, students from the poorest households are not being taught by the most effective teachers**

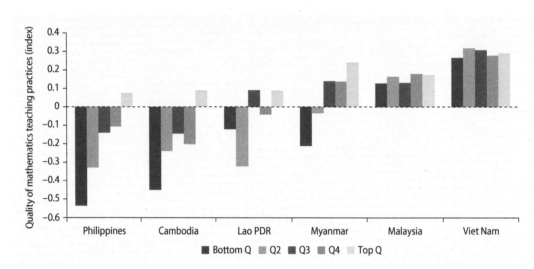

Source: World Bank estimates, based on 2019 Southeast Asia Primary Learning Metrics (SEA-PLM) data (UNICEF and SEAMEO 2020).
Note: The figure shows the quality of mathematics teaching practices (index), by household socioeconomic status quintile (Q)—a nationally derived measure based on (a) highest parental occupation of either parent, (b) highest education level of either parent, and (c) family's home resources through the home resources scale (UNICEF and SEAMEO 2020, 66). The average value of the teaching practices index is normalized to zero; schools reporting poorer-than-average teaching practices are thus shown to have negative values in the figure.

Evidence on teacher professional development from high-income countries shows that concrete, classroom-based programs make the most difference to teachers (Darling-Hammond et al. 2009; Walter and Briggs 2012).

The limited data available from East Asian and Pacific countries suggest that a significant percentage of the region's teachers are trained each year (figure 3.7). Nevertheless, the data also suggest that the quality of training is often low and ineffective in raising teachers' capabilities or students' learning outcomes. For example, World Bank analysis of 2019 Southeast Asia Primary Learning Metrics (SEA-PLM) student assessment data finds only a weak association between current teacher in-service training and student performance on these standardized assessments.

New survey data collected for this report indicate that the in-service training programs in many East Asian and Pacific middle-income countries lack the key elements of effective programs found elsewhere in the world. A global analysis of high-impact in-service teacher training programs indicates that effective programs have four key features (Popova et al. 2022):

- A focus on *content* knowledge (that is, subject-matter knowledge in the subject a teacher teaches)
- Opportunities to practice with *colleagues*
- *Continued* support through follow-up visits focused on training content
- *Career* incentives through promotion or increased salary.

Four "C's" distinguish top in-service training programs

The new data collected for this report show, however, that the largest government-funded in-service teacher training programs in nine East Asian and Pacific middle-income countries do not consistently employ the practices shown to improve student learning.[7] Figure 3.8

FIGURE 3.7 **Large percentages of primary teachers receive in-service training in a given school year, in Indonesia, Viet Nam, and the Philippines**

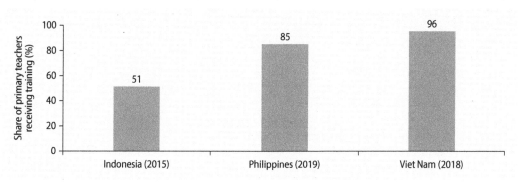

Source: Education statistics, UNESCO Institute for Statistics database (UIS.Stat), http://data.uis.unesco.org/Index.aspx.

FIGURE 3.8 **Teacher training programs in nine middle-income East Asian and Pacific countries tend not to employ the practices linked to improved student learning**

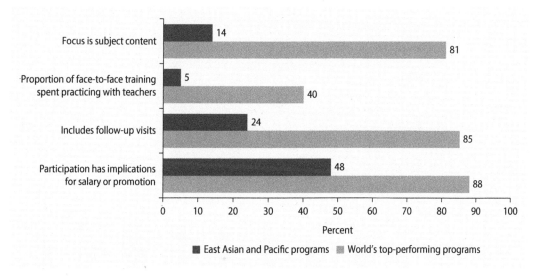

Sources: Popova et al. 2022 (for top performers worldwide); World Bank calculations, based on 2022 In-Service Teacher Training Survey Instrument (ITTSI) data for 65 programs in nine middle-income East Asian and Pacific countries.
Note: Percentages represent the proportion of programs containing a given feature, except for "practicing with teachers," where the percentage is the proportion of time training courses devote to this activity. The nine East Asian and Pacific countries are Cambodia, Fiji, Lao PDR, Mongolia, the Philippines, Thailand, Timor-Leste, Tonga, and Viet Nam. Orange bars designate "top performers" from a global study of training programs in 14 countries (Popova et al. 2022). Brown bars designate percentages of only the 65 training programs in nine East Asian and Pacific countries. Detailed data were collected on large-scale teacher professional development programs conducted in countries between January 2018 and June 2022 to observe the landscape of in-service teacher training both before and during the COVID-19 pandemic.

compares the top-performing in-service training programs worldwide with the largest government-funded programs in East Asia and Pacific regarding their use of four effective practices (the four "C's"):

- *Content knowledge*: Only 14 percent of East Asian and Pacific teacher training programs focus on improving teachers' content knowledge, whereas 81 percent of top-performing programs aim to do so. Given the weak grasp of curriculum content in the region, improving teacher content knowledge is foundational to improving instructional practice (Filmer, Molina, and Wane 2020).

- *Practice with colleagues*: Top-performing programs provide opportunities for teachers to practice what they learn with other teachers during face-to-face training sessions. This enables teachers to try out the new ideas and activities and identify ways to use them in their classrooms. The region's government-funded programs allocate only 5 percent of overall training time to practice with other teachers. By comparison, the world's top-performing training programs allocate, on average, 40 percent of training time to practice with other teachers.
- *Continued follow-up support*: Follow-up visits provide opportunities for trainers to reconnect with teachers after the initial period of training has ended and to respond to teachers' questions that arise from having tried to implement new ideas and activities. Eighty-five percent of top-performing programs include follow-up visits with teachers, compared with only 24 percent of programs in East Asia and Pacific.
- *Career incentives*: Only half of in-service teacher training programs in the region are linked to salary or promotion. By comparison, 88 percent of top-performing programs link training to pay or promotion. A high proportion of the region's training programs (47 percent) have the objective of fulfilling continuing education requirements or teacher certification, but these programs are not directly linked to career incentives. This reduces teachers' motivation to participate in training and, if they do, to take it seriously.

The region's countries vary widely in their use of the "four C's"

Few large in-service teacher training programs surveyed in East Asian and Pacific countries include all four key practices associated with effective training, and the largest programs in general include only one or two of them, with significant country-to-country variation (figure 3.9). Thailand and Timor-Leste are the only countries surveyed where some programs incorporate all four practices. In contrast, most programs in Fiji and Lao PDR do not incorporate any of these effective practices. Overall, most in-service training programs surveyed lack a

FIGURE 3.9 Few in-service teacher training programs in selected East Asian and Pacific countries demonstrate the full set of effective practices at scale

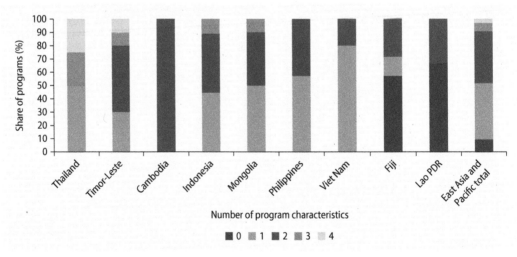

Source: Calculations from 2022 In-Service Teacher Training Survey Instrument (ITTSI) data.
Note: The figure shows the percentages of in-service teacher training programs within nine middle-income East Asian and Pacific countries that included either 0, 1, 2, 3, or 4 of the four characteristics associated with effective programs: content knowledge focus, face-to-face practice with colleagues, continued support through follow-up visits, and career incentives for participation. The "East Asia and Pacific total" bar aggregates the percentages of all 65 programs from the nine countries.

subject focus, which can partially explain the continuing poor knowledge base of teachers in the region. The most common effective practice incorporated in the region's large teacher training programs is allocating time for teachers to practice new techniques and ideas with one another; except for Fiji and Lao PDR, 90 percent or more of countries' largest programs include this feature, although as shown in figure 3.8, the amount of time spent practicing is well below best practice and likely too little to have much impact on teachers' classroom skills.

Lower learning outcomes due to teacher behavior

Students' learning outcomes are often lower because of teacher absences and poor classroom management. Students can only learn from their teachers if the teachers are in the classroom. Across six Southeast Asian countries—Cambodia, Lao PDR, Malaysia, Myanmar, the Philippines, and Viet Nam—an average of 14 percent of surveyed students report that their teachers are often absent (figure 3.10). Across 15 Pacific Island countries, 36 percent of students attend a school whose principal reports that instruction was hindered by teacher absenteeism (EQAP 2022). In contrast, data from Japan, the Republic of Korea, and Shanghai, China, show teacher absence rates of 1 percent or less, and data from Singapore show only 3 percent absenteeism (OECD 2018).

Moreover, even when teachers are present in class, many do not use the time efficiently. More than three-fifths of surveyed students in the six Southeast Asian countries report that their teachers take a long time to settle the class down. A separate survey in Indonesia found that, on average, almost one in five teachers (19 percent) were absent from school and nearly one-quarter (24 percent) were not in class during unannounced visits to schools managed by the Ministry of Religious Affairs. Moreover, in 20 percent of schools, the teacher was absent from class 40 percent of the time or more. Although a recent study in Indonesia suggests that absences are often for legitimate reasons, time away from the classroom nevertheless impedes learning (Yarrow et al. 2020).

Even when teachers are present, the amount of class time dedicated to foundational learning (mathematics and language) is often low, hindering student learning. Although there is variation across countries, less than one-third of fifth graders in Lao PDR, Malaysia, Myanmar, and the Philippines report having daily mathematics and language lessons (figure 3.11).

FIGURE 3.10   **Students in six Southeast Asian countries report that their teachers are frequently absent or late to class**

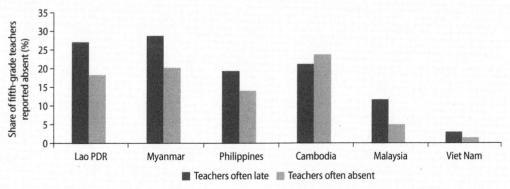

Source: World Bank calculations, using the 2019 Southeast Asia Primary Learning Metrics (SEA-PLM) dataset (UNICEF 2020).

FIGURE 3.11   **Across much of Southeast Asia, few of the fifth graders report having daily mathematics and language lessons**

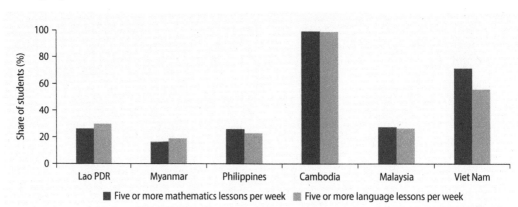

Source: World Bank estimates, based on Southeast Asia Primary Learning Metrics (SEA-PLM) data, available from UNICEF 2020.
Note: Responses were to this question: "How much time do you typically spend per week studying the following subjects in regular lessons at school?"

Daily lessons might not be provided for multiple reasons. Some factors could be related to teacher capacity issues, as discussed earlier (for example, not recognizing the importance of daily mathematics and language lessons). Others might relate to incentives or the lack thereof (for example, if the curriculum is overloaded, or if administrators check only whether the curriculum is completed and not whether students are learning). Nevertheless, the lack of daily mathematics and language lessons has measurable costs in terms of student learning.

World Bank analysis of the 2019 SEA-PLM data indicates that moving from the status quo to daily mathematics and language lessons would have a sizable positive impact on student learning outcomes. Taken together with measures to ensure full-time presence of teachers in school, it is estimated that daily mathematics and language lessons could raise fifth graders' average SEA-PLM score by approximately 6.2 points, the equivalent of about two-thirds of a year of learning.

Systems that appraise teacher performance are nonexistent or weak in the region. Such assessments, which could form a basis for incentivizing improvements, often lack focus on how effectively teacher performance promotes classroom learning. In Papua New Guinea, for example, teacher appraisal is linked to promotion and to associated salary increases. However, although Papua New Guinea's policy states that it is "performance-based," the underlying principles defining performance are not rooted in practices linked to student outcomes or teacher practice and behavior. The teacher appraisal tool used by inspectors is largely focused on teacher qualifications and certification (PNGTSC 2017). In Cambodia, teacher assessments similarly lack focus on classroom practices or student learning, with uneven implementation across the country (box 3.2).

Viet Nam is an exception among the region's middle-income countries, with teacher appraisal undertaken routinely and tied to training as well as salary increments. Teachers are graded on a scale of 1 (lowest) to 4 (highest) on the annual appraisal undertaken by the Ministry of Education and Training. Teachers who score 1 or 2 are provided training and expected to improve. Should teachers not undertake their annual tasks or duties satisfactorily, their pay raise is delayed by 6–12 months (Viet Nam, Ministry of Home Affairs 2021).

BOX 3.2   **The gap between how Cambodian teachers perform in the classroom and how they are evaluated**

Teaching practice in Cambodia is teacher-focused rather than student-centered. On the surface, teachers use class time reasonably well. The teacher in a typical Cambodian classroom spends about 54 percent of time in active instruction, 34 percent in passive instruction, 6 percent in management activities, and 6 percent off task (Tandon and Fukao 2015). Although these percentages are broadly in line with global good-practice indicators for classroom instruction, postobservation summaries indicate that less than one-third of teachers use teaching aids effectively. And whereas recitation is prevalent, teachers tend to ask questions of the same few students rather than interacting with all students. In only 20 percent of classes do teachers ask questions that require students to use their imaginations or think creatively, and students ask questions of teachers in only 17 percent of classes.

Moreover, the evaluation of teachers does not include an assessment of their classroom practices. Teachers are formally evaluated using a form that reflects the values of government civil servants, such as "working for the national benefit" and "solidarity." The teacher evaluation form includes four questions, which rate teachers on a scale of 1–20 on how much they display (a) "initiative and result orientation"; (b) "professional ethics, responsibility, and work discipline"; (c) efforts to take "into account the national benefit"; and (d) "solidarity, moral, and social activities." There are no formal scoring guidelines, no accounting for classroom practices, and no benchmarks on student learning. Moreover, the data that exist (from the 2010s) show that the frequency of teacher evaluation was very uneven. On average, teachers were evaluated using this form every one or two years. However, one-quarter of teachers—mostly in remote areas—reported never having been evaluated (figure B3.2.1). Moreover, nearly half of teachers in remote areas reported that they were unfamiliar with the form used to evaluate them.

FIGURE B3.2.1   **Teacher evaluations in Cambodia are usually infrequent or irregular, if they happen at all**

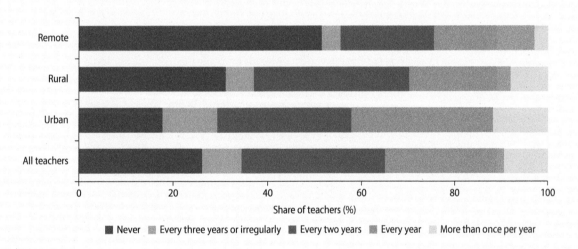

Source: Tandon and Fukao 2015.

Even in contexts where evaluation systems focus on teaching competencies, performance incentives remain weak. For instance, Malaysia has a sophisticated teacher evaluation system and ample resources to assess each of its nearly 400,000 teachers that is linked to teaching competencies and includes target setting and periodic performance review processes. However, anecdotal evidence suggests that the system struggles to identify ineffective teachers, whether because of poor teaching practices, lack of content knowledge, late arrival, or teacher absenteeism.

Notes

1. In the 2013/14 school year, Cambodia attempted to attract higher-performing grade 12 graduates (those with A, B, and C grades) into teacher preservice colleges by providing them automatic entry into programs. The policy was revoked after a year of implementation, resulting in little change in the academic profile of those entering TTCs (Tandon and Fukao 2015). To our knowledge, there is no analysis of grade levels among more recent entrants to teacher training colleges in Cambodia. However, anecdotal evidence suggests that a grade of D or E would no longer be sufficient to gain admission.
2. The pandemic and the military coup has considerably disrupted the education sector in Myanmar (see World Bank (2023) for more details). It is estimated that 30 percent of the teachers have been dismissed by the military government for participating in civil disobedience movement. Moreover, public schools have experienced violent attacks in the ongoing conflict.
3. As also noted in the figure 3.4 note, the data for Indonesia are based on a nationally representative sample of Ministry of Religious Affairs schools as well as a smaller sample of schools under the control of Ministry of Education, Culture, Research, and Technology (MoECRT) (which, at the time of the 2019 survey, was the Ministry of Education and Culture).
4. Although the assessment data presented here were collected in 2012, most of the teachers tested at that time are likely still teaching, and no new data on teachers' subject content knowledge are currently available. The same caveat applies to 2015 data on teachers' subject content knowledge in the Philippines, discussed later.
5. In Malaysia, English teachers are tested annually for their English proficiency. In 2021, 17,558 out of 33,024 (53 percent) of English teachers who sat for the English proficiency test reached the minimum-level mastery of the Common European Framework of Reference (CEFR) for Languages, "C1" (Malaysia MOE 2020).
6. "Learning poverty," a concept and indicator developed by the World Bank and the United Nations Educational, Scientific and Cultural Organization (UNESCO) Institute for Statistics, is defined as the inability to read and understand a simple, age-appropriate text by age 10.
7. Together with government counterparts, surveys were carried out on large-scale in-service teacher training programs in nine middle-income countries across the region: Cambodia, Fiji, Lao PDR, Mongolia, the Philippines, Thailand, Timor-Leste, Tonga, and Viet Nam. The methodology and survey instrument follows Popova et al. (2022). Detailed data were collected on teacher professional development programs conducted in countries between January 2018 and June 2022 to observe the landscape of in-service teacher training both before and during the COVID-19 pandemic.

References

Béteille, T. 2022. *Vibrant or Stuck?* Unpublished background paper for this report, World Bank, Washington, DC.

Carneiro, P., P. Glewwe, A. Guha, and S. Krutikova. 2022. "Unpacking the Black Box of School Quality." Unpublished manuscript. https://drive.google.com/file/d/1MQDGSL5nan1v7Mry29XgJ6T5P7NQZbIf/view?pli=1.

Coflan, A., A. Ragatz, A. Hasan, and Y. Pan. 2018. "Understanding Effective Teaching Practices in Chinese Classrooms: Evidence from a Pilot Study of Primary and Junior Secondary Schools in Guangdong, China." Policy Research Working Paper 8396, World Bank, Washington, DC.

Darling-Hammond, L., R. C. Wei, A. Andree, N. Richardson, and S. Orphanos. 2009. "Professional Learning in the Learning Profession: A Status Report on Teacher Development in the United States and Abroad." Report, National Staff Development Council, Washington, DC.

Dolton, P., and O. Marcenaro-Gutierrez. 2011. "Teachers' Pay and Pupil Performance." CentrePiece 16 (2): 20–22.

EQAP (Education Quality & Assessment Programme). 2022. *Pacific Islands Literacy & Numeracy Assessment 2021 Regional Report.* Suva, Fiji: Pacific Community. https://pilna.eqap.spc.int/2021/regional.

ILO (International Labour Organization). 2019. 2019 Labour Force Surveys from ILOSTAT, https://www.ilo.org/surveyLib/index.php/catalog/LFS/?page=1&ps=15&repo=LFS.

Lai, K. 2019. "Teacher Practices in Mongolia: Results from the *Teach* Classroom Observation Study." Unpublished manuscript, World Bank, Washington, DC.

Malaysia MOE (Ministry of Education). 2020. "Annual Report 2020: Malaysia Education Blueprint (2013–2025)." Report, RMOE, Putrajaya, Malaysia.

Molina, E., S. F. Fatima, T. Iva, and T. Wilichowski. 2018. "Teacher Practices in Mindanao: Result of the Teach Classroom Observation Study." Report No. 134535, World Bank, Washington, DC.

Namit, K. 2018. "RISE PNG Elementary Teachers' Math Subject Knowledge Assessment Report." Unpublished paper, Save the Children, Port Moresby, New Guinea.

OECD (Organisation for Economic Co-operation and Development). 2018. *TALIS 2018 Results (Volume II): Teachers and School Leaders as Valued Professionals,* Annex C., table II.2.60, "Teachers' Absenteeism, by School Characteristics: Results Based on Responses of Lower Secondary Principals," Version 2, Last updated March 11, 2020. Paris: TALIS, OECD Publishing. https://doi.org/10.1787/19cf08df-en.

OECD (Organisation for Economic Co-operation and Development). 2019. *TALIS 2018 Results (Volume I): Teachers and School Leaders as Lifelong Learners.* Paris: TALIS, OECD Publishing. https://doi.org/10.1787/1d0bc92a-en.

OECD (Organisation for Economic Co-operation and Development). 2021. *Education in Brazil: An International Perspective.* Paris: OECD Publishing.

PNGTSC (Papua New Guinea Teaching Service Commission). 2017. "HR Policy Information and Operations Manual." Manual prepared by PNGTSC, published by AusAID, Australian Government, Canberra.

Popova, A., D. Evans, M. E. Breeding, and V. Arancibia. 2022. "Teacher Professional Development Around the World: The Gap between Evidence and Practice." *The World Bank Research Observer* 37 (1): 107–36.

Tanaka, N., and L. Sondergaard. 2023. "Analysis of Teacher Stock versus Flow in Primary Education in East Asia and the Pacific Middle-Income Countries: A Simple Model and Results from Simulation between 2020 and 2030." Policy Research Working Paper 10479, World Bank, Washington, DC.

Tandon, P., and T. Fukao. 2015. *Educating the Next Generation: Improving Teacher Quality in Cambodia.* Directions in Development Series. Washington, DC: World Bank.

UNICEF (United Nations Children's Fund). 2020. South-East Asia Primary Learning Metrics (SEA-PLM) 2019 dataset, https://www.seaplm.org/index.php?option=com_content&view=article&id=54&Itemid=438&lang=en.

UNICEF and SEAMEO (United Nations Children's Fund and Southeast Asian Ministers of Education Organization). 2020. *SEA-PLM 2019 Main Regional Report: Children's Learning in 6 Southeast Asian Countries.* Bangkok: UNICEF and SEAMEO.

Vietnam, Ministry of Home Affairs. 2021. "Modifications and Amendments of the Regulations on Periodic Salary Increase, Salary Advancement and Seniority Allowances for Staff, Public Servants, Civil Servants and Employers." Circular 03/2021/TT-BNV, June 29, 2021, Ministry of Home Affairs, Hanoi, Vietnam.

Walter, C., and J. Briggs. 2012. "What Professional Development Makes the Most Difference to Teachers?" Report, University of Oxford Department of Education, Oxford University Press.

World Bank. 2015. "Myanmar Public Expenditure Review 2015: Realigning the Union Budget to Myanmar's Development Priorities." Public expenditure review, World Bank, Yangon, Myanmar.

World Bank. 2016. "Assessing Basic Education Service Delivery in the Philippines: Public Education Expenditure Tracking and Quantitative Service Delivery Study." Report No. AUS6799, World Bank, Washington DC.

World Bank. 2018. "Delivery of Education Services in Lao PDR: Results of the SABER Service Delivery Survey, 2017." Report, World Bank, Washington, DC.

World Bank. 2019. "Using EGRA for an Early Evaluation of Two Innovations in Basic Education in Timor-Leste: The New Curriculum and the Professional Learning and Mentoring Program." Report No. 147764, World Bank, Washington, DC.

World Bank. 2020. "The Promise of Education in Indonesia." Report No. 154388, World Bank, Washington, DC.

World Bank. 2023. "Education in Myanmar: Where Are We Now?" World Bank, Washington, DC https://thedocs.worldbank.org/en/doc/716418bac40878ce262f57dfbd4eca05-0070012023/original/State-of-Education-in-Myanmar-July-2023.pdf.

Yarrow, N., R. Afkar, E. Masood, and B. Gauthier. 2020. "Measuring the Quality of MoRA's Education Services." Report, World Bank, Jakarta, Indonesia.

Strengthening Teaching for Improved Learning | 4

Introduction

Strengthening the quality and effectiveness of teaching in the East Asia and Pacific region will require action on several fronts. This chapter focuses on global evidence and country experiences that have been effective in raising the quality of teaching for improved student learning.[1] Building on the conceptual framework presented in chapter 3, the discussion focuses on three key areas (figure 4.1):

- Attracting and selecting more effective teachers
- Enhancing teachers' capacity to teach—that is, strengthening their subject knowledge and pedagogical skills as well as improving the tools they use
- Encouraging greater teacher effort.

An important element of all three areas involves improving the information base upon which informed policy choices can be made and implemented.

Countries throughout East Asia and Pacific will need to recruit more new teachers over the next decade—in some countries, significantly more. Hence, improved selection and recruitment will be important. Although all countries in the region can expect to continue to recruit primary-school teachers, the number will likely vary considerably.

Projections suggest that 16 out of 22 countries in the region will need more teachers in 2030 than in 2020, with 10 out of 12 Pacific Island countries being in this position (Tanaka and Sondergaard 2023), as shown in figure 4.2. Among those countries with the highest projected increases, Cambodia could have 26 percent more teachers in 2030 than in 2020; on current trends, 11,000 of the current 42,000 teachers are expected to leave the profession by 2030 and will need replacing, and a further 11,000 teachers will need to be hired to put the country on track to reach an overall pupil-teacher ratio of 25 to 1 by 2030. Papua New Guinea will have an estimated 42 percent more teachers overall by 2030, with 10,000 leavers to be replaced and an additional 14,000 teachers to be hired.

However, strengthening the quality of teaching in the region will require a strong focus on existing teachers because, in *all countries*, most of those who will be teaching in 2030 have already been recruited.[2] The average teacher attrition rate is less than 3 percent in the region, according to calculations from the World Bank's Education Statistics (EdStats) data.

FIGURE 4.1   **Policy to strengthen teaching for public basic education has several entry points**

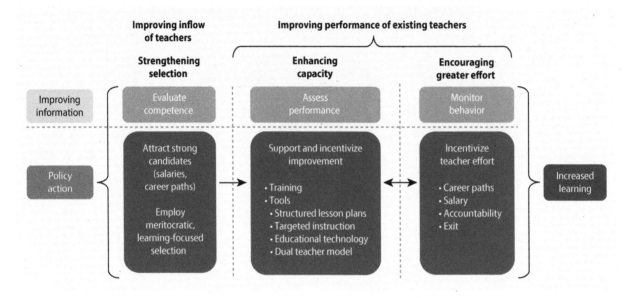

FIGURE 4.2   **In East Asia and Pacific, the primary-school teacher workforce is projected to grow in about two-thirds of the countries by 2030**

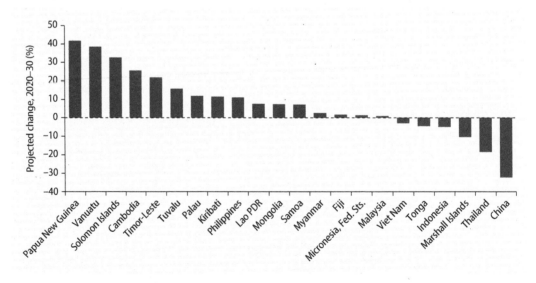

Source: Tanaka and Sondergaard 2023.
Note: The figure shows the projected percentage change in the number of primary-school teachers needed between 2020 and 2030, by country. Simulations use the United Nations' *World Population Prospects 2022* (medium scenario) for children of primary-school age (UN DESA 2022) and the following assumptions: (a) countries will reach a net enrollment rate of 100 percent at least by 2030; (b) countries will lower pupil-teacher ratios to 25 to 1 (or maintain current levels if below that ratio) by 2030; and (c) teacher attrition rates are the average country-reported attrition rates for the past five years (if reported in the United Nations Educational, Scientific and Cultural Organization [UNESCO] Institute for Statistics database), or if countries are not reporting attrition rates, we use the average attrition rate over the past five years of the countries that do report.

In China, Indonesia, Malaysia, the Marshall Islands, the Federated States of Micronesia, Mongolia, the Philippines, and Tonga, three-quarters or more of teachers expected to be employed in 2030 are already part of those countries' teaching corps (figure 4.3). Even in countries that will need to increase the number of teaching positions, the large stock of teachers means that existing teachers will make up most of the teaching workforce at the start of the next decade. For example, although Cambodia may recruit 22,000 more teachers in the decade to 2030, more than 30,000 currently employed teachers are still expected to be in the profession at that time.

Therefore, it would take a long time for countries to realize improvements in the overall quality of the teacher workforce (and hence in student learning) by focusing predominantly on strengthening selection and recruitment of new teachers. To have an observable impact on learning outcomes over the next 10–15 years, the region's policy makers must make more concerted efforts to raising the performance of existing teachers.

Mechanisms to make teaching more attractive and selective

High-performing education systems in East Asia have been effective in making teaching attractive through a combination of mechanisms. For example, teaching is a highly attractive career in Shanghai, China, driven by several factors: competitive pay, conducive working conditions, and clear career progression structures (Liang et al. 2016). Shanghai's Teacher's Law stipulates that teachers' average salary should be equal to or higher than the national average salary of civil servants. Permanent full-time teachers also receive medical and retirement benefits. Working conditions are attractive, with regular inspections to ensure that infrastructure and sanitation

FIGURE 4.3   **Most of those expected to be teaching in East Asia and Pacific by 2030 have already been recruited**

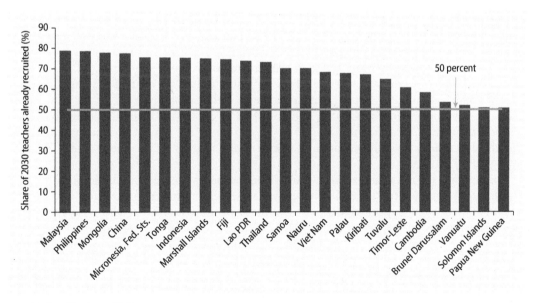

Source: Tanaka and Sondergaard 2023.
Note: The figure shows the percentage of primary-school teachers projected to be teaching in 2030 who had already joined the teaching workforce by 2020. Simulations use the United Nations' *World Population Prospects 2022* (medium scenario) for children of primary age (UN DESA 2022) and the following assumptions: (a) countries will reach a net enrollment rate of 100 percent at least by 2030; (b) countries will lower pupil-teacher ratios to 25 to 1 (or maintain current levels if below that ratio) by 2030; and (c) teacher attrition rates are the average country-reported attrition rates for the past five years (if reported in the United Nations Educational, Scientific and Cultural Organization [UNESCO] Institute for Statistics database), or if countries are not reporting attrition rates, we use the average attrition rate over the past five years of the countries who do report.

conditions are met, and teachers receive personal computers to assist them with their work. Pupil-teacher ratios are also low: 16 to 1 at the primary level. Finally, teachers have the opportunity to progress professionally through an explicit five-tier structure, based on a careful measurement of their performance.

High-performing East Asian countries also use rigorous and meritocratic selection processes to recruit teachers. To achieve selectivity, Singapore uses rigorous filtering mechanisms to determine who enters teaching at the time that candidates enter their preservice education (World Bank 2018). Before becoming a teacher, candidates must undergo preparatory training, which has two components: a compulsory contract teaching stint to affirm interest and ascertain suitability, and a subsequent study phase to earn the proper qualifications. The study phase lasts between nine months and two years, depending on the level of teaching (kindergarten, primary school, secondary school, and so on). Admitted candidates get paid beginning on day one. Teachers also receive a generous benefits package, including bonuses and payouts at defined points in their careers. Moreover, when teachers enter the profession, they can choose one of three career tracks—the master teacher track, the leadership track, or the specialist track—based on an initial assessment. Levels within each track are mapped to a range of coordinated experiences and training to prepare teachers for roles with greater responsibility. Movement along each track (or between tracks, if teachers choose) is based on an appraisal system that uses multiple sources of information to assess teachers.

Japan and Shanghai also apply rigorous criteria after teacher candidates complete their preservice education but before they become teachers. Common features of this approach include establishing high standards for the academic requirements to enter teaching such that only high-performing students apply, as well as successful completion of (a) written tests on general and subject-specific skills, (b) an interview, and (c) mock teaching exercises in real classroom settings. The credibility of the process depends on the technical quality of teacher tests, having a clear and objective grading system in place, and fairness and rigor in the interview and mock teaching sessions.

As a result of their rigorous, merit-based screening processes, the high-performing education systems in East Asia accept only a small share of aspiring teachers. In Japan, only 14 percent of all applicants to education programs are accepted, and only about 30–40 percent of graduates are hired (CIEB n.d.); newly hired teachers represent only 5 percent of the applicant pool (World Bank 2018). In the Republic of Korea, teacher education programs admit only the top 10 percent of high school graduates, and only 1 in 20 passes the arduous exams to become a teacher (Ferreras, Kessel, and Kim 2015). In Singapore, the government recruits from the top third of graduates of universities and polytechnic schools to become teachers (Tan and Wong 2007).

Among the region's middle-income countries, Indonesia has recently undertaken reforms to make the teacher recruitment process more selective and meritocratic. In 2020, the country introduced a more rigorous recruitment process for those who wish to become government contract teachers. Prospective teachers are assessed on their content knowledge; there is a minimum passing score, and the examination is managed through an electronic process. These changes have made the teacher selection process more competitive. Nearly 1.2 million candidates took the test to become government contract teachers in September and December 2021. The government announced that just under 300,000 candidates passed, for a pass rate of 25 percent (Haryanto 2021).

Despite political pressures,[3] the new arrangements represent a more robust approach to teacher selection in Indonesia; those who passed made up only about 59 percent of the number the education ministry said it intended to hire (Haryanto 2021). Sustained political and institutional commitment to maintaining teacher quality will be critical to Indonesia's—and other countries'—success in raising the quality of incoming teachers. As discussed in chapter 7, political forces continue to impede meritocratic selection of teachers in many countries in the region.

Training and tools to enhance teaching capacity

The evidence on what low- and middle-income countries can do to improve learning outcomes in basic education has expanded greatly (see, for example, World Bank [2020a]). This evidence uses different types of data and methodological approaches, each with their own strengths and limitations (box 4.1). For example, randomized controlled trials (RCTs) of specific projects are important to identifying effective interventions, but further information may be needed to assess whether evaluated programs can be as effective at a national scale. Large national and cross-country datasets can help identify patterns within or across countries, but additional analysis may be needed to understand the underlying causes of these correlations.

Wherever possible, the report seeks to compare evidence using different data and methodologies—and different country contexts—to assess the robustness of the policy conclusions. Where strong evidence from East Asia and Pacific is not available, evidence from other middle-income comparators or high-income countries is presented.

BOX 4.1   How should policy makers interpret the evidence from education evaluations?

Policy researchers use a variety of quantitative methods to evaluate educational interventions. However, the more precise the evidence—especially the ability to make causal inferences that a particular intervention led to a particular outcome—the harder it may be to generalize the finding across diverse settings. So, how should policy makers interpret the accumulating evidence? This box describes different analytical approaches along with the strengths and limitations of each.

Randomized controlled trials

One approach to evaluating the impact of a specific project or program involves randomized controlled trials (RCTs), which can establish a causal effect if properly implemented (that is, if exposure to the intervention is truly random). However, RCTs are generally carried out on small-scale inventions, which makes it difficult to know how well findings from a particular study apply in other settings (that is, RCTs may lack *external validity*). Moreover, RCTs are expensive, so they are not often used to evaluate the impact of a specific intervention in more than one setting.

A challenge related to the external validity of RCTs involves making inferences from small-scale pilot projects about regional or national impacts. A global review by Evans and Yuan (2020) finds that the effect size of smaller studies of education interventions (fewer than 500 students) is roughly twice the effect size of larger studies (more than 5,000 students). Other studies document similar patterns (Pritchett and Sanderfur 2013; Stern, Jukes, and Piper 2020; Vivalt 2020). The high levels of expertise and monitoring that are provided during implementation of small-scale studies, as well as the technical support and encouragement to teachers and administrators, often translate to fidelity of implementation to the original program design that can break down when pilot programs are expanded.

Global and country-level datasets

Another approach is to use the large datasets that are representative at the country level (national assessments) or at the international level—for example, the Programme for International Student Assessment (PISA) of the Organisation for Economic Co-operation and Development; the Trends in International Mathematics and

box continues next page

BOX 4.1   **How should policy makers interpret the evidence from education evaluations?**
(Continued)

Science Study (TIMSS) of the International Association for the Evaluation of Educational Achievement; or the Southeast Asia Primary Learning Metrics (SEA-PLM) assessments.

With these datasets, learning outcomes can be tracked over time and statistical associations (correlations) established between these outcomes and characteristics at the system, school, parent, teacher, or student level. These types of analyses do not usually establish that a certain characteristic *causes* a better (or worse) learning outcome, much less the causal effect of specific policy interventions. Nevertheless, patterns that are consistent and statistically significant on a large scale can provide an important guide to policy.

Quasi-experimental approaches

A third approach comprises quasi-experimental approaches—for example, difference-in-differences, regression discontinuity designs, or instrumental variables. These use large datasets and identify effects that can be interpreted as causal under specific conditions. Quasi-experimental methods are less precise than RCTs, but the results are more generalizable. Relative to simple associations, these analyses are commonly less detailed but can be given a causal interpretation.

Checks for robustness of findings

Although each approach has its own strengths and limitations, certain approaches can help analysts and policy makers assess the robustness of the findings on a particular intervention. For example, where multiple impact evaluations have been carried out on a specific type of program, statistical meta-analyses can be used to assess the expected impact of that intervention across the universe of such interventions. In addition, it is possible to "triangulate" analytical findings across different methodological approaches and types of data. Where findings are consistent across types of analyses, policy makers can have greater confidence in the robustness of the findings.

Training content and methods get results when they match teachers' needs

For training to be effective, it must be guided by data and evidence for several reasons:

- Data are needed on teachers' knowledge and pedagogical skills to match the content and dosage of the training to teachers' needs. The government of Malaysia, for example, has used assessment data on teachers' English language skills to inform whom to train and how much training was needed (see box 4.2).
- Training methodologies should seek to ensure, not assume, that all teachers understand the subject material they are supposed to teach. Too often, training on a new curriculum is about informing teachers of what is in the curriculum rather than ensuring they understand it or can convey it effectively to their students.
- The design of training should be informed by what works. As discussed in chapter 3, analysis of high-impact in-service teacher training programs from around the world indicates that effective programs have four key features (also called the "four C's"): (a) a *content* knowledge focus, (b) practice with *colleagues*, (c) *continued* support through follow-up visits focused on training content, and (d) *career* incentives through promotion or increased salary.

Moreover, a growing body of rigorous evaluation evidence from the region and beyond can help guide policy makers in designing better education policies.

Impact evaluations have revealed interventions with positive outcomes

Evidence from impact evaluations of teacher training programs in East Asia and Pacific that combine the four "C's" highlight their effectiveness in raising student learning. For instance, the Tonga "Come Let's Read and Write" (CLRW) program provided training focused on content and a new method to teach reading, follow-up in the form of regular coaching focused on subject content, plus instructional materials. The program operated during the 2015/16, 2016/17, and 2017/18 school years. Average reading scores improved by 0.19 standard deviations after one year of intervention and 0.33 standard deviations after two years[4] (figure 4.4, panel a), increasing the proportion of second-grade students who could read from 18 percent to 29 percent (Macdonald et al. 2018). Effects for girls and boys were similar.

Even relatively short-duration programs can yield significant results. The Sa Aklat Sisikat (SAS) program in the Philippines provided teachers with a two-day training in 2009 to incorporate the teaching of reading throughout the curriculum. It targeted fourth-grade teachers in public schools in Tarlac Province and provided them with storybooks, a teacher's manual, and corresponding reading materials. The initial training focused on practice with other teachers and emphasizing Socratic, progressive methods built around questions, discussions, acting out stories, and playing. It included three follow-up visits to teachers in their classrooms.

Despite being of relatively short duration—the main component of the program was a read-a-thon over 31 days—the program improved reading skills by 0.13 standard deviations (Abeberese, Kumler, and Linden 2014), as shown in figure 4.4, panel b. A follow-up evaluation of the program three months later found significant improvements in student learning outcomes, albeit somewhat smaller (0.06 standard deviations). This highlights the importance of follow-up and continuity in teacher support to ensure that the full benefits of teacher training methods persist.

FIGURE 4.4   **Rigorous impact evaluations of in-service teacher training programs in East Asia and Pacific show that well-designed, well-implemented training can lead to better learning outcomes**

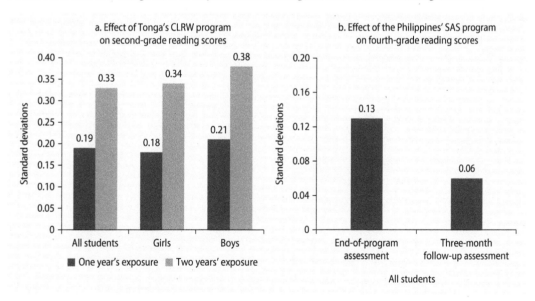

Sources: Macdonald et al. 2018 (panel a); Abeberese, Kumler, and Linden 2014 (panel b).

Note: Panel a shows the improvement (in standard deviations) in reading scores from the Tonga Early Grade Reading Assessment (TEGRA) of second-grade students at one and two years after their teachers received training through the Come Let's Read and Write (CLRW) program. The estimated effect size for all students lies outside the range estimates for girls and boys. This is likely due to the fact that the gender-specific effects were estimated separately from the all-student effects. Panel b shows the improvement (in standard deviations) in reading scores from a bespoke reading skills assessment, based in part on a national reading examination created and administered annually by the Philippine Department of Education after teachers received a two-day training through the Sa Aklat Sisikat (SAS) program and subsequently led fourth-grade students in a 31-day read-a-thon. The follow-up assessment was conducted three months later.

Effective teacher training programs have positive financial returns, with benefits far out-weighing costs. Programs in East Asia and Pacific have found benefit-cost ratios ranging from 7.5 to 1 to 12.3 to 1. For the Tonga CLRW program, for example, the present value of per pupil program costs is $116, compared with the $1,425 present value of the per pupil benefits from higher future earnings projected from increased cognitive skills obtained through the program (figure 4.5).[5] In the case of the Philippines SAS program, the corresponding figures are costs of $85 per student, set against $640 in benefits.

These findings are consistent with recent evidence from outside the East Asia and Pacific region. Evans and Yuan (2019) estimate that the present value of pupils' future earnings as a result of effective teacher training programs globally ranges from $959 owing to the India PicTalk program (25th percentile) to $24,369 owing to Brazil's new curriculum training pro-gram (75th percentile), with a median present value of $1,338 on future earnings per indi-vidual pupil.

Several governments' training programs are designed for effectiveness
Several promising examples of large-scale government training programs in the region include all four features (the four C's) of effective programs—although, for the most part, their impact on student learning has not been demonstrated through rigorous evaluation:

- *In Thailand,* the Academic Olympiad and Development of Math and Science Education Program was designed and implemented by the government with the POSN Foundation.[6] The program, which trained 6,444 teachers in 2021, its 11th year of implementation, tar-gets teachers by subject, grade (10–12), and skills gaps.[7] The training is formally linked with teacher opportunities for promotion and provides follow-up support to teachers as needed.
- *In Timor-Leste,* a training program to support the introduction of the 3rd Cycle Mathematics and Science Curriculum Revision seeks to improve teachers' laboratory expe-rience. In its second year of implementation, the government-designed and -implemented training program provided teachers with 15 days of training as well as teaching manuals

FIGURE 4.5   **Effective teacher training programs in East Asia and Pacific yield positive rates of return on investment**

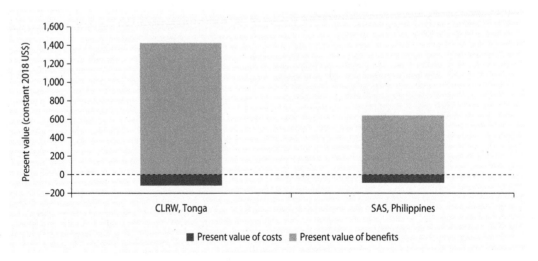

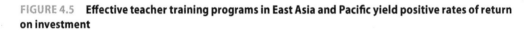

Sources: Macdonald et al. 2018 (for Tonga's CLRW program); World Bank estimates (for the Philippines' SAS program).
Note: Figure shows the estimated present value of costs and benefits per student (in US dollars) of three countries' teacher training interventions. Benefits are estimated as the effects on future earnings per student from increases in either cognitive skills or educational attainment. CLRW = Come Let's Read and Write; SAS = Sa Aklat Sisikat.

and teaching kits.[8] The program incentivizes teachers to perform by offering them in-kind gifts for improving teaching outcomes after program participation, and it includes multiple follow-up visits (more than 30 throughout the year) as well as phone calls and text messages to monitor and support teachers.

- *In Malaysia,* the large-scale Professional Upskilling for English Language Teachers (ProELT) program to improve English language teaching skills is particularly noteworthy for its strong focus on establishing a robust baseline of performance, using that baseline to target the program and tailor learning resources to individual teachers' language capabilities, and conducting a postprogram assessment and survey to identify the level of success—in teachers' proficiency and students' learning—and the reasons for it (box 4.2).

BOX 4.2 **Malaysia's push to upgrade English language skills of teachers and students**

A core ambition of Malaysia Education Blueprint 2013–25 is to improve students' mastery of the English language. However, when the Blueprint was written in 2011, it was not known how many teachers needed training, how fast an upgrade of teachers' skills could be achieved, and at what cost. So, in 2012, all 24,075 teachers who had been specifically trained as English language teachers were tested. The testing found that 15,465 (65 percent) of these teachers fell short of the required minimum proficiency level ("C1" on the Common European Framework of Reference for Languages, CEFR), as shown in figure B4.2.1.

FIGURE B4.2.1 **Most Malaysian English language teachers lacked minimum English proficiency in 2012**

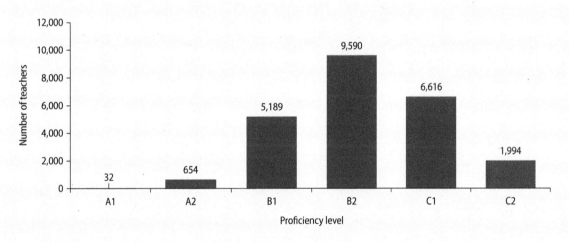

Source: Malaysia MOE 2014, Exhibit 3-11.
Note: The English language proficiency of 24,075 Malaysian English language teachers was measured using the British Council's Aptis English language test and reported against Common European Framework of Reference for Languages (CEFR) proficiency levels—which range from "A1" (the lowest, basic user) to "C2" (highest). "C1" designates the minimum level for CEFR language "proficient user."

In response, the Ministry of Education (MOE) set up a program called Professional Upskilling for English Language Teachers (ProELT) to train the 14,479 teachers who did not yet meet required minimum proficiency levels but had some English language proficiency (testing at CEFR level B1 or B2). The aim was to raise the level of language proficiency by one level (from B1 to B2 or from B2 to C1). To reach and support teachers who were spread across the country and busy teaching, ProELT combined face-to-face and virtual learning modules, which could be flexibly scheduled over a 12-month period, although teachers had to complete 240 hours of face-to-face interaction and another 240 hours of self-paced digital learning (online and/or offline). Moreover, the resources and training materials were designed to match the teachers' language proficiency levels.

box continues next page

BOX 4.2   Malaysia's push to upgrade English language skills of teachers and students
(Continued)

From 2012 to 2015, two cohorts of teachers (totaling approximately 14,000) took the ProELT course, with the cohorts being trained by native English speakers from the British Council. Subsequent cohorts were smaller, averaging 1,000–2,000 per year, and training was taken over by local providers with non-native English language speakers, with an independent panel to assess the quality of training.

The MOE's English Language Teaching Centre (ELTC) with Universiti Kebangsaan Malaysia (UKM) conducted an impact study of the first cohort that participated in ProELT, which showed that ProELT participants improved in three areas:

- *Teachers' proficiency improved:* They used more extensive vocabulary, lengthier sentences, and clearer language instructions, and had improved pronunciation and fluency. They also had greater confidence while giving classroom instructions and speaking in front of others, and they reduced the use of languages other than English in the classroom.
- *Teachers' pedagogy improved:* More student-focused lessons allowed for student autonomy, varied strategies and approaches, and more self-reflection as teachers became more aware of their teaching routines.
- *Students' English-language use increased:* Students reduced their classroom use of their first language and were more willing to participate in classroom activities.

A second evaluation, done by ELTC in 2015, focused on the impact of ProELT on student outcomes. The study focused on 242 teachers who completed ProELT and 463 students from 15 primary and 5 secondary schools. Classroom observations showed most of the teachers were motivated to deliver a more creative approach to teaching and learning. Their students—tested before and after the teachers had taken ProELT—showed a 4 percent improvement in achievement on tests that contained cloze passages[a] and essay writing administered over a three-month period.

Sources: MOE Malaysia Education Blueprint 2013–2025 annual reports, various years.
a. Cloze procedure is a reading comprehension activity that involves a passage of text with missing words that need to be filled in from a list of words. Pupils use the surrounding words and context in the passage to identify the correct or an appropriate word from the list.

Coaching and mentoring are key elements of effective follow-up
One key feature of effective training programs is follow-up—such as through visits to teachers once they return to their schools. Such follow-up can support teachers in implementing the content of the training. Coaching and mentoring can be effective tools for strengthening teaching by supporting teachers, either one-on-one or in teacher groups, to address their ongoing classroom challenges and be responsive to their specific capacity issues. Coaching and mentoring are analogous to the approach that teachers strive to take with students when they respond to students' individual needs.

Implementing coaching and mentoring at scale is likely to be a challenge for many East Asian and Pacific countries, given the lack of experience with this approach in the region and therefore the lack of qualified coaches and mentors. However, it will be essential to develop such systems to improve the performance of teachers and realize the full benefits of training programs.

Coaching and mentoring have been shown to be effective at raising learning outcomes in middle-income country contexts, although no rigorous evaluations have been carried out in East Asian and Pacific countries to date. Elsewhere, in Peru, a program under which specially trained government employees at the district level visited teachers monthly raised reading comprehension by 0.25 standard deviations and mathematics performance by 0.38 standard deviations (Castro, Glewwe, and Montero 2019). Other effective programs in middle-income countries include those in Kenya and South Africa (table 4.1).

Table 4.1 **Coaching and mentoring programs have been effective in raising student learning outcomes in middle-income country settings**

Acompañamiento Pedagogico Multigrado, Peru	Tusome Early Grade Reading Activity, Kenya	Early Grade Reading Study (EGRS I and II), South Africa
Student learning improved by 0.25 standard deviations (SDs) in reading comprehension and 0.38 SDs in mathematics.	Student learning improved by 0.63 SDs and 0.76 SDs across a range of Kiswahili reading tasks, in grade 1 and grade 2, respectively.	Student learning improved by 0.24 SDs in mother tongue reading proficiency (EGRS I), by 0.31 SDs in English oral language proficiency, and by 0.13 SDs in English reading proficiency (EGRS II).

Source: Wilichowski and Popova 2021.
Note: The table presents examples of effective one-to-one support programs for teachers of primary grades in selected middle-income countries.

The details of coaching programs can vary in the ratio of pedagogical leaders to teachers (from 1 to 11 in low-structured programs to 44 to 1 in highly structured programs); the frequency of visits (typically one per month); and the amount of time that coaches and teachers spend together per visit (typically about one hour, including both classroom observation and feedback). Effective programs also commonly include additional group training to discuss and practice pedagogical methods and encourage the exchange of ideas (Wilichowski and Popova 2021).

Beyond specific coaching and mentoring programs, the high-performing education systems in East Asia have developed cultures of "continuous improvement" in which observation of teachers by other education professionals and feedback on their classroom practices is encouraged, with the objective of improving teaching and enhancing student learning (World Bank 2018). Japan's "lesson study" is the epitome of this approach—although the approach has been adopted elsewhere in the region. Lesson study brings together teachers of different skill and experience levels to discuss techniques and formulate sample teaching plans. Several high-performing systems in the region also foster extensive collaboration with networks and learning communities of teachers. Indeed, Japan, Korea, Singapore, and Shanghai, China, all have policies that encourage regular observation of teachers and critiquing of their classroom practices by other education professionals to improve teaching and enhance student learning.

Tools to support teachers include scripted lessons, targeted instruction, technology, and the dual teacher model

Teachers can be supported in being more effective with several different tools, such as (a) structured lessons plans, (b) targeted instruction, (c) educational technology (EdTech), and (d) the dual teacher model.

Structured lesson plans range from scripts to guides

Structured lesson plans (also called structured pedagogy) range from highly scripted lessons that teachers simply follow carefully, reading from a prepared script, to guides that teachers can depend on while also having the freedom to deviate according to their skills and confidence. Where teachers lack pedagogical skills or subject knowledge, the lesson scripts can be more prescriptive, as they lead the teacher, and thus the student, through a series of activities designed by the best teachers. Scripted lessons need to be linked to materials that are available to students, including textbooks.

Experience across middle-income countries, including Cambodia and the Philippines, shows that providing these teacher guides—on which teachers need training for their most effective use—leads to significant learning gains. Such gains can be equivalent to an additional half year or more of learning, raising student language scores by 0.23 standard deviations (figure 4.6) and mathematics scores by 0.14 standard deviations on average (Snilstveit et al. 2015).

FIGURE 4.6 **Structured pedagogy can be effective in raising student learning outcomes**

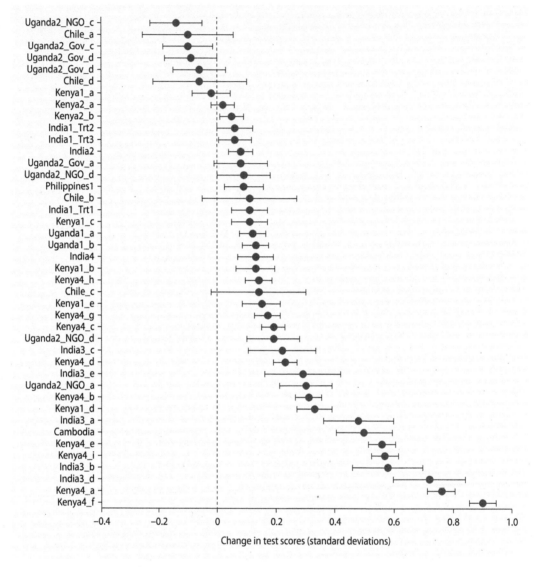

Change in test scores (standard deviations)

Source: Adapted from Snilstveit et al. 2015.
Note: The figure shows the impact on language arts test scores in grades 1–3 from structured pedagogy interventions in a sample of six middle-income countries, two of which (Cambodia and the Philippines) are in the East Asia and Pacific region. Brown dots designate the effect sizes for language arts (in standard deviations), and whiskers designate the 95 percent confidence interval. The black dashed line represents zero impact of the intervention. Negative values mean that students performed worse than they would have without the intervention. Numbers, letters, and abbreviations following country names in the listed interventions distinguish between the various studies reviewed by Snilstveit et al. (2015), who found that that most structured pedagogy interventions are positive (that is, to the right of the black dashed line) and that this is true for a range of interventions across a range of countries.

Although the impact of structured lesson plans on learning is almost always found to be positive, the size of the effect varies, with large impacts for language arts in Cambodia (0.50 standard deviations) but smaller effect sizes in the Philippines (0.09 standard deviations).

Evaluation of Papua New Guinea's Reader Booster Programme found particularly large effects of highly scripted lessons on student reading skills. The program provided teachers with training on a highly structured teaching method that they could apply one hour per day within the teaching time allocated to reading. Importantly, the curriculum provided flexibility for teachers on how to use the time allocated for language learning, and so this program was designed as a targeted remedial reading program for use in language teaching time during the regular school day. The program targeted the reading skills of initial sounds and familiar words and had positive impacts (0.6–0.7 standard deviations) on these skills for third-grade students (Macdonald and Vu 2018). The program also had positive impacts on other reading skills including reading comprehension, oral comprehension, and oral reading fluency.

Targeted instruction helps children learn by meeting them where they are

Targeted instruction—an approach sometimes known as teaching at the right level (TaRL)[9]—helps teachers address the major challenge that, in any given classroom, children have achieved different levels of learning. Teachers in East Asia and Pacific commonly face the challenge that in any given classroom the children they are trying to teach have a wide range of achievement levels; given the high rates of learning poverty, many students will be behind the expected levels of progression embedded in the national curriculum.[10] Moreover, teachers are often pushed to complete the curriculum without regard to the actual progress of their students.[11] Teaching children at different achievement levels has been made even more critical given pandemic-related learning losses.

Targeted instruction involves grouping students by learning levels, rather than age or grade, and engaging them in activities appropriate to their levels of academic achievement, often in small groups. This can be done both in school (by setting aside one hour a day when all children change classrooms) or through out-of-school catch-up camps.

International evidence indicates that targeted instruction is highly effective, whether implemented by government teachers or external organizations. In the Indian state of Haryana, for example, regular schoolteachers using the model led to students being 5 percentage points more likely to be able to read a story; in the Indian state of Uttar Pradesh, an in-school program run by an external organization resulted in students being 25 percentage points more likely to be able to read a story (Banerjee et al. 2017).

Targeted instruction is also highly cost-effective—delivering, on average, the equivalent of more than three years of high-quality schooling per $100 spent (Angrist et al. 2020). Although targeted instruction is an intervention focused on students, it is implemented by teachers in their classrooms, and as such, in-service training programs can play an important role in preparing teachers to use the approach. Two implementation considerations: A targeted instruction program must be built on evidence of students' knowledge and progress, so that students can be grouped and instruction targeted appropriately. In addition, targeted instruction requires flexible organization at the school level since it requires that children in different grades study the same subject at the same time; as such, it is not a strategy for teaching all subjects all the time.

Educational technologies can strengthen classroom teaching and learning

Educational technologies provide another set of useful tools for strengthening teaching and learning in the classroom. Interest in and use of educational technologies grew dramatically during COVID-19–related school closures. Different types of digital technologies have potential in several areas for policy action, and there is some emerging evidence about where technology can be useful and how to deploy it effectively. For example, evidence shows that the use of technology can implement remote coaching support and provide a platform for structured lesson plans and computer-assisted learning.

However, the findings also indicate that these technologies are most effective when teachers use them to teach more effectively. In this respect, the experience of the pandemic is both misleading and illustrative. During the pandemic, technology (and distance learning more generally) was used to try to provide learning opportunities for students in their homes; however, often, technology was used to provide learning materials directly to students and was not mediated or supported by teachers. It is perhaps for this very reason that those learning opportunities proved largely ineffective in helping students learn at a significant pace.

Remote coaching support. Technology has been used to provide coaching at a distance, although initial evidence suggests it has been less effective than in-person coaching. By providing remote support, coaches can reduce their travel time and hence provide support to more teachers, and they can also communicate directly albeit remotely. This can also help address shortages of trained coaches. In Brazil and Chile, for example, coaches observe videos of teachers teaching and provide remote feedback.

An evaluation in South Africa found virtual coaching to be less effective than in-person coaching, however. After three years, *in-person* support to teachers improved their students' English oral language and reading proficiency by 0.31 standard deviations and 0.13 standard deviations, respectively, whereas *remote* support improved English oral language proficiency by only 0.12 standard deviations, had no impact on English reading proficiency, and had an unintended negative effect on home language literacy (Cillers et al. 2022). The remote program was also found to be less cost-effective, in part because of the limited development of the required technology infrastructure. Moreover, the evidence suggests that successful remote programs must ensure more frequent interactions between teachers and coaches than in-person programs, in part to generate the appropriate accountability and support that is characteristic of in-person programs (Wilichowski and Popova 2021).

Platforms for structured lesson plans. Technology can help with structured lesson plans as they can be loaded onto a website or tablet for offline use. This type of EdTech enables teachers to keep track of progress and update content regularly as needed. For example, the Tusome Early Grade Reading Activity in Kenya is a highly structured national program that provides teachers with structured teaching guides and trains "pedagogical leaders" to help teachers use the guides. These pedagogical leaders are commonly government employees who receive tablets loaded with pedagogical resources and have a Global Positioning System (GPS) to support and track visits to teachers. A separate implementation firm provides additional support. A recent impact evaluation of this program found that student learning improved by 0.63 and 0.76 standard deviations across a range of Kiswahili reading tasks in grades 1 and 2, respectively (Wilichowski and Popova 2021).

Computer-assisted learning. As a supplement to traditional classroom instruction, computer-assisted learning (CAL) has proven highly effective. CAL refers to interventions in which students engage in self-directed learning with the assistance of a computer software program. In general, CAL software packages aim to improve student learning in a specific subject area through drills and exercises that give students opportunities to practice material learned in class and by providing immediate feedback. The evidence suggests that CAL is most effective in improving learning outcomes when it is used to complement classroom learning—and hence part of improved teaching practice—and not as a substitute for instruction by a teacher. Thus, CAL may be best used as a remedial platform for students to review material already taught in class (Linden 2008).

CAL has demonstrated success in a variety of country contexts. Evidence from East Asian and Pacific countries shows that most CAL interventions have had positive impacts on learning outcomes, and in some instances, the improvements have been large (figure 4.7). Evaluation evidence from India similarly shows positive impacts of CAL on student learning: increases of 0.37 standard deviations in mathematics performance and of 0.23 standard deviations in Hindi achievement over just a 4.5-month period as part of a teacher-supported after-school tutoring program (Muralidharan, Singh, and Ganimian 2019).

In principle, adaptive CAL could support targeted instruction, although more evidence is needed on its effectiveness. In the past decade, CAL platforms with adaptive features have become increasingly available. These platforms use algorithms and artificial intelligence to adjust learning content, sequence, and difficulty based on individual learners' performance in much the same way that a teacher can teach at the right level.

FIGURE 4.7   Computer-assisted learning programs have helped improve student learning in selected East Asian and Pacific economies

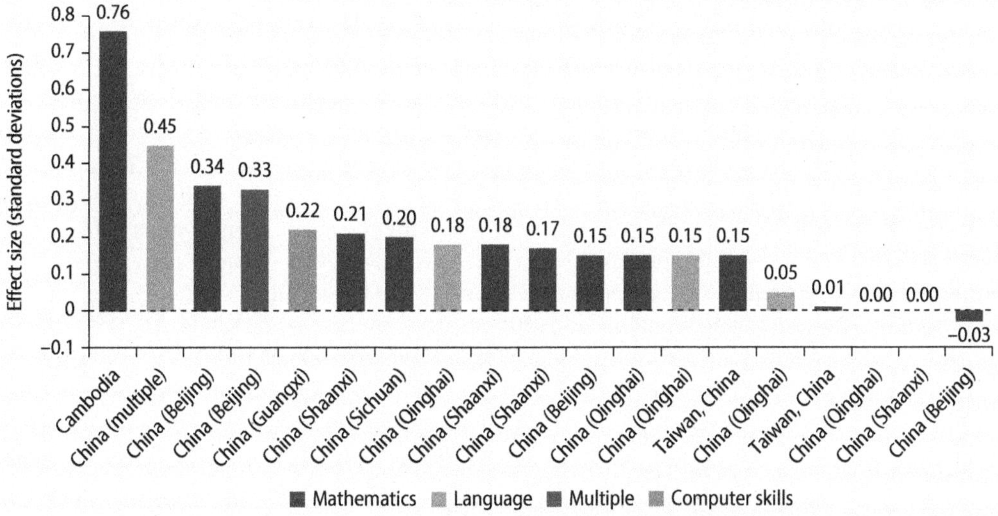

Source: Adapted from Yarrow et al., forthcoming.
Note: The figure shows the impact (in standard deviations) of computer-assisted learning programs on student performance, by subject area. Parentheses indicate Chinese provinces.

Evidence on the effectiveness of adaptive platforms is still relatively thin. Although one seminal study in India exhibited significant positive effects (Muralidharan, Singh, and Ganimian 2019), the evaluation also included group-based tutoring with a teacher and, as such, it was difficult to separate out the impacts of each intervention component. In one instance in China, a remedial, game-based CAL platform was not found to improve academic outcomes relative to a pencil-and-paper workbook group (Ma et al. 2020). And several studies have found no significant differences between adaptive platforms and nonadaptive platforms regarding student learning outcomes (Eau, Judah, and Shahid 2019; Klaveren, Vonk, and Cornelisz 2017; Vanbecelaere et al. 2019), including one recent study conducted in rural China (Feng et al. 2023). The available evidence is that CAL—and thus adaptive CAL—is most effective when linked to the curriculum and in-classroom activities and that effective CAL includes engagement of a teacher in focusing and encouraging students and answering their questions.

The dual teacher model can extend the reach of good teaching
Remote instruction, sometimes called the dual teacher model, has also contributed to improved student learning in several middle-income countries. The dual teacher model extends the reach of the best teachers by enabling them to provide content and model elements of effective pedagogy in school environments where teacher capacity is lacking. This approach, in which expert teachers provide content through either prerecorded or livestreamed sessions, has had significant positive impacts on learning in several rural contexts where high-quality teachers are in short supply, including in China, Ghana, India, Mexico, and Pakistan (Beg et al., 2019; Borghesan and Vasey, forthcoming; Johnston and Christopher 2017; Li et al., 2023; Naik et al. 2020).

Impacts have been found in multiple subject areas across a range of grade levels. In the East Asia and Pacific region, a study of seventh to ninth graders in China found improvements in student learning of 0.23 standard deviations in language and 0.18 standard deviations in mathematics (Bianchi, Lu, and Song 2022). It is noteworthy that three of the cited studies—in China, India, and Mexico—were scaled-up interventions implemented by governments, not small pilot programs. And notably, in contrast to the remote instruction during COVID-19–related school closures, these remote instruction interventions all took place in the classroom during the regular school day, and they involved a teacher's classroom presence with the students in addition to the remote teacher who transmitted prerecorded or livestreamed lectures.

In sum, although EdTech shows some promise in supporting teaching and learning, the evidence also highlights that much more still needs to be learned on how to harness educational technologies effectively. EdTech is a tool, and the evidence suggests it is most effective as a supplement to good teaching, not as a substitute. Moreover, emerging experience, including from the COVID-19 pandemic, suggests that in and of itself—in the absence of engaged, effective teachers and adequate affordable educational technologies—EdTech is unlikely to have a significant positive impact on learning outcomes in the region (box 4.3).

BOX 4.3   The promise and perils of educational technology

During the COVID-19 pandemic, the use of educational technology (EdTech) increased substantially in East Asia and Pacific. By May 2021, more than 70 percent of the region's countries had reported the establishment of online platforms and the provision of take-home packages across all education levels (UNICEF 2021). While the evidence indicates that EdTech has the potential to contribute to better teaching and stronger learning outcomes, it also highlights that EdTech is most effective when it is well integrated with the curriculum and used as a supplement to classroom teaching rather than as a substitute. Successful EdTech interventions include support to teachers (for example, training in their use) and are well connected with other parts of the teaching process.

Growth in the use of technology during the pandemic also highlighted some risks associated with EdTech that must be addressed if EdTech is to serve as a tool for improving teaching and learning that is both effective and inclusive. For example, the pandemic exposed prepandemic gaps in access and the ability to use educational technologies. Across East Asia and Pacific, 32 percent of children had no internet connectivity at home (UNICEF and ITU 2020). Students in poor or remote rural households have significantly less access to internet—or even access to computers for schoolwork—than those in wealthy or urban households. Even when households had access to a computer or mobile phone, the effectiveness of EdTech as a learning tool was often impeded because multiple children needed to use a single device or parents' lack of knowledge or ability to help their children with EdTech tools (World Bank 2020b).

Moreover, some EdTech approaches that appear promising have yet to contribute to learning outcomes, at least in middle-income country contexts. For example, e-readers would seem to have potential to support student learning if integrated into the curriculum. Some aspects of the technology—such as the ability to make text larger, provide web links to additional material, or provide the same text in many different languages—may be helpful for certain learners and contexts. Evidence from a small-scale study in Korea showed gains in learning associated with the introduction of digital textbooks as a supplement to other, printed material (Lee et al. 2023). However, a study in Lagos, Nigeria, found that e-readers with material aligned with the curriculum led to increased student learning only in the absence of textbooks, whereas e-readers with reading material that was not related to the curriculum led to decreases in student learning in both reading and mathematics (Habyarimana and Sabarwal 2018).

To enable countries to benefit from the promise of EdTech, it will be important to ensure that technologies are well integrated with school curricula and support rather than being used to replace teachers. In addition, it will be important to address identified risks associated with access and use, including through experimentation, evaluation, and adjustment of approaches when needed.

Incentives to motivate greater teacher effort

Even teachers who have mastered their subject content and have the right pedagogical knowl-edge and tools must be in the classroom and *use* their knowledge and the tools to enable their students to learn more and acquire the foundational skills. Teacher motivation to engage in effective practice is therefore an important consideration, especially given, as noted earlier, that teachers often work under difficult circumstances. The COVID-19 pandemic reinforced the chal-lenges many teachers face.

The high-performance systems in East Asia and Pacific have ways to enable the best teachers to share their good practices and help other teachers improve their practice. Conversely, policy makers must decide how to address the challenge of teachers who continue to perform below expectations, even after having been supported to improve. This section examines several types of incentives that could motivate teachers to perform effectively. Bruns and Luque (2015) identify three broad categories: professional rewards, financial incentives, and accountability pressure.

Professional rewards bolster teacher effort

Professional rewards include well-equipped, congenial working conditions; intrinsic motivation;[12] recognition and prestige; and mastery and professional growth. Data collected from Finland's high-performing education system indicates that teachers there have high intrinsic motivation fostered by a high degree of autonomy and relatively low classroom teaching hours, enabling teachers to work jointly outside of class hours (OECD 2013).

However, few evaluations exist from middle-income East Asian and Pacific countries that would help policy makers identify effective policies in the regional context. One of the few studies from the region analyzes how promotion incentives among primary- and middle-school teachers in China affect teacher effort (Karachiwalla and Park 2017). The authors find that teachers' effort, as reflected in teacher time use and student test scores, increases with their prospects of promotion and associated pay increases. This evidence is consistent with the evidence discussed earlier that effective teacher training programs commonly include incen-tives linked to career progression or higher earnings (Popova et al. 2022).

Financial incentives seek to pay for performance

One popular financial incentive policy used in some countries is performance pay.[13] Across countries in the region, public support for performance pay systems varies, with substan-tial support in some middle-income countries—for example, 74 percent of those surveyed in Indonesia and 51 percent in Malaysia (figure 4.8).

The intuitive appeal is clear: if teachers were paid in line with student outcomes, then teach-ers should be motivated to work harder and more effectively to achieve those outcomes. This proposal may also appeal to policy makers because it does not involve making fundamental changes to teacher pay scales (unlike many career-based incentives), and these programs can be suspended more easily if ineffective. Pay-for-performance programs implicitly operate on the presumption that it is teachers' *motivation*, not their *capabilities*, that is the binding con-straint to their effective performance.

Global evidence on performance pay programs is mixed and suggests that their overall impact on student learning is small. The literature on the longer-term effectiveness of teacher performance pay finds few examples of positive impacts on learning at scale. The best-known example is the National System of School Performance Assessment (SNED) in Chile. SNED is a group incentive program in which schools compete against their peers on the basis of their

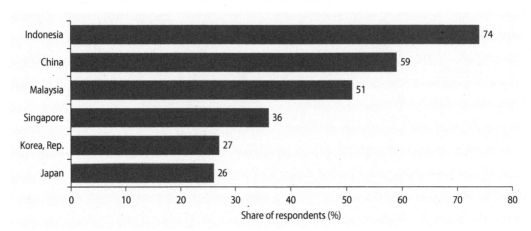

FIGURE 4.8 **Public support for teacher performance pay is high in middle-income East Asian countries**

Source: Varkey Foundation 2018.
Note: The figure shows the shares of surveyed members of the general public in selected East Asian countries who answered, "Strongly agree" or "Tend to agree" to the question, "Should teachers be rewarded in pay according to their pupils' results?"

average performance and in which monetary rewards are mainly distributed equally among all teachers in the winning schools. Evaluation evidence shows a significant effect on schools' performance of 0.14–0.25 standard deviations for language and mathematics scores (Contreras and Rau 2012).

Overall, however, most evaluations show no significant impact or very small impacts on student performance, as shown in figure 4.9 (Pham, Springer, and Nguyen 2017; see also Breeding, Béteille, and Evans 2021). This may partially explain the much lower public support for performance pay among high-performing countries in East Asia—only 26 percent and 27 percent in Japan and Korea, respectively (figure 4.8)—and why few programs have been sustained over time in low- and middle-income countries.

Accountability mechanisms show mixed impacts on teacher conduct

More evidence is available about the effect of accountability mechanisms on teacher conduct than about the performance pay effects, although the link to improved learning outcomes has yet to be consistently established.

School-based management gives parents and communities a bigger voice
The most common and evaluated accountability mechanism is school-based management (SBM), especially those "strong" forms in which parents and community members have a voice in the hiring and firing of teachers. SBM can help change the dynamics at the school level, by increasing parental involvement or effecting changes in teacher behavior (especially reducing absenteeism), and at the pupil level by lowering repetition and dropouts. However, the evidence about the relationship between SBM implementation and student learning (for example, on standardized tests) is mixed. A recent evaluation that took advantage of a randomized assignment of primary schools under the Quality School Program (Programa Escuelas de Calidad, or PEC) in the Mexican state of Colima found no impact on learning outcomes after eight years (Garcia-Moreno, Gertler, and Patrinos 2019).

In contrast, an Indonesian program that empowered communities to hold teachers accountable and that used cameras in classrooms to monitor teacher presence increased both teaching hours and, consequently, learning outcomes by 0.17–0.20 standard

FIGURE 4.9 **Most pay-for-performance schemes have little effect on student learning**

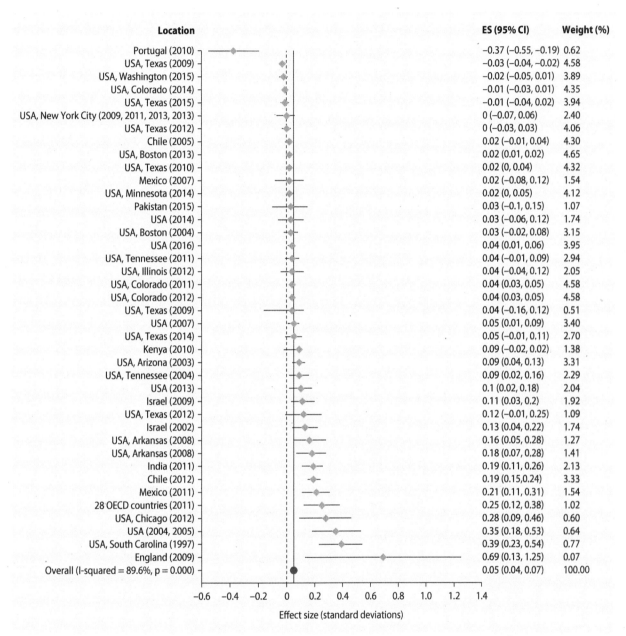

Location	ES (95% CI)	Weight (%)
Portugal (2010)	–0.37 (–0.55, –0.19)	0.62
USA, Texas (2009)	–0.03 (–0.04, –0.02)	4.58
USA, Washington (2015)	–0.02 (–0.05, 0.01)	3.89
USA, Colorado (2014)	–0.01 (–0.03, 0.01)	4.35
USA, Texas (2015)	–0.01 (–0.04, 0.02)	3.94
USA, New York City (2009, 2011, 2013, 2013)	0 (–0.07, 0.06)	2.40
USA, Texas (2012)	0 (–0.03, 0.03)	4.06
Chile (2005)	0.02 (–0.01, 0.04)	4.30
USA, Boston (2013)	0.02 (0.01, 0.02)	4.65
USA, Texas (2010)	0.02 (0, 0.04)	4.32
Mexico (2007)	0.02 (–0.08, 0.12)	1.54
USA, Minnesota (2014)	0.02 (0, 0.05)	4.12
Pakistan (2015)	0.03 (–0.1, 0.15)	1.07
USA (2014)	0.03 (–0.06, 0.12)	1.74
USA, Boston (2004)	0.03 (–0.02, 0.08)	3.15
USA (2016)	0.04 (0.01, 0.06)	3.95
USA, Tennessee (2011)	0.04 (–0.01, 0.09)	2.94
USA, Illinois (2012)	0.04 (–0.04, 0.12)	2.05
USA, Colorado (2011)	0.04 (0.03, 0.05)	4.58
USA, Colorado (2012)	0.04 (0.03, 0.05)	4.58
USA, Texas (2009)	0.04 (–0.16, 0.12)	0.51
USA (2007)	0.05 (0.01, 0.09)	3.40
USA, Texas (2014)	0.05 (–0.01, 0.11)	2.70
Kenya (2010)	0.09 (–0.02, 0.02)	1.38
USA, Arizona (2003)	0.09 (0.04, 0.13)	3.31
USA, Tennessee (2004)	0.09 (0.02, 0.16)	2.29
USA (2013)	0.1 (0.02, 0.18)	2.04
Israel (2009)	0.11 (0.03, 0.2)	1.92
USA, Texas (2012)	0.12 (–0.01, 0.25)	1.09
Israel (2002)	0.13 (0.04, 0.22)	1.74
USA, Arkansas (2008)	0.16 (0.05, 0.28)	1.27
USA, Arkansas (2008)	0.18 (0.07, 0.28)	1.41
India (2011)	0.19 (0.11, 0.26)	2.13
Chile (2012)	0.19 (0.15, 0.24)	3.33
Mexico (2011)	0.21 (0.11, 0.31)	1.54
28 OECD countries (2011)	0.25 (0.12, 0.38)	1.02
USA, Chicago (2012)	0.28 (0.09, 0.46)	0.60
USA (2004, 2005)	0.35 (0.18, 0.53)	0.64
USA, South Carolina (1997)	0.39 (0.23, 0.54)	0.77
England (2009)	0.69 (0.13, 1.25)	0.07
Overall (I-squared = 89.6%, p = 0.000)	0.05 (0.04, 0.07)	100.00

Effect size (standard deviations)

Source: Pham, Springer, and Nguyen 2017.
Note: Orange diamonds indicate the effect size (ES), in standard deviations, and the whiskers indicate the 95 percent confidence interval (CI). Both ES and CI values are shown numerically under the "ES (95% CI)" column. The year(s) of the analysis is shown within parentheses after locations. Weights are from random effects analysis. Correlation between multiple outcomes within a study, r, is 0.5. OECD = Organisation for Economic Co-operation and Development.

deviations (Gaduh et al. 2020). Notably, however, this program addressed multiple failures in the local accountability system, and improvements in learning were observed even without cameras. It is also noteworthy that the program was relatively small and in locations with specific characteristics, which raises questions about the potential scalability of the intervention (box 4.4).

BOX 4.4 **Strengthening teacher performance and accountability: Lessons from an Indonesian experiment**

The Teacher Performance and Accountability interventions (called KIAT Guru in Indonesian) showed that strong accountability to school communities can shift teacher behavior and improve student learning. There were two core components: (a) a social accountability mechanism (SAM) to formulate local education service standards and a user committee to monitor their adherence; and (b) a pay-for-performance mechanism linking results to the amount of a remote-area teacher allowance received from the government. Monitoring indicators were either teacher presence or a wide variety of indicators, including teacher presence plus locally formulated education service performance. The intervention design included testing different combinations of the SAM, number of monitoring indicators, and links to teachers' pay.

Student learning outcomes improved under all combinations, but the effects were largest when SAM was combined with teacher pay based on presence in school, proven by pictures taken by teachers at the beginning and end of a school day using a tamper-proof camera application. The SAM alone and the SAM with a wide variety of indicators improved Indonesian language and mathematics outcomes by 0.07 and 0.11 standard deviations, respectively. However, SAM plus monitoring teacher presence solely (rather than a wider range of indicators) yielded student learning impacts that were up to twice as large (0.17 and 0.20 standard deviations).

The strength and coherence of the accountability system seems to be central to explaining the results. A follow-up study conducted one year after the project facilitators left the villages showed that student outcomes where SAM was combined with monitoring teacher presence continued to be better and statistically significant compared with other combinations and the control group, whereas the SAM-only intervention was no longer statistically significant compared with the control group. This result suggests that when the community has weak authority over teachers, the presence of project facilitators provided additional support for the community. The provision of the camera monitoring seemed to increase the community's authority, and the use of a narrow but verifiable set of indicators (for example, just teacher presence) works better in this context than using a set of more comprehensive but subjective indicators. The data produced under the "teacher monitoring by camera" intervention was reported directly to the district and national government, which maintained some of the pressure for sustained teacher and parental efforts.

A second phase of the program provided some insight into the institutionalization of the accountability mechanism (though the formal impact evaluation was disrupted by the COVID-19 pandemic). The new user committees continued to be effective because national, subnational, and local governments issued decrees and the committees received a small amount of funding from the village government to keep conducting monitoring and monthly meetings with the schools. In contrast, the previously existing school committees, which are appointed by the school principal and received no funding from the village government, appear to have been less effective.

Finally, in considering this intervention's scalability to other contexts, it is worth noting that the 270 schools involved were located across five districts in two different provinces that were remote and disadvantaged, were willing to participate, had significant problems of teacher absenteeism, and were not in conflict-prone areas.

Sources: Elaborations of Gaduh et al. 2021; Hwa et al. 2022.

Appraisal systems are fundamental to accountability

Incentives for teachers to improve their capacity and practice—or even to focus on student learning outcomes—remain weak or nonexistent without effective appraisal systems. Weak systems of teacher assessment also mean that countries can neither support their teachers to improve nor create a systematic process by which teachers who consistently perform poorly can be taken out of classroom settings.

Improving the effectiveness of individual teachers starts with identifying their capacity.[14] In Viet Nam, for example, where teacher absenteeism is significantly lower than elsewhere in the region, teachers take part in regular internal and external evaluations that hold them accountable for teaching quality. Teachers may be dismissed for misconduct, child abuse, absenteeism, or consistently poor performance.

Although many countries have teacher appraisal systems, they can be difficult to implement effectively. Teacher appraisal can serve several functions: It can be a tool for quality assurance when aimed at ensuring that required standards are met or recommended practices followed (summative appraisal). It can also provide an opportunity for teachers to reflect on their teaching practice and on their strengths and weaknesses and to identify areas for improvement (formative appraisal). And it can yield important information to support schools, teachers, and external authorities in their decisions on career advancement and professional development. A meta-analysis of 800 studies of educational interventions and student achievement in high-income countries, including in East Asia and Pacific, found that appraisal of teachers' classroom practice, when done in a constructive rather than punitive manner, can be a highly effective mechanism for strengthening student performance (Hattie 2009).

At the core of successful appraisal systems that improve student learning are robust procedures whereby principals, other evaluators, and teachers invest sufficient time in the appraisal; evaluators possess the required expertise, in terms of both pedagogical knowledge and assessment techniques; and teachers judge the system as fair and trustworthy so that they accept and use the results of the assessment (Schleicher 2020). Such features of successful appraisal systems can be found in high-income country settings. However, as discussed earlier, many appraisal systems in middle-income East Asia and Pacific make few links between student learning and teacher performance. Significant reform and reorientation of the region's teacher appraisal systems are thus needed before they can be an effective tool for strengthening teaching and, thus, students' learning outcomes.

Arranging for teachers' exits takes planning but also reinforces standards

Although appraisals should emphasize improvement in the performance of existing teachers, some teachers may not improve their performance to acceptable levels because they are either unable or unwilling to enhance their capacity despite support to improve. Arranging the exits of teachers, especially those with the status of civil servants, is not, and should not be, easy and takes considerable time and political commitment. However, where it is feasible to identify persistent weak performers, inducing their exit would strengthen incentives for other teachers to improve their performance—by demonstrating that the system sets standards for capacity and behavior, assesses performance against those standards, and acts when they are not met.

Better data and information for better education policy making

The previous sections have identified several actions that countries in East Asia and Pacific can take to significantly improve the quality of teaching in their primary-school classrooms. A major deficit among the region's countries, however, is the lack of reliable data and systematic information about key features of teaching quality. As highlighted at the beginning of this chapter (figure 4.1), having adequate, real-time information is at the core of policy makers' abilities to diagnose the problems related to teaching and learning and to design policies that effectively address the identified problems. This section outlines the key role of teacher appraisal systems to enable better gathering of this information, which can be used to inform the design of effective training programs and provide career progression for teachers.

The improvement in the competence of teachers of English in Malaysia is a good example of the effective use of data (see box 4.2). Policy makers identified a concern about learning outcomes—in this case, about students' English language performance, using data from existing national assessments and examinations. The government recognized that improving student performance would be possible only if English teachers were more effective. To test this hypothesis, it assessed the language competence of all 24,000 English language teachers. Notably, the government secured the services of an expert organization that already had a robust tool to assess language competence, so policy makers could be confident of the results. Using the assessment results, the government identified the groups of teachers who required priority attention along with the specific actions to address the capacity needs of these groups. After implementing the improvement program, teachers were reassessed using the same evaluation instrument. This enabled policy makers to see the extent to which the program was successful.

The Malaysia example illustrates several important aspects of data collection and use: the data were (a) collected in a systemic and robust way, focused on the particular problem; (b) collected regarding teachers' knowledge; (c) collected before and after the intervention; and (d) used to design the intervention for improvement. Importantly, the government also published the results of the program. Data about students' learning were not gathered as systemically or robustly before and after the intervention, however. This would have been helpful because policy makers could have demonstrated the link between better teaching and greater student learning and measured the effectiveness of the program as its implementation changed over time.

The situation that Malaysian policy makers found themselves in when first seeking to improve the learning of English—lacking systematic information about teaching quality—pervades countries in East Asia and Pacific. Few countries in the region collect systematic information about key features of effective teachers, such as whether teachers have the content knowledge they need to teach or have the pedagogical knowledge and tools to do so successfully. Moreover, the region's education systems do not collect regular information about teachers' presence in the classroom at times when they should be teaching. All this information should be at the core of teacher appraisal systems, but this is rarely the case. Fortunately, instruments already exist to measure these teacher attributes; what is needed, however, is a commitment from policy makers to use these instruments to regularly assess all teachers.

These teacher appraisal systems would then enable education systems to identify the areas in which their cadre of teachers needs additional support. This would provide the basis for the design of large-scale teacher training programs including ongoing coaching support, which can be used to collect information on teachers' progress on a continuing basis. Appraisal systems would enable the customization of training for teachers. Teacher appraisal systems could also identify the most effective teachers, who could serve as coaches and mentors for other teachers and who could prepare tools (scripted lessons, video lessons, or dual teaching lessons) to support a much larger number of teachers to provide better teaching. Finally, teacher appraisal systems are the foundation of career progression for teachers, one of the key incentives for improved performance.

Notes

1. This chapter focuses on *what* is required to strengthen teaching to improve student learning; a forthcoming World Bank report, "Making Teacher Policy Work: Small Changes, Big Results," focuses on the operationalization of this agenda by discussing *how* to implement this agenda effectively.

2. The projections presented here likely underestimate the proportion of 2030 teachers who have already been recruited for several reasons: First, evidence suggests that countries have difficulty reducing the

number of teaching positions as student numbers fall (Sondergaard et al. 2012). Second, the number of teachers who are recruited will also depend on other things such as the government's ability to finance additional teachers, the availability and interest of people to join the profession, and the speed of government recruitment procedures. Experience suggests that constraints in all three of these areas dampen new-teacher recruitment. Third, the simulations assume that countries seek to obtain an ambitious pupil-teacher ratio of 25 to 1 by 2030, and higher ratios would mean that fewer teachers are recruited.

3. For the September 2021 round of exams, about 91,000 applicant teachers passed the tests based on the original scoring criteria, meaning a pass rate of 14.9 percent. Based on pressure from Parliament, the ministry agreed to a scoring change that resulted in approximately 82,500 additional honorarium teachers passing the test, for a total (revised) passing rate of 28.5 percent.

4. Many evaluations of education interventions report their results as standard deviation changes in test scores. This enables intervention effect sizes to be compared across studies, even when the unit of analysis or the assessment instrument is not the same.

5. The benefits may be even larger if increased cognitive skills of students also translate into students completing more years of schooling. In the case of Tonga, when making this additional assumption, the estimated benefits would increase by $560. The present value of future earnings is derived from Mincerian earnings functions, which model individuals' future earnings. In the case of Tonga, the relationship between cognitive skills and earnings is estimated using the Tonga Household Income and Expenditure Survey (Abeberese, Kumler, and Linden 2014; Evans and Yuan 2019; Macdonald and Vu 2018; Montenegro and Patrinos 2014).

6. The Promotion of Academic Olympiads and Development of Science Education (POSN) Foundation was formed in 1999.

7. Thailand training program participation figures are from 2022 In-Service Teacher Training Survey Instrument (ITTSI) data for 65 programs in nine middle-income East Asian and Pacific countries.

8. Timor-Leste training program information is from 2022 In-Service Teacher Training Survey Instrument (ITTSI) data for 65 programs in nine middle-income East Asian and Pacific countries.

9. Teaching at the right level (TaRL), pioneered by Pratham, a nongovernmental organization (NGO) in India, is perhaps the most widely known and used version of targeted instruction in low- and middle-income countries.

10. "Learning poverty," a concept and indicator developed by the World Bank and the United Nations Educational, Scientific and Cultural Organization (UNESCO) Institute for Statistics (further discussed in chapter 1), is defined as the inability to read and understand a simple, age-appropriate text by age 10.

11. In many cases, also, the curriculum is too ambitious for the progress that the majority of students can be reasonably expected to make.

12. There is growing interest in teachers' *intrinsic* motivation ("the desire to engage in an activity for its own sake or for satisfying one's values, curiosity, purpose, or challenge") given that a teacher's job in the classroom is complex and requires adaptation, flexibility, and the ability to make lots of choices—things that are hard to measure and promote through extrinsic rewards. Most teachers are also alone in their classrooms. However, little evidence is yet available either about how to measure or encourage intrinsic motivation or about its link to better student learning outcomes.

13. Financial incentives include teacher performance pay and salary increases for performance. Pay-for-performance programs provide financial incentives—monetary bonuses or in-kind gifts beyond standard teacher salaries—as a direct reward to teachers for improved performance. These may be based on measures of individual teacher performance or group-based performance, and they are provided to improve teacher performance and recruitment or to retain high-quality teachers (Bruns and Luque 2015).

14. Several robust and validated classroom observation tools have been used on a large scale in low- and middle-income countries. These tools can provide evidence that mentors and coaches can use to support teachers and that education systems can use to design large-scale training programs. The World Bank has developed such a tool that is publicly available. For more information on this free classroom observation tool—*Teach* Primary—see https://www.worldbank.org/en/topic/education/brief/teach-helping-countries-track-and-improve-teaching-quality.

References

Abeberese, A. B., T. J. Kumler, and L. L. Linden. 2014. "Improving Reading Skills by Encouraging Children to Read in School: A Randomized Evaluation of the Sa Aklat Sisikat Reading Program in the Philippines." *Journal of Human Resources* 49 (3) 611–33.

Angrist, N., D. K. Evans, D. Filmer, R. Glennerster, F. H. Rogers, and S. Sabarwal. 2020. "How to Improve Education Outcomes Most Efficiently? A Comparison of 150 Interventions Using the New Learning-Adjusted Years of Schooling Metric." Policy Research Working Paper 9450, World Bank, Washington, DC.

Banerjee, A., R. Banerji, J. Berry, E. Duflo, H. Kannan, S. Mukerji, Marc Shotland, and M. Walton. 2017. "From Proof of Concept to Scalable Policies: Challenges and Solutions, with an Application." *Journal of Economic Perspectives* 31 (4): 73–102. https://doi.org/10.1257/jcp.31.4.73.

Beg, S. A., A. M. Lucas, W. Halim, and U. Saif. 2019. "Beyond the Basics: Improving Post-Primary Content Delivery through Classroom Technology." Working Paper 25704, National Bureau of Economic Resarch, Cambridge, MA.

Bianchi, N., Y. Lu, and H. Song. 2022. "The Effect of Computer-Assisted Learning on Students' Long-Term Development." *Journal of Development* 158: 102919.

Borghesan, E., and G. Vasey. Forthcoming. "The Marginal Returns to Distance Education: Evidence from Mexico's Telesecundarias." Accepted for publication in *American Economic Journal: Applied Economics*. https://gabriellevasey.github.io/MarginalReturns_BorghesanVasey.pdf.

Breeding, M., T. Béteille, and D. K. Evans. 2021. "Teacher Pay-for-Performance: What Works? Where? And How?" Brief, Report No. 158606, World Bank, Washington, DC.

Bruns, B., and J. Luque. 2015. *Great Teachers: How to Raise Student Learning in Latin America and the Caribbean.* Washington, DC: World Bank.

Castro, J. F., P. Glewwe, and R. Montero. 2019. "Work with What You've Got: Improving Teachers' Pedagogical Skills at Scale in Rural Peru." Working Paper No. 158, Peruvian Economic Association, Lima.

CIEB (Center on International Education Benchmarking). n.d. "Japan: Teacher and Principal Quality." Top-Performing Countries Report, National Center on Education and the Economy, Washington, DC. https://ncee.org/country/japan/.

Cillers, J., B. Fleisch, J. Kotzé, N. Mohohlwane, S. Taylor, and T. Thulare. 2022. "Can Virtual Replace In-Person Coaching? Experimental Evidence on Teacher Professional Development and Student Learning." *Journal of Development Economics* 155: 102815.

Contreras, D., and T. Rau. 2012. "Tournament Incentives for Teachers: Evidence from a Scaled-Up Intervention in Chile." *Economic Development and Cultural Change* 91 (1): 219–46.

Eau, G., K. Judah, and H. Shahid. 2019. "How Can Adaptive Platforms Improve Student Learning Outcomes? A Case Study of Open Educational Resources and Adaptive Learning Platforms." https://papers.ssrn.com/sol3/papers.cfm?abstract_id=3478134.

Evans, D. K., and F. Yuan. 2017. "The Economic Returns to Interventions that Increase Learning." Background paper for *World Development Report 2018: Learning to Realize Education's Promise.* Washington, DC: World Bank.

Evans, D. K., and F. Yuan. 2019. "Equivalent Years of Schooling: A Metric to Communicate Learning Gains in Concrete Terms." Policy Research Working Paper 8752, World Bank, Washington, DC.

Evans, D. K., and F. Yuan. 2020. "How Big Are Effect Sizes in International Education Studies?" Working Paper 545, Center for Global Development, Washington DC.

Feng, T., Y. Ma, C. Liu, P. Loyalka, R. Fairlie, and S. Rozelle. 2023. "The Effectiveness of Adaptive Computer Assisted Learning in Rural China." REAP Working Paper. Stanford University, Stanford, CA.

Ferreras, A., C. Kessel, and M.-H. Kim. 2015. *Mathematics Curriculum, Teacher Professionalism, and Supporting Policies in Korea and the United States: Summary of a Workshop.* Washington, DC: National Academies Press.

Gaduh, A., M. Pradhan, J. Priebe, and A. D. Susanti. 2020. "Scores, Camera, Action? Incentivizing Teachers in Remote Areas." RISE Working Paper Series 20/035, Research on Improving Systems of Education (RISE), Oxford, UK. https://doi.org/10.35489/BSG-RISE-WP_2020/035.

Gaduh, A., M. Pradhan, J. Priebe, and D. Susanti. 2021. "Scores, Camera, Action: Social Accountability and Teacher Incentives in Remote Areas." Policy Research Working Paper 9748, World Bank, Washington, DC.

Garcia-Moreno, V., P. Gertler, and H. A. Patrinos. 2019. "School-Based Management and Learning Outcomes: Experimental Evidence from Colima, Mexico." Policy Research Working Paper 8874, World Bank, Washington, DC.

Habyarimana, J., and S. Sabarwal. 2018. "Re-Kindling Learning: eReaders in Lagos." Policy Research Working Paper 8665, World Bank, Washington, DC.

Haryanto, A. 2021. "Number of Vacant Teacher Positions and Opportunities for Teacher Selection Phase 2" (PPPK Guru 2021: Jumlah Formasi yang Belum Terisi & Peluang Tahap II). https://tirto.id /pppk-guru-2021-jumlah-formasi-yang-belum-terisi-peluang-tahap-ii-gkev.

Hattie, J. A. 2009. *Visible Learning: A Synthesis of Over 800 Meta-Analyses Relating to Achievement.* Oxford, UK: Routledge.

Hwa, Y.-Y., S. K. Lumbanraja, U. A. Riyanto, and D. Susanti. 2022. "The Role of Coherence in Strengthening Community Accountability for Remote Schools in Indonesia." RISE Working Paper Series 22/090, Research on Improving Systems of Education (RISE), Oxford, UK. https://doi.org/10.35489 /BSG-RISE-WP_2022/090.

Johnston, J., and K. Christopher. 2017. "Effectiveness of Interactive Satellite-Transmitted Instruction: Experimental Evidence from Ghanaian Primary Schools." CEPA Working Paper No. 17-08, Stanford Center for Education Policy Analysis, Stanford, CA.

Karachiwalla, N., and A. Park. 2017. "Promotion Incentives in the Public Sector: Evidence from Chinese Schools." *Journal of Public Economics* 146: 109–28.

Klaveren, C. V., S. Vonk, and I. Cornelisz. 2017. "The Effect of Adaptive versus Static Practicing on Student Learning: Evidence from a Randomized Field Experiment." *Economics of Education* 58: 175–87.

Lee, S., J.-H. Lee, and Y. Jeong. 2023. "The Effects of Digital Textbooks on Students' Academic Performance, Academic Interest, and Learning Skills." *Journal of Marketing Research* 60 (4). https:// doi.org/10.1177/00222437221130712.

Li, H., Z. Liu, F. Yang, and L. Yu. 2023. "The Impact of Computer-Assisted Instruction on Student Performance: Evidence from the Dual-Teacher Program." SSRN Electronic Journal. https://doi .org/10.2139/ssrn.4360827.

Liang, X., H. Kidwai, M. Zhang, and Y. Zhang. 2016. *How Shanghai Does It: Insights and Lessons from the Highest-Ranking Education System in the Worrld.* Directions in Development Series. Washington DC: World Bank.

Linden, L. L. 2008. "Complement or Substitute? The Effect of Technology on Student Achievement in India." Research paper, Columbia University, New York.

Ma, Y., R. W. Fairlie, P. Loyalka, and S. Rozelle. 2020. "Isolating the 'Tech' from EdTech: Experimental Evidence on Computer Assisted Learning in China." Working Paper 26953, National Bureau of Economic Research, Cambridge, MA.

Macdonald, K., S. Brinkman, W. Jarvie, M. Machuca-Sierra, K. McDonall, S. Messaoud-Galusi, S. Tapueluelu, and B. T. Vu. 2018. "Intervening at Home and Then at School: A Randomized Evaluation of Two Approaches to Improve Early Educational Outcomes in Tonga." Policy Research Paper 8682, World Bank, Washington, DC.

Macdonald, K., and B. T. Vu. 2018. "A Randomized Evaluation of a Low-Cost and Highly Scripted Teaching Method to Improve Basic Early Grade Reading Skills in Papua New Guinea." Policy Research Working Paper 8427, World Bank, Washington, DC.

Malaysia MOE (Ministry of Education Malaysia). 2014. "Annual Report 2013: Malaysia Education Blueprint 2013–2025." MOE, Putrajaya, Malaysia.

Montenegro, C. E., and H. A. Patrinos. 2014. "Comparable Estimates of Returns to Schooling around the World." Policy Research Working Paper 7020, World Bank, Washington, DC.

Muralidharan, K., A. Singh, and A. J. Ganimian. 2019. "Disrupting Education? Experimental Evidence on Technology-Aided Instruction in India." *American Economic Review* 109 (4): 1426–60.

Naik, G., C. Chitre, M. Bhalla, and J. Rajan. 2020. "Impact of Use of Technology on Student Learning Outcomes: Evidence from a Large-Scale Experiment in India." *World Development* 127: 104736.

OECD (Organisation for Economic Co-operation and Development). 2013. "Education Policy Outlook: Finland." Country education profile, OECD, Paris. https://www.oecd.org/education/EDUCATION%20 POLICY%20OUTLOOK%20FINLAND_EN.pdf.

Pham, L. D., M. G. Springer, and T. Nguyen. 2017. "Teacher Merit Pay and Student Test Scores: A Meta-Analysis." Study, Vanderbilt University, Nashville, TN.

92   FIXING THE FOUNDATION

Popova, A., D. Evans, M. E. Breeding, and V. Arancibia. 2022. "Teacher Professional Development Around the World: The Gap between Evidence and Practice." *The World Bank Research Observer* 37 (1): 107–36.

Pritchett, L., and J. Sanderfur. 2013. "Context Matters for Size: Why External Validity Claims and Development Practice Don't Mix." CGD Working Paper 336, Center for Global Development, Washington, DC.

Schleicher, A. 2020. "Teaching and Learning International Survey (TALIS 2018): Insights and Interpretations." Paper, Organisation for Economic Co-operation and Development, Paris.

Snilstveit, B., J. Stevenson, D. Phillips, M. Vojtkova, E. Gallagher, T. Schmidt, H. Jobse, M. Geelen, M. G. Pastorello, and J. Eyers. 2015. "Interventions for Improving Learning Outcomes and Access to Education in Low- and Middle-Income Countries: A Systematic Review." Systematic Review 24, International Initiative for Impact Evaluation (3ie), London.

Sondergaard, L., M. Murthi, D. Abu-Ghaida, C. Bodewig, and J. Rutkowski. 2012. *Skills, Not Just Diplomas: Managing Education for Results in Eastern Europe and Central Asia.* Directions in Development Series. Washington, DC: World Bank.

Stern, J., M. Jukes, and B. Piper. 2020. "Is It Possible to Improve Learning at Scale? Reflections on the Process of Identifying Large-Scale Successful Education Interventions." Center for Global Development blog, March 2. https://www.cgdev.org/blog/it-possible-improve-learning-scale-reflections-process-identifying-large-scale-successful.

Tan, S. K. S., and A. F. L. Wong. 2007. "The Qualifications of the Teaching Force: Data from Singapore." In *A Comparative Study of Teacher Preparation and Qualification in Six Nations,* edited by R. E. Ingersoll, 71–82. Philadelphia: Consortium for Policy Research in Education.

Tanaka, N., and L. Sondergaard. 2023. "Analysis of Teacher Stock versus Flow in Primary Education in East Asia and the Pacific Middle-Income Countries: A Simple Model and Results from Simulation between 2020 and 2030." Policy Research Working Paper 10479, World Bank, Washington, DC.

UN DESA (United Nations Department of Economic and Social Affairs). 2022. *World Population Prospects 2022: Summary of Results.* New York: United Nations.

UNICEF (United Nations Children's Fund). 2021. "Reopening with Resilience: Lessons from Remote Learning during COVID-19 in East Asia and the Pacific." Report, UNICEF, New York.

UNICEF and ITU (United Nations Children's Fund and International Telecommunication Union). 2020. "How Many Children and Young People Have Internet Access at Home? Estimating Digital Connectivity during the COVID-19 Pandemic." Report, UNICEF, New York.

Vanbecelaere, S., K. Van den Berghe, F. Cornillie, D. Sasanguie, B. Reynvoet, and F. Depaepe. 2019. "The Effectiveness of Adaptive versus Non-Adaptive Learning with Digital Educational Games." *Journal of Computer Assisted Learning* 36 (4): 502–13.

Varkey Foundation. 2018. *Global Teacher Status Index 2018.* Surrey, UK: The Varkey Foundation.

Vivalt, E. 2020. "How Much Can We Generalize from Impact Evaluations?" *Journal of the European Economic Association* 18 (6): 3045–89.

Wilichowski, T., and A. Popova. 2021. "Structuring Effective 1-1 Support: Technical Guidance Note." Report No. 157088, World Bank, Washington, DC.

World Bank. 2018. *Growing Smarter: Learning and Equitable Development in East Asia and Pacific.* Washington DC: World Bank.

World Bank. 2020a. "Cost-Effective Approaches to Improve Global Learning: What Does Recent Evidence Tells Us Are 'Smart Buys' for Improving Learning in Low- and Middle-Income Countries?" Recommendations of the Global Education Evidence Advisory Panel, World Bank, Washington, DC.

World Bank. 2020b. *Realizing the Future of Learning: From Learning Poverty to Learning for Everyone, Everywhere.* Washington, DC: World Bank.

World Bank. Forthcoming. "Making Teacher Policy Work: Small Changes, Big Results." Report, World Bank, Washington, DC.

Yarrow, N., C. Abbey, S. Shen, and K. Alyono. Forthcoming. "Using Education Technology to Improve K–12 Student Learning in East Asia and Pacific: Promises and Limitations." Report, World Bank, Washington, DC.

Spending for Improved Learning and Greater Equity | 5

Introduction

Countries in middle-income East Asia and Pacific can improve teaching and learning by implementing the types of interventions highlighted in chapter 4, but this will require more resources as well as more *effective* spending given the scarcity of resources available for education. Moreover, to address the inequalities in students' learning outcomes within countries, it will be important to ensure that additional resources are channeled to the classrooms where disadvantaged students learn. So, what is the state of play regarding public—and private—education spending in the region? And what is the scope for making that spending more effective?

Public spending on education varies considerably across the countries of the region. Several East Asian countries spend very few public resources—below global recommended benchmarks[1] and below the average of middle-income countries. A second group of countries are average spenders. And a third group, mainly Pacific Island countries, spend substantially above the recommended global benchmarks. Across these three groups of countries, spending varies widely, from around 2 percent of gross domestic product (GDP) (in Cambodia, the Lao People's Democratic Republic, and Myanmar) to over 10 percent (in Kiribati, the Marshall Islands, and the Solomon Islands), as shown in figure 5.1.[2]

When measured in terms of public spending *per student* as a percentage of per capita GDP, most middle-income East Asian countries spend well below what would be expected given their levels of development. Spending lags predicted values by 2 percentage points in Viet Nam and as much as 19 percentage points in Lao PDR (Yarrow et al., forthcoming).

Factors in the region's varied public education spending

The countries' different levels of public spending on education reflect their varying budget priorities as well as differences in the overall size of government. For instance, in three of the low-spending countries—China, Lao PDR, and Myanmar—low education spending reflects policy makers' choices to allocate a relatively small proportion of overall government spending to education.[3]

FIGURE 5.1   **Public spending on education (2016–19) is below 4 percent of GDP in most East Asian countries, while many Pacific Island countries spend over 6 percent**

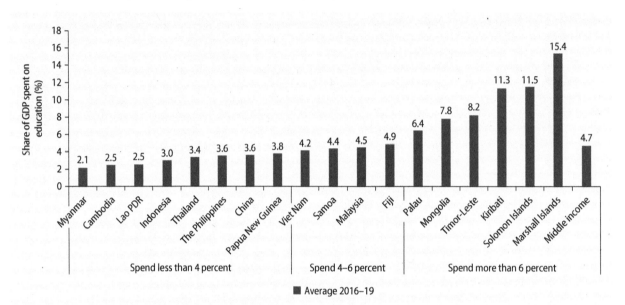

Sources: UIS 2022 except for Timor-Leste and Papua New Guinea, whose data are from the World Bank's BOOST databases for each respective country (https://www.worldbank.org/en/programs/boost-portal/country-data).
Note: The figure shows average public spending on education, as a share of GDP, in only middle-income countries for which a full set of 2012–19 data are available from UIS (2022). For this reason, the following countries are excluded: the Federated States of Micronesia, Papua New Guinea, Tonga, and Vanuatu. The "Middle income" bar on the far right represents the average of middle-income countries globally. GDP = gross domestic product.

These three countries allocate less than 12 percent of their budgets to education, compared with the global middle-income average of 16 percent (UIS 2022). In contrast, the Marshall Islands, Mongolia, Papua New Guinea, and the Solomon Islands allocate more than 20 percent of government expenditures toward education (figure 5.2).

At the same time, the overall size of government spending matters. For example, Myanmar's and Lao PDR's spending on education is low at least in part because these countries' overall government spending is relatively small as a share of GDP: only 17 percent and 22 percent, respectively (UIS 2022).

Private spending—a boost that leaves most children behind

In some of the region's middle-income countries, private (household) spending on education is considerable but tends to be concentrated among the wealthiest 40 percent of households, making it a weak substitute for public education spending for much of the population. It is substantial in Myanmar, making up almost 60 percent of total spending on education (figure 5.3). But elsewhere, private spending makes up a relatively smaller proportion than the average observed in middle-income countries globally (Zheng and Sondergaard, forthcoming). Within the region, this share is lowest in Pacific Island countries, where generous public spending on education helps reduce the need for private resources.

Across much of the region, wealthier households allocate a larger share of their total budget toward their children's education than do poorer households (Zheng and Sondergaard, forthcoming), as shown in figure 5.4, panel a.[4] As such, the bulk of private education

FIGURE 5.2　Differences in public spending on education (2016–19) across East Asian and Pacific countries partly reflect varying budget priorities

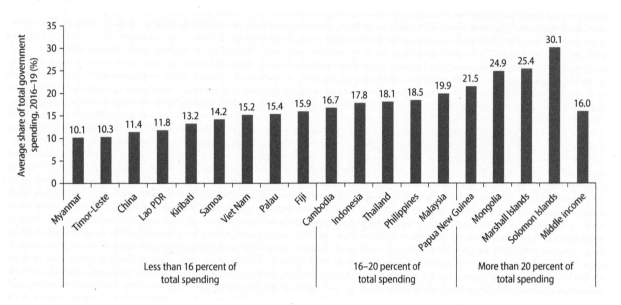

Sources: UIS 2022 except for Timor-Leste and Papua New Guinea, whose data are from the World Bank's BOOST databases for each respective country (https://www.worldbank.org /en/programs/boost-portal/country-data).
Note: The figure shows the average share of total government spending allocated toward education. It includes only middle-income countries for which a full set of 2016–19 data are available from UIS (2022). For this reason, the following countries are excluded: the Federated States of Micronesia, Papua New Guinea, Tonga, and Vanuatu. The "Middle income" bar on the far right represents the average of middle-income countries globally.

FIGURE 5.3　In most East Asian and Pacific countries, private spending makes up a relatively modest contribution toward overall spending

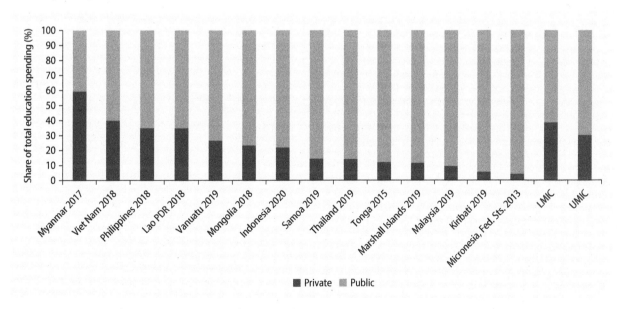

Source: Zheng and Sondergaard, forthcoming.
Note: LMIC = lower-middle-income country average; UMIC = upper-middle-income country average.

FIGURE 5.4   **The wealthiest households undertake the bulk of private education spending across East Asia and Pacific**

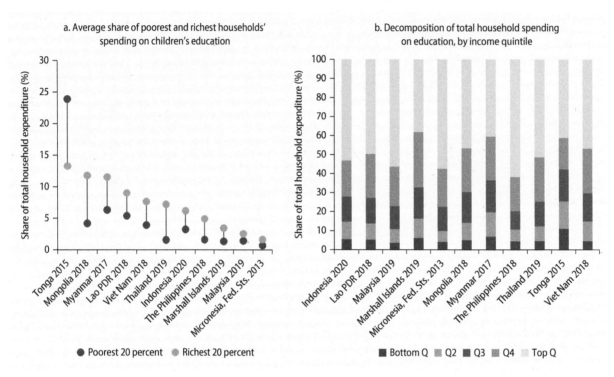

Source: Zheng and Sondergaard, forthcoming.
Panel a shows the average private (household) spending on education as a share of total household expenditure by the poorest and richest 20 percent of households.
Panel b decomposes the country's total private (household) spending on education, by household income quintile (Q).

spending in the region comes from the wealthiest 40 percent of households (figure 5.4, panel b). This reflects the greater likelihood of wealthier households to send their children to private schools or university and to spend more on extracurricular activities and private tutoring services.

Role of public spending in addressing education inequality

Importantly, public spending on education helps level the educational playing field in middle-income East Asia and Pacific in two ways: First, by providing tuition-free basic education, governments significantly lower financial barriers to enroll and learn. Second, intergenerational mobility is higher in countries with higher government expenditure on education (figure 5.5). Specifically, in countries where governments spend more on education as a share of GDP, children's educational attainment is less tied to their parents' educational attainment than in countries with lower public spending on education (van der Weide et al. 2021).

Looking across the region, however, the picture is mixed regarding the extent to which public resources are distributed in ways that reduce the inequalities in teaching quality and learning outcomes between poorer and wealthier localities and households. In Papua New Guinea, public spending per student varies widely across provinces, with provinces with higher poverty rates spending less per student than provinces with lower poverty rates (World Bank, forthcoming), as shown in figure 5.6, panel a. Analysis carried out

FIGURE 5.5   **Higher public spending on education correlates with higher equality of educational opportunity for children**

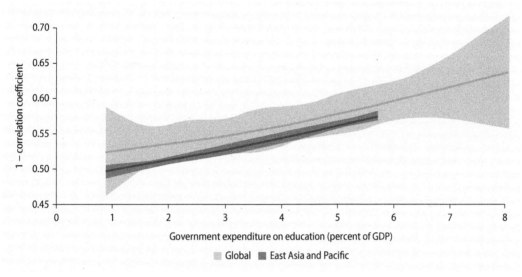

Source: World Bank estimates, based on data from van der Weide et al. 2021.
Note: The figure shows the relationship between (a) relative mobility (defined by "1 − correlation coefficient," where the correlation is between respondents' years of schooling and the years of schooling of their most educated parent); and (b) government expenditure on education (as a share of GDP) globally and in East Asia and Pacific. The orange-shaded and brown-shaded areas denote the 95 percent confidence interval for their respective regression lines. The regression lines and 95 percent confidence intervals were based on data on all countries' cohorts born in the 1960s, 1970s, and 1980s. We matched each cohort with the data on government spending when the cohort, on average, was about to enter school. For instance, the cohort born in the 1980s was matched with the GDP per capita from 1990, at which point the cohort, on average, was five years old. Plots control for a second-order polynomial of GDP per capita GDP = gross domestic product.

FIGURE 5.6   **Whereas some East Asian countries allocate more public funds per student to poorer localities, others do not**

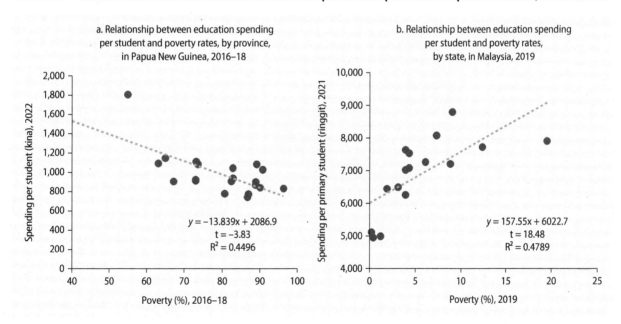

Sources: World Bank, forthcoming (panel a); World Bank calculations based on publicly available data from Malaysia's Ministry of Education, Public Service Department, and Department of Statistics (panel b).
Note: Results are shown from 20 of the 22 provinces in Papua New Guinea and from all 16 states and federal territories in Malaysia. Papua New Guinea's poverty rate is the share of the population that is poor using a measure of multidimensional deprivation (based on 2016–18 Demographic and Health Survey data). Malaysia uses an absolute poverty measurement following the cost of basic needs approach, which establishes a minimum requirement level known as poverty line income (PLI) comprising two categories: food PLI and nonfood PLI.

for this report similarly shows that poorer subnational entities in the Philippines and Thailand also tend to spend less on a per student basis than their wealthier counterparts. Malaysia, in contrast, distributes more public education spending toward localities with greater needs (figure 5.6, panel b). Similar "pro-poor" patterns are seen in Indonesia and Myanmar.

Less learning for the money in many East Asian and Pacific countries than in peer countries

For every middle-income country in the region (except Viet Nam), there is a peer at a similar income level that achieves a lower rate of learning poverty—often at lower levels of public spending.[5] For example, Malaysia, Mongolia, and Thailand each has a income per capita peer in Europe and Central Asia: Kazakhstan, Moldova, and Serbia, respectively. Yet these peers have achieved significantly lower rates of learning poverty (figure 5.7).

The gap is particularly striking between Kazakhstan and Malaysia, with learning poverty rates of 2 percent and 42 percent, respectively. Moreover, Kazakhstan and Moldova achieve lower learning poverty with lower levels of public spending on education (as a share of GDP) than Malaysia and Mongolia, spend respectively.

At the same time, Viet Nam is the world's best-performing lower-middle-income country regarding learning poverty—with an impressive teacher workforce at the heart of this achievement. With a gross national income (GNI) per capita of only US$9,280 (in 2018 purchasing power parity [PPP] terms) and with public spending at 4.1 percent of GDP, Viet Nam achieves

FIGURE 5.7   **Many East Asian and Pacific countries have peers at the same income level that achieve lower learning poverty rates while often spending less**

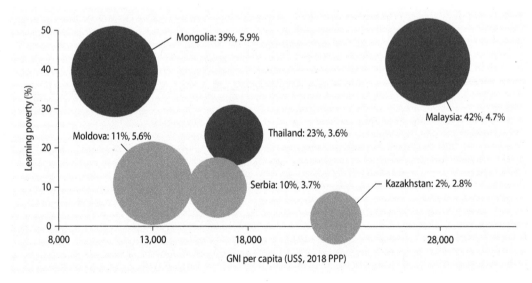

Sources: World Bank estimates, based on UIS 2022 and World Bank and UIS 2022.
Note: The figure compares the performance of each of three East Asian countries—Mongolia, Thailand, and Malaysia (brown bubbles)—with a per capita income peer in Europe and Central Asia (orange bubbles): Moldova, Serbia, and Kazakhstan, respectively. Percentages following each country label are the country's learning poverty rate, followed by its share of public spending on education (as a share of GDP). Bubble size indicates the relative size of the country's average 2015–18 public spending on education (as a share of GDP). "Learning poverty" refers to the percentage of 10-year-olds who cannot read and understand a simple, age-appropriate text. Mongolia's data on learning poverty are dated (from 2007) because Mongolia has not participated in any international assessments of its primary students since then. GDP = gross domestic product; PPP = purchasing power parity.

a learning poverty rate of only 18 percent, similar to that of Turkey (with a per capita income three times larger than Viet Nam). All of Viet Nam's global income peers have learning poverty rates well above 60 percent.

Several recent papers document how Viet Nam has achieved such impressive levels of student learning, including Glewwe et al. (2021).[6] Differences in observed child and household characteristics explain only a little about the learning gaps (in both literacy and mathematics) between Viet Nam and India or between Viet Nam and Peru. However, one observed school variable has a large explanatory effect: the pedagogical skills of primary-school mathematics teachers. This metric explains about 10–12 percent of the gap between Viet Nam and India (Glewwe et al. 2021). In the case of Peru, the metric explains most (65–84 percent) of the gap. In short, the quality of teaching matters.

Simply allocating more money to do more of the same is unlikely to improve learning outcomes in the region. Two of the region's countries, Indonesia and Thailand, have participated in the Programme for International Student Assessment (PISA) since 2000. In both countries, budgetary allocations have grown rapidly (on a per child basis, in constant US dollars) over these two decades—more so in Indonesia than in Thailand (figure 5.8, panel b). However, students' reading skills have not improved in either country (OECD 2022). In fact, reading scores have deteriorated over the period in Thailand (figure 5.8, panel a). Looking at these two countries' experiences across two decades, the current approach to education designed to produce children who can read is clearly not working; a transformation is needed.

Based on the patterns observed in figure 5.7, it is tempting to conclude that the region's countries can pay for learning-enhancing education reforms simply by eliminating inefficiencies in the system. That is, if Kazakhstan—which is near Malaysia's income level but spends only 2.8 percent of GDP on education, compared with Malaysia's 4.7 percent—can ensure that 98 percent of its 10-year-olds learn to read (that is, the learning poverty rate is just

FIGURE 5.8 More of the same is unlikely to result in better learning outcomes in East Asia and Pacific

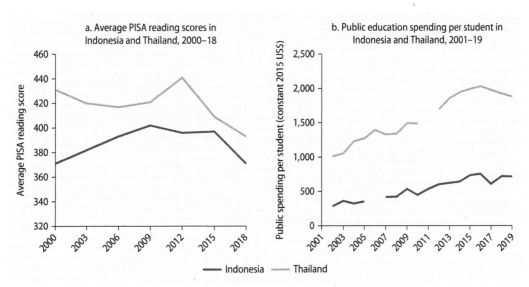

Sources: OECD 2022 (panel a); World Bank calculations based on UIS 2022 (panel b).
Note: PISA = Programme for International Student Assessment. The UNESCO Institute for Statistics (UIS) defines "Spending per student is spending on students of compulsory school age, which is children ages 6–14 years in Thailand and children ages 7–15 years in Indonesia (UIS 2016)." Data on public spending per child is not available for Indonesia in 2006 and Thailand in 2011.

2 percent), should not Malaysia be able to achieve the same by spending less than it currently spends, or at the very least, without additional resources? Similarly, at the same level of income and spending approximately the same on education, should not Thailand be able to replicate Serbia's learning poverty rate simply by shifting its existing resource allocations to more efficient uses? The answer is not that straightforward.

Technical and political challenges to improving spending efficiency

To begin with, the underlying causes of inefficient spending vary across countries. And they are often difficult to identify without in-depth analysis of the sector. In Thailand, for example, such analysis showed how it is possible to provide higher-quality education for the approximately 1 million (largely poor) students who are enrolled in small village primary schools that are relatively costly but of poor quality (World Bank 2015). Specifically, spatial analysis of the school network showed that chronic teacher shortages, affecting nearly half of Thai basic education classrooms, could be addressed through school consolidation. Simulations suggested that consolidation of small village schools could be implemented in a way (a) to ensure that all classrooms would be adequately staffed without having to hire more teachers, and (b) to result in better learning outcomes for the more than 1 million students enrolled in such schools (figure 5.9, panel a).

However, school consolidation would involve the politically difficult task of convincing parents to close their village schools and allow their children to travel up to 6 kilometers away to a larger—and higher-quality—school. Conducting a full consolidation of the school network would be a major logistical and political challenge: it would involve 58 percent of all schools, affecting the lives of more than 1.8 million students and 35 percent of the teacher workforce.

FIGURE 5.9 **The underlying causes of inefficiencies in public education spending differ widely across East Asian and Pacific countries**

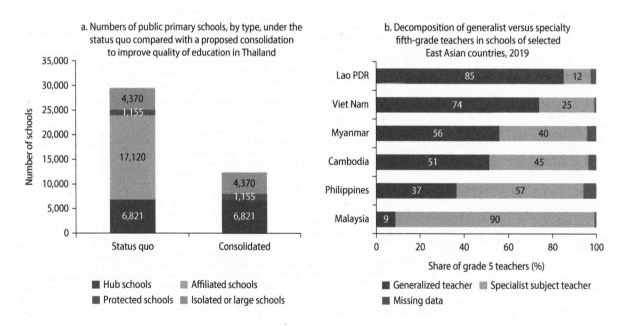

a. Numbers of public primary schools, by type, under the status quo compared with a proposed consolidation to improve quality of education in Thailand

b. Decomposition of generalist versus specialty fifth-grade teachers in schools of selected East Asian countries, 2019

Source: World Bank 2015 (panel a); teacher questionnaire administered as part of Southeast Asia Primary Learning Metrics (SEA-PLM) 2019, available from UNICEF AND SEAMEO 2020 (panel b). Panel a: "Affiliated schools" are those identified under the simulation to be merged into nearby "hub schools." "Protected schools" are small (averaging 20 students or less per grade on average) and isolated (more than 6 kilometers from any other school). "Isolated schools" are non-small (averaging more than 20 students per grade) and isolated, and "large schools" have enrollments of 500 or more students.

The underlying causes of Malaysia's education spending inefficiencies are very different from those of Thailand—although also politically difficult to address. Unlike Thailand, Malaysia already has a relatively efficient school network, with few opportunities for creating larger schools and classes (without creating unacceptably large travel times for students). At the same time, Malaysia's model of delivering primary education has relatively high unit costs, mainly because each primary-school teacher is specialized in teaching one or two subjects, resulting in a large number of teachers per class (figure 5.9, panel b). Malaysia's policy choices about the use of specialist teachers result in a relatively costly model of delivering primary education. It is beneficial to its teaching workforce but does not deliver commensurate results in terms of student learning.

That said, changing the current policies—in the interest of increasing the quality of teaching and learning—would be politically difficult. In the Thailand case, for example, resources would be needed to invest in those schools receiving more students (to create a larger library, build more toilets, perhaps add some classrooms, and so on) as well as in those schools that would be closed (to move equipment and materials to the new schools, carry out the consultations with parents and the community, and help teachers relocate, among other things). In both Thailand and Malaysia, it may be that some teachers cannot shift to the new ways of working and may need help to exit the profession.

Moving forward

For *all countries* in the region, most of the reforms discussed in the chapters thus far will be new, will require spending additional resources, or both. All middle-income East Asian and Pacific countries will need to invest resources in improving the *measurement* of students' foundational learning—particularly, by strengthening teachers' capacities to measure learning progress in the classroom; by ensuring that national assessments are conducted regularly and yield results that are comparable over time; and, preferably, by participating in international assessments to benchmark their progress. All countries will also need to review and revamp their in-service teacher training and their coaching and mentoring programs to align with the principles of effective practice and to reach all teachers on a regular basis.

In addition, given the heterogeneity *within* countries in student learning outcomes and teaching practices, countries must more carefully consider the distribution of public resources for education within their country. For students from disadvantaged backgrounds to succeed, they will need access to high-quality teaching. And attracting and retaining such talent in remote areas will require more, not fewer, resources on a per student basis in these areas.

However, as the cautionary tales of Malaysia and Thailand show, simply spending more, by itself, is unlikely to result in better learning. Better teaching will be needed to raise student learning outcomes. Indeed, improving teacher performance represents the most important opportunity to increase the efficiency of education spending. As discussed in chapter 4, strengthening teacher training that builds on evidence of effective interventions will yield positive returns on additional investment. The precise needs for reforms and education investments will differ from country to country, however. To be effective, measures to strengthen teaching and improve student learning must be well grounded in each country's situation and challenges.

Notes

1. The Education 2030 Framework for Action recommends that countries' public spending lie within the band of 4–6 percent of gross domestic product (GDP). The Framework was adopted by 184 United Nations Educational, Scientific and Cultural Organization (UNESCO) member states on November 4, 2015, in Paris (UNESCO 2015).

2. For more details on public education spending in the Pacific, see World Bank (2023). In brief, relatively large allocations to education as a share of GDP in many Pacific Island countries reflect mainly three factors: First, given their small size and their vast dispersion, the unit cost of delivering education is exceptionally large. Second, the high-spending countries have large sources of revenue, either from tax revenue (for example, from fisheries) or from donor grant resources. Third, most Pacific Island countries spend a relatively large share of public resources subsidizing nonpublic educational institutions, especially at the secondary and tertiary levels.
3. As discussed in World Bank (2022): Myanmar Budget Brief (November 2022), following the military coup, budgetary allocations to education have continued to shrink in Myanmar. In FY2022, education accounted for just 5.6 percent of the total government spending, the lowest since FY2012.
4. The exception is Tonga, where the poorest households spend a larger proportion of their household income (24 percent) on education than richer households (13 percent). Because wealthy households have larger overall budgets, they still spend more household resources on education, in absolute terms, than poor households.
5. "Learning poverty," a concept and indicator developed by the World Bank and the UNESCO Institute for Statistics (further discussed in chapter 1), is defined as the inability to read and understand a simple, age-appropriate text by age 10.
6. The findings of Glewwe et al. (2021) draw upon Young Lives data, a longitudinal study of poverty and inequality that has been following the lives of 12,000 children in Ethiopia, India (Andhra Pradesh and Telangana), Peru, and Viet Nam since 2001. For more details about these data, see the description in Glewwe et al. (2021) and the Young Lives website: https://www.younglives.org.uk/.

References

Glewwe, P., Z. James, J. Lee, C. Rolleston, and K. Vu. 2021. "What Explains Vietnam's Exceptional Performance in Education Relative to Other Countries? Analysis of the Young Lives Data from Ethiopia, Peru, India and Vietnam." RISE Working Paper 21/078, Research on Improving Systems of Education (RISE), Oxford, UK.

OECD (Organisation for Economic Co-operation and Development). 2022. PISA 2018 Database, OECD, Paris. https://www.oecd.org/pisa/data/2018database.

UIS (United Nations Educational, Scientific and Cultural Organization [UNESCO] Institute for Statistics). 2022. SDG 4 Data Explorer (browser). http://sdg4-data.uis.unesco.org/.

UNESCO (United Nations Educational, Cultural and Scientific Organization). 2015. "Education 2030 Incheon Declaration and Framework for Action: Towards Inclusive and Equitable Quality Education and Lifelong Learning for All." Final draft for adoption at the World Education Forum, UNESCO, Paris.

UNICEF (United Nations Children's Fund). 2020. South-East Asia Primary Learning Metrics (SEA-PLM) 2019 dataset. https://www.seaplm.org/index.php?option=com_content&view=article&id=54&Itemid=438&lang=en.

van der Weide, R., C. Lakner, D. G. Mahler, A. Narayan, and R. Ramasubbaiah. 2021. "Intergenerational Mobility around the World." Policy Research Working Paper 9707, World Bank, Washington, DC.

World Bank. 2015. "Thailand: Wanted: A Quality Education for All." Report No. AUS13333, World Bank, Bangkok.

World Bank. 2023. "Raising Pasifika: Strengthening Government Finances to Enhance Human Capital in the Pacific. A Public Expenditure Review of Nine Pacific Island Countries." World Bank, Washington, DC.

World Bank, forthcoming. "PNG Education Budget Brief 2023." World Bank, Washington, DC.

World Bank and UIS (UNESCO Institute for Statistics). 2022. "Learning Poverty Global Database: Historical Data and Sub-Components." https://datacatalog.worldbank.org/search/dataset/0038947.

Yarrow, N., P. Cahu, M. E. Breeding, and R. Afkar. Forthcoming. "What I Really Think: Policymaker Views on Education Data in East Asia Pacific." Report, World Bank, Washington, DC.

Zheng, S., and L. M. Sondergaard. Forthcoming. "Private Spending on Education and Enrollment in Non-Government Schools." Report, World Bank, Washington, DC.

Tailoring Education Reform to Country and Within-Country Circumstances

6

Introduction

Middle-income countries in East Asia and Pacific are diverse, and reforms will thus need to reflect different circumstances across and within countries. In general, countries with high learning poverty (such as Cambodia, the Lao People's Democratic Republic, Myanmar, and the Philippines) must focus on fostering systemic improvements and supporting all teachers.[1] Countries with more moderate learning poverty (such as China, Palau, Thailand, and Viet Nam) can take more targeted, selective approaches, focusing on specific challenges and areas for improvement, including remedial support for lagging school districts. The Pacific Island countries face additional challenges—small size, significant population dispersion, and linguistic diversity—that make education reform particularly costly and logistically difficult to implement (World Bank 2023).

Identifying country-specific challenges and priorities for reform

Existing data highlight the considerable diversity in learning challenges and outcomes across the region's middle-income countries. Table 6.1 reflects this diversity, presenting country-specific data on several key issues discussed in the report, including (a) learning poverty, (b) public spending on education, (c) current teacher capacity, (d) teacher behavior, (e) the availability of relevant diagnostic data, (f) the expected persistence of the current teacher stock, and (g) projected changes in the size of countries' teaching corps. The measure of teacher capacity—the percentage of qualified teachers in primary education—is a poor proxy for teacher content knowledge and teaching practices. However, in the absence of systematic country-level teacher assessments, it represents the best available measure.

The first eight data columns of table 6.1 take the form of a heat map, with, for each measure, red-shaded cells indicating countries in the bottom tercile of countries; yellow-shaded cells, the middle tercile; and green-shaded cells, the top tercile. The cells in the two rightmost data columns are in varying shades of orange: the darker the orange, (a) the lower the country's persistence of current teacher stock, or (b) the larger the projected increases in future teaching positions. Throughout the table, the gray-shaded cells indicate missing data. In the leftmost column, countries are listed in order of 2021 per capita income.

TABLE 6.1 Countries in East Asia and Pacific confront different policy challenges based on their current circumstances

Country	Country context — GDP per capita 2021 (US$)[a]	Learning deficit — Learning poverty rate (%)[b]	Fiscal resources spent — Government expenditure on education (% GDP)[c]	Fiscal resources spent — Government expenditure on education (% total spending)[d]	Teacher capacity — Share of qualified teachers in primary education (%)[e]	Teacher behavior — Teachers are often absent (%)	Data availability — Participation in international assessments[f]	Data availability — Quality of EMIS (score 1–6)[g]	Selection vs. capacity (flow vs. stock) — Teacher persistence to 2030 (%)	Selection vs. capacity (flow vs. stock) — Projected change in teacher positions by 2030 (%)
Palau	13,251	10	6.8	15.7			1		68	0.12
China	11,188	18	3.5	11.2			1		77	−0.32
Malaysia	10,827	42	4.2	17.7	95.7	4.9	2	4.5	79	0.01
Thailand	6,270	23	3	13.7	98.9		0	4.5	73	−0.19
Fiji	4,708	41	5.1	16.8	100		1	4	74	0.02
Tonga	4,630	72	8	11.9	92.5		1	2	75	−0.05
Mongolia	4,121	39	4.9	16.5	93.7		0		78	0.07
Tuvalu	4,019	73			100		1	2.5	65	0.16
Samoa	3,972	61	4.7	15.6			1	2.5	70	0.07
Indonesia	3,856	53	2.8	17.3	87.5		0	3.5	75	−0.05
Philippines	3,413	91	3.2	17.5	99.8	14	2	3.5	79	0.11
Marshall Islands	3,397	62	15.8	24.8			1	3	75	−0.1
Viet Nam	3,373	18	4.1	14		1.4	2	4.5	68	−0.03
Micronesia	2,720	53	9.7	18.1	90.8		1	3	76	0.01
Papua New Guinea	2,655	72	3.6	21.1	71.8		1	1	51	0.42
Vanuatu	2,613	58	1.8	5.6			1	3	52	0.38
Lao PDR	2,582	98	2.3	14	90.2	18.3	2	3	74	0.08
Solomon Islands	2,081	58	11.1	30.1	79.6		1	2.5	51	0.33
Timor-Leste	1,626	71	8.1	10.9	76.5		1	3	61	0.22
Kiribati	1,474		12.4	12.4	99.7		1	2.5	67	0.11
Cambodia	1,400	90	2.2	11.8	100	23.7	2	3	58	0.26
Myanmar	1,292	89	2.1	10.6	91.3	20.2	2	1		

Source: Compilation from World Bank databases; teacher absence data from UNICEF 2020.

Note: Red cells indicate countries in the bottom tercile; yellow cells, the middle tercile; and green cells, the top tercile. Gray cells indicate missing data. In the two rightmost columns, the darker the orange, (a) the lower the country's persistence of current teacher stock, or (b) the larger the projected increase in future teaching positions. GDP = gross domestic product.

a. GDP per capita is in constant 2015 US$, using 2021 or latest data.
b. Learning poverty is the percentage of children who cannot read and understand a simple, age-appropriate text by age 10.
c. Government expenditure on education, as a percentage of GDP, uses 2019 or the latest prepandemic data.
d. Expenditure on education, as a percentage of total government expenditure, uses 2019 or the latest prepandemic data.
e. The percentage of qualified teachers in primary education—a proxy for existing teacher capacity—uses 2019 or latest available data.
f. Participation in international assessments of primary students measures participation in any of the past three years (2019–21). 2 = yes, data are publicly available; 1 = yes, data are not publicly available; 0 = no.
g. Quality of education management information systems (EMIS) ranges from 1 (poor quality) to 6 (high quality).

The data reveal several patterns to frame policy makers' decisions:

- *Should policy makers prioritize teacher selection or existing teachers' capacity?* Data indicate that teacher persistence is generally lowest, and the projected increase in teaching positions generally highest, in the region's lowest-income, highest learning-poverty countries. Although all countries in the region will need to focus on strengthening the capacity of existing teachers, those that expect to recruit a significant number of new teachers have an important opportunity to raise teaching quality by strengthening teacher selection.
- *How serious a problem is existing teacher capacity?* Teacher capacity, as proxied by percentage of qualified primary-school teachers, also tends to be lowest in the region's lowest-income countries and is generally associated with higher rates of learning poverty. As noted earlier, in the absence of more direct measures of teachers' content knowledge and pedagogical practices, it is hard to know just how much this qualification measure captures, and it underlines the need for more and better data on teaching quality. Nonetheless, the association with learning poverty is concerning.
- *How serious a problem is teacher behavior?* Few countries have available, let alone comparable, data on teacher behavior. But among those with available data, the country with the lowest learning poverty rate—Viet Nam—also has, by far, the lowest rate of teacher absenteeism. Understanding the situation in other countries and the reasons for high teacher absenteeism are urgent tasks for the region's governments. Investments in better-quality training and tools for teachers will be ineffective if teachers are not in their classrooms and motivated to use them.
- *Are governments spending enough on education?* Whether measured as a share of gross domestic product (GDP) or as a share of total government expenditure, public spending levels tend to be lowest in the region's lowest-income, highest learning-poverty countries. Whereas low public education spending as a share of GDP may partly reflect a country's overall ability to mobilize public resources, low education spending as a share of total government spending reflects explicit decisions about the priority given to spending on education relative to other sectors.

Where adequate data exist, they can help policy makers identify specific priorities for reform in their respective countries. For example, countries like Cambodia, Papua New Guinea, and Vanuatu, which expect substantial growth in their teacher workforces, need to emphasize strengthening teacher selection more than countries like Fiji, Malaysia, and the Philippines, which project stable or negative growth in the size of the teaching corps. Where data indicate that current teacher capacity is particularly low, as in the Solomon Islands, Timor-Leste, and Vanuatu, more intense training and coaching as well as greater use of tools like highly scripted lessons and the dual teacher model will be needed to adequately support teachers. And countries such as Cambodia, Kiribati, and Myanmar, where data reveal that learning poverty is high and public spending on education is low, must direct additional public resources to education to support reform initiatives.

Addressing within-country inequalities through reforms

All of the region's middle-income countries, regardless of their learning poverty levels, will need to address differences within their countries in teaching quality and learning outcomes across socioeconomic groups and across different parts of the country. Even in Viet Nam, among the region's best-performing middle-income countries, learning outcomes are substantially lower among children from the poorest households than among their better-off peers (as shown in chapter 1, figure 1.3).

Countries commonly struggle to recruit, deploy, and retain high-quality teachers in poor and remote areas. In Papua New Guinea, for example, teacher vacancy rates in the Western Province, which has a large proportion of difficult-to-reach schools, are twice as high as in the Southern Highlands, where schools are generally accessible: 34 percent versus 17 percent. Student-teacher ratios are also higher: 48 to 1 in the Western Province, compared with 34 to 1 in the Southern Highlands. And in Thailand, similarly, Bangkok has fewer problems attracting higher-caliber teachers than do remote, mountainous regions, such as Mae Hong Son Province in northern Thailand. In Bangkok, nearly 20 percent of teachers have at least a bachelor's degree, compared with less than 10 percent in Mae Hong Son.[2]

Reducing basic learning inequalities within countries will require the region's governments to allocate additional resources to recruit, deploy, incentivize, and build the capacity of teachers in lagging regions and school districts. Such efforts will be critical to ensuring a more equitable allocation of well-trained, effective teachers to disadvantaged schools. In addition to better designed and implemented professional development programs, special measures will be needed to support teachers in lagging areas (as further discussed in chapter 4), including more intensive use of highly scripted lessons, enhanced coaching and mentoring, and increased use of dual teacher models to extend the reach of a country's best teachers.

Countries can also reduce basic learning inequalities within countries by identifying and learning from "positive deviants": localities or schools that deliver better learning outcomes than what would be expected given their spending levels and the socioeconomic backgrounds of their student populations. Such analysis can help identify what teachers and administrators are doing in these locations to deliver better outcomes. Recent work by the United Nations Children's Fund (UNICEF) in Lao PDR reinforces the importance of teachers having stronger subject content knowledge and superior pedagogical skills (UNICEF 2022). This research also shows that principals of higher-performing schools are more likely to observe and provide feedback to their teachers, fostering an environment of accountability and ongoing improvement.

Summary

Effectively diagnosing and addressing countries' learning challenges requires adequate data. However, the data needed to diagnose problems and support evidence-based, targeted policy making within countries remains scarce in much of East Asia and Pacific, as table 6.1 shows. In some countries, like Malaysia and Viet Nam, relatively sophisticated databases contain up-to-date information about each teacher and his or her current and past employment, qualifications, and training. In other countries, including Pacific Island countries, even basic information on teachers is missing. In Papua New Guinea, for example, the most recent digitized teacher data are from 2018.

Virtually no middle-income country in the region collects data on teachers' content knowledge and teaching practices. Few countries collect regular information on teachers' presence in the classroom at times when they should be teaching. Developing stronger information and teacher appraisal systems will be critical to enabling more targeted education reforms to strengthen teaching.

Building country-level, evidence-based reform programs will be critical to raising learning outcomes in the region. However, addressing the technical and financial challenges in education reform may well be ineffective if attention is not also paid to the political economy of reform. Global evidence and experience suggest that political economy challenges—not only among senior policy makers but also along the long education service delivery chains from countries' capitals to local classrooms—can impede even the best-conceived reforms (World Bank 2018). The next chapter discusses the political economy of education reform in East Asia and Pacific and highlights several principles that have enabled policy makers in some middle-income country contexts to implement quality-enhancing education reforms.

Notes

1. "Learning poverty," a concept and indicator developed by the World Bank and the United Nations Educational, Scientific and Cultural Organization (UNESCO) Institute for Statistics (further discussed in chapter 1), is defined as the inability to read and understand a simple, age-appropriate text by age 10.
2. Data on teachers' education levels are from World Bank calculations using 2011 Office of the Basic Education Commission (OBEC) data (World Bank 2015).

References

UNICEF (United Nations Children's Fund). 2020. "Country Results," South-East Asia Primary Learning Metrics (SEA-PLM) 2019 dataset, SEA-PLM Secretariat, Bangkok. https://www.seaplm.org/index .php?option=com_content&view=article&id=56&Itemid=441.

UNICEF (United Nations Children's Fund). 2022. "Policy Brief 1: Investing in Teacher Capacity—The Key to Effective Learning." Policy brief, Data Must Speak: Positive Deviance Research in Lao PDR Initiative, UNICEF Lao PDR, Vientiane.

World Bank. 2015. "Thailand: Wanted: A Quality Education for All." Report No. AUS13333, World Bank, Bangkok.

World Bank. 2018. *World Development Report 2018: Learning to Realize Education's Promise.* Washington, DC: World Bank.

World Bank. 2023. "Raising Pasifika: Strengthening Government Finances to Enhance Human Capital in the Pacific. A Public Expenditure Review of Nine Pacific Island Countries." World Bank, Washington, DC.

The Political Economy of Education Reform | 7

Introduction

What impedes effective reforms to improve learning outcomes in East Asian and Pacific countries? Is it a lack of information or knowledge? A misalignment of incentives? A lack of implementation capacity? This chapter examines policy makers' perceptions of countries' learning deficits as well as the political economy of enacting quality-enhancing education reforms. It analyzes how both policy maker perceptions and political forces commonly impede meaningful efforts to strengthen teaching and improve student learning in middle-income East Asia and Pacific.

The first hurdle for policy makers: Recognizing the crisis

Surveys of senior government officials around the world suggest they are not aware of the magnitude of their countries' foundational learning deficits. A recent survey of over 1,000 senior government officials working on education in 40 low- and middle-income countries, including two Pacific Island countries, asked officials to estimate the share of 10-year-old children in their countries who cannot read (Crawfurd et al. 2021). These estimates were then compared with the actual shares of children who cannot read, based on formal assessments of students' reading skills. Officials systematically overestimated student learning outcomes—and in some cases, substantially so (see their estimates are below the red line in figure 7.1, panel a). Overall, 80 percent of officials surveyed provided estimates that were below actual rates of learning poverty.

A follow-up survey, focused specifically on the East Asia and Pacific region, found similar gaps between policy makers' perceptions and actual learning poverty levels. In five of the seven East Asian and Pacific countries where surveys were carried out—Indonesia, the Lao People's Democratic Republic, Mongolia, the Philippines, and Vanuatu—policy makers' estimates of 10-year-olds' reading levels exceeded the evidence by significant margins (figure 7.1, panel b).

Policy makers may also have other educational priorities. Crawfurd et al. (2021) find, for example, that senior officials tend to prioritize socialization and nation-building goals for education over building foundational literacy (figure 7.2, panel a). This view has some historical

FIGURE 7.1   **Policy makers do not (or choose not to) recognize the magnitude of their countries' learning deficits**

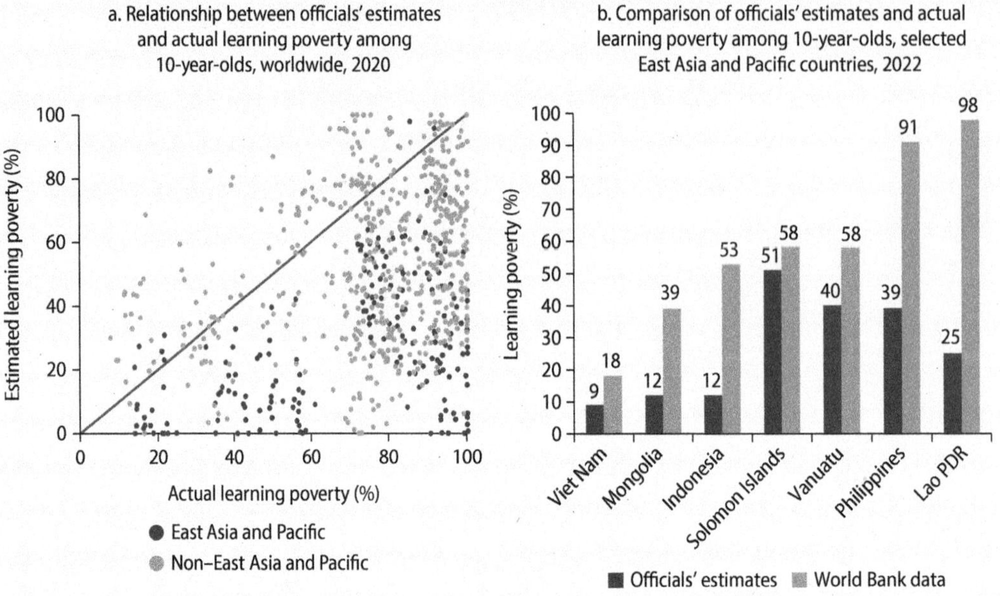

a. Relationship between officials' estimates and actual learning poverty among 10-year-olds, worldwide, 2020

b. Comparison of officials' estimates and actual learning poverty among 10-year-olds, selected East Asia and Pacific countries, 2022

● East Asia and Pacific
● Non–East Asia and Pacific

■ Officials' estimates   ■ World Bank data

Sources: World Bank calculations, based on Crawfurd et al. 2021 and 2022 Center for Global Development–World Bank survey (panel a); and Yarrow et al., 2023 (panel b).
Note: "Learning poverty" refers to the percentage of 10-year-olds who cannot read and understand a short, age-appropriate text. Panel a: The survey of over 1,000 senior government education officials in 40 low- and middle-income countries, including two Pacific Island countries, asked respondents to estimate the share of 10-year-old children in their countries who can read. The remaining percentage is the learning poverty rate. The study compared these estimates with the actual shares of children who can read, based on formal assessments of students' reading skills. Panel b: The survey reported policy makers' perceptions and compared them with literacy levels in seven East Asian and Pacific countries: Indonesia, Lao PDR, Mongolia, the Philippines, the Solomon Islands, Vanuatu, and Viet Nam. Vanuatu and Solomon Islands LP rates are interim estimates/not WB official data (from Cahu and Sondergaard).

precedent in the region. During the Suharto period in Indonesia, for example, a core objective of the education system was to inculcate students with the state ideology, Pancasila;[1] and nation-building has been a key objective of other education systems as well, such as in Cambodia and Lao PDR (Béteille 2022).

In addition, when faced with a hypothetical choice between different types of education projects, the surveyed policy makers expressed a preference for investing in technical and vocational education and training (TVET) projects over projects to increase foundational literacy (Crawfurd et al. 2021), as shown in figure 7.2, panel b. Their focus on TVET may result from the higher risk of unemployment among unskilled youth, who are hence of concern to politicians and policy makers. Yet it is precisely because such youth had not acquired foundational skills as young children that they lack productive skills as adults. The lack of a sense of crisis regarding basic learning outcomes, combined with a focus on other priorities, has likely diluted policy makers' focus on strengthening basic learning outcomes.

Political influences on teacher hiring and promotions

Evidence from countries around the world highlights how the misalignment of incentives between key actors along the education service delivery chain can get in the way of improving teaching and learning, even when sound technical solutions and financial resources have been identified (World Bank 2018). Incentive misalignments that cause reforms to fail can happen at any number of points along the chain from central government policy makers who design

FIGURE 7.2 **Policy makers place a lower priority on foundational learning**

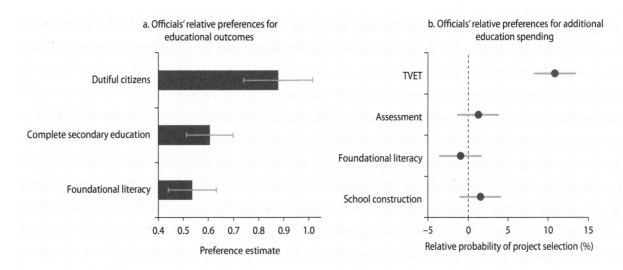

Source: Estimates based on data obtained from Crawfurd et al. 2021.
Note: Whiskers indicate 95 percent confidence intervals. Panel a describes the extent to which, in an education system, the share of children having a specific characteristic—either being dutiful citizens, having completed secondary school, or mastering foundational literacy—increases the probability that the respondents would prefer that specific state of the world (versus the average state of the world). For example, when the share of children with foundational literacy goes from 0 percent to 100 percent in an education system, it increases the probability that people prefer that state of the world by about 54 percentage points. The findings result from a survey in which respondents were asked which state of the world they would prefer between two hypothetical scenarios, each of which contained randomly varied levels of three education outcome attributes: (a) the share of the population with foundational literacy, (b) the share completing secondary school, and (c) the share who are dutiful citizens. The results show that officials value all three outcomes but value a higher proportion of "dutiful citizens" the most. As shown in panel b, the figure shows the probability that surveyed individuals preferred the projects listed in the figure relative to a project focusing on information technology. Respondents were asked to choose between two hypothetical aid projects, from making six binary choices between two projects. The five project areas were information technology, school construction, foundational literacy, assessment, and TVET—presented with randomly varying total dollar budgets and numbers of full-time technical advisers (1–3). TVET = technical and vocational education and training.

reforms to local politicians and administrators who manage the reform and to teachers who deliver lessons in the classroom.

As a result, quality-enhancing reforms such as decentralization, school choice, and accountability measures often fail because they can threaten jobs, reallocate responsibilities, require more effort from education workers, change benefits, or reduce job tenure security. These changes incentivize different actors along the service delivery chain to obstruct such reform efforts.

Teachers' unions have limited influence in East Asia and Pacific

A large empirical literature argues that teachers' unions exert great influence over education policy—and that this influence does not necessarily result in reforms aimed at raising education quality (see, for example, Carnoy 2007; Eberts and Stone 1987; Hoxby 1996; Moe 2001). The debilitating effect of teachers' unions on performance-oriented education reform across North America and Europe is well documented, as is their impact in Sub-Saharan Africa and South Asia (Moe and Wiborg 2017). However, although powerful teachers' unions are seen as hindering quality-oriented reforms in several regions (including South Asia, Latin America and the Caribbean, and Sub-Saharan Africa), political resistance from teachers' unions does not appear to impede reform in middle-income East Asia and Pacific (Béteille 2022; Moe and Wiborg 2017).

Indeed, teachers' unions in middle-income East Asian countries appear to have relatively little independent influence on education policy at present. In several countries, teachers'

FIGURE 7.3 **Officials in East Asia do not see political resistance from labor unions as a barrier to improving learning outcomes**

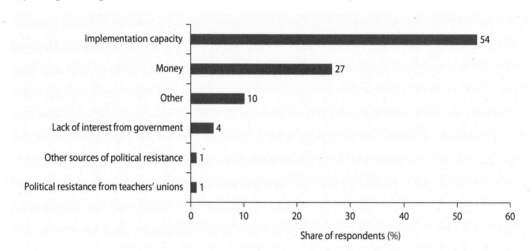

Source: World Bank calculations, 2022 Center for Global Development—World Bank survey. More detailed information about the survey can be found in Yarrow et al. 2023.
Note: Survey respondents were asked to select, from several options, what they viewed as the most important barrier to improving student learning outcomes. The respondents included 188 officials either from the Ministry of Education, the Ministry of Finance, or serving as members of parliament in five middle-income East Asian countries: Indonesia, Lao PDR, Mongolia, the Philippines, and Viet Nam. "Other sources of political resistance" refers to sources other than teachers' unions. Percentages do not add up to 100 because of rounding.

unions are closely aligned with government. In Lao PDR and Viet Nam, for example, teachers are part of professional unions that generally promote and support government policy. In Indonesia, which has multiple teachers' unions, the largest one, the Indonesian Teachers Union (PGRI), was set up by the government and maintains close ties with the bureaucracy. In Cambodia and the Philippines, teachers' unions were powerful historically, but their influence has declined over time (Bertelsmann Stiftung 2022a, 2022c; Hickey and Hossain 2019). The current lack of teachers' union influence is reflected in the findings of the recent Center for Global Development–World Bank survey of policy makers in the region conducted for this report. When the officials were asked about the main obstacles to improving learning outcomes, political resistance on the part of teachers' unions hardly featured (figure 7.3).

Patronage-based politics impede reforms

Political interests, nevertheless, play a key role in teacher hiring and promotion decisions. Although teachers' unions have not been an obstacle to education reform in East Asia and Pacific, politics—as expressed in the power dynamics between individuals—remains a key explanation for the region's poor teaching quality. The politicization of teachers, along with patronage relationships between politicians, administrators, and teachers, perpetuates situations in many countries whereby unqualified teachers are hired and low-quality, poorly performing teachers are shielded from accountability.

Across regions, including East Asia and Pacific, politicians and bureaucrats use their ability to create jobs, their access to information on job vacancies, and their role in the selection of teachers to establish systems of patronage, with the objective of securing teachers' loyalty (Béteille 2009; Hickey and Hossain 2019; Rosser and Fahmi 2018). As a result, teachers not only receive jobs or transfers of their choice but are also protected by their political patrons from breaches of accountability, such as absenteeism.

These relationships may not have been as detrimental to education systems if patronage hires performed well. However, evidence indicates the opposite: patronage hires, having circumvented meritocratic selection procedures, tend to be of lower quality (Béteille and Evans 2021; Pierskalla and Sacks 2020) and lack the capacity to implement reforms according to plan (as shown in figure 7.3).

Creating patronage relationships with teachers is beneficial to politicians in part because of the sheer size of the teaching corps. Education systems in East Asia, as elsewhere, employ large numbers, if not the largest number, of employees in the public sector. In Cambodia, Lao PDR, and Indonesia, for example, education workers make up over 40 percent of the government's workforce, according to the World Bank's Worldwide Bureaucracy Indicators database.[2] Teachers can influence the votes of family and friends, and because of their large numbers, the effect can be consequential (Béteille 2009). Moreover, teachers are located countrywide and are perceived by politicians as important community leaders who can garner constituents' votes (ACDP Indonesia 2015). Indeed, in Indonesia, teachers are often used as vote canvassers for candidates for district heads (Pierskalla and Sacks 2020). Elections often happen in school buildings, and teachers are regularly put in charge of polling booth stations, which allows them to monitor or potentially to manipulate votes.

Bureaucrats can also benefit from these patronage relationships because these relationships create possibilities to exact rents. Teachers can channel rents up the system, as is common in countries across the region, through informal (and often illegal) collections from parents (see figure 7.4).

Politicians induce teacher loyalty through their control of teacher deployments and redeployments, since teachers often prefer postings in better-resourced schools and in more-developed locations. In Indonesia, for example, district heads cultivate loyalty through control over the redeployment of permanent teachers across job types and schools. This control includes both rewards and sanctions. District heads might facilitate desirable teaching assignments in return for effective political support. Conversely, they might reassign to isolated areas the teachers who had supported losing candidates. So, patronage-based deployment decisions

FIGURE 7.4   **Corrupt practices remain a significant feature of many of the region's education systems**

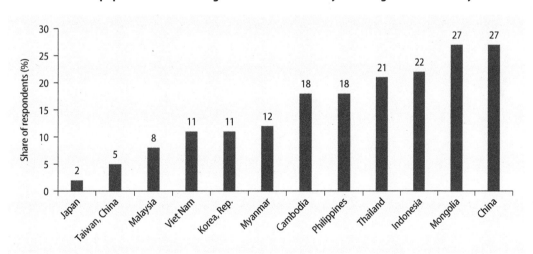

Source: Transparency International 2020.
Note: The figure shows the share of survey respondents who, within the last 12 months, said they both (a) had contact with education services, and (b) had to pay a bribe, give a gift, or do a favor for a teacher or school official for services from a school.

contribute to the inefficient and inequitable allocation of teachers across urban and rural areas and across wealthier and poorer school districts.

How widespread and influential are patronage practices?

Establishing the extent of widespread patronage that undermines the pursuit of good teaching in the region is challenging, given that most of such practices happen in the shadows. Nevertheless, several recent studies highlight its importance. An analysis of state effectiveness in the region found that political connections remain a potent force in civil service recruitment and promotions in most low- and middle-income East Asian countries despite efforts to increase meritocratic hiring (Mason and Shetty 2019).

In addition, recent survey evidence from Indonesia, Lao PDR, Mongolia, the Philippines, and Viet Nam paints a similar picture, specifically regarding the hiring of teachers. Senior government officials were asked whether a teacher candidate with good test scores but with no political connections was more, equally, or less likely to get a teaching job than a candidate who lacked good test scores but was well connected politically. In four of the five countries surveyed (Lao PDR, Mongolia, the Philippines, and Viet Nam), more than half the officials said they thought the politically connected candidate had at least an equal if not better chance of being selected than the candidate with good test scores (figure 7.5, panel a). Only in Indonesia did the majority of officials surveyed (65 percent) say that they thought the

FIGURE 7.5 **Informal mechanisms play an important role in teacher selection and promotions, making performance-based reform difficult in East Asia and Pacific**

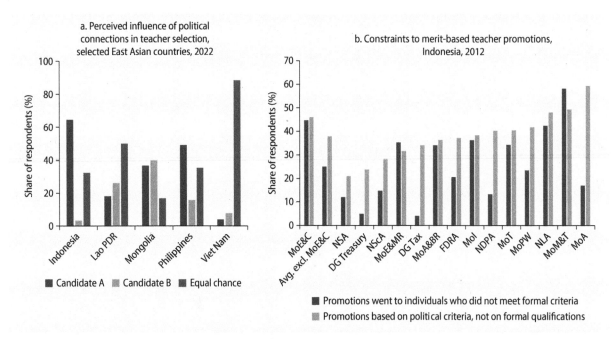

Source: World Bank calculations, 2022 Center for Global Development—World Bank survey. More detailed information about the survey can be found in Yarrow et al. 2023 (panel a); and Keefer 2012 (panel b).
Note: Panel a: In the survey, senior government officials were asked, regarding teacher candidates in the capital city of their countries, "Who is most likely to get the job? Candidate A has good test scores but is not well connected politically. Candidate B does not have good test scores but is well connected politically." Panel b shows data from the 2012 Indonesia Survey of Public Servants (Keefer 2012), which surveyed 3,903 public servants from three employee ranks across 15 government institutions about the effects of the Bureaucratic Reform allowances on the performance, efficiency, and morale of public servants in Indonesia. Each percentage (bar) shown represents responses from that same agency or ministry. DG Treasury = Directorate General Treasury, Ministry of Finance; DG Tax = Directorate General Tax, Ministry of Finance; FDRA = Food and Drug Regulatory Agency; MoA = Ministry of Agriculture; MoA&BR = Ministry of Administrative and Bureaucratic Reform; MoE&C = Ministry of Education and Culture; MoE&MR = Ministry of Energy and Mineral Resources; MoI = Ministry of Industry; MoM&T = Ministry of Manpower and Transmigration; MoPW = Ministry of Public Works; MoT = Ministry of Transportation; NDPA = National Development Planning Agency; NLA = National Land Agency; NSA = National Statistics Agency; NScA = National Science Agency.

candidate with good test scores was most likely to get the job. The more recent survey results suggest there is hope: Indonesia's new teacher policy reforms focusing on meritocracy and performance appear to be bearing fruit.

A separate study on Indonesia found that the Ministry of Education and Culture[3] was more likely than most government ministries to circumvent formal processes in giving promotions, with political reasons listed as most important (figure 7.5, panel b). Moreover, a study of teacher hiring around election time in Indonesia, using detailed teacher census data, found a significant increase in the hiring of contract teachers during election years relative to nonelection years (Pierskalla and Sacks 2020).

How does teacher patronage undermine reform?
Patronage-based hiring and promotion of teachers have deep ramifications for incentives to improve education quality and accountability. They create a quid pro quo that can push education systems into low-performance equilibriums (Béteille 2009, 2022). When formal policies and regulations are undercut by relationship-based political dynamics, implementing reforms to increase teacher performance and accountability—for which there may be no clear rewards—becomes difficult, with adverse effects on quality, efficiency, and equity (World Bank 2018). As such, patronage hiring and promotion consumes scarce resources that could otherwise be used to strengthen basic learning outcomes.

Not all the middle-income countries in East Asia and Pacific have succumbed to the types of politicization of teachers and patronage that have impeded efforts to improve education quality and basic learning outcomes. In just a few decades, Viet Nam has achieved an impressive record in basic education and learning—not only expanding schooling rapidly but also recording high levels of learning at the primary level, with Programme for International Student Assessment (PISA) scores in 2012 and 2015 that rivaled those in high-income countries.

In Viet Nam, teacher hiring and promotions are meritocratic. Teacher appraisal is carried out regularly and is free from systematic capture. And teachers who score poorly during appraisal receive training opportunities to help improve their performance. Together, the unique structure of Viet Nam's political and education systems—coupled with a deep societal commitment to learning—have enabled achievement of learning outcomes that significantly exceed what would be expected given the country's level of per capita income (box 7.1).

How limited parental voice also impedes reform

Parents in most of the region have little say on the conduct of school activities and little ability to influence quality-enhancing reforms. Moreover, they frequently lack the information necessary to assess where reforms would be most beneficial. In contrast to politicians, administrators, and teachers, for whom the benefits of patronage relationships are observable in the short term, parents may not be able to assess the gains from improving the quality of education, because the ultimate returns to quality will only be realized once students enter the labor market. As a result, parents are often loosely organized and unable to promote the needed reforms to the education system. This is true even though nearly every education system in middle-income East Asia has a framework for school-based management and school management committees (or their counterparts) with the stated goal of giving parents a voice in school decisions and operations. In practice, however, these entities rarely give parents much say, because information and decision-making power is vested with teachers, school principals, and local and regional administrators whose interests often do not align with improving learning outcomes.

In Indonesia, for instance, the main institutional mechanisms for parental participation in education decision-making are school communities and local education boards, with schools having access to funding and controlling voluntary teachers' appointments. However, these

---

BOX 7.1 **Viet Nam's strong learning outcomes have benefited from teaching built on a societal commitment to education, meritocratic hiring, and regular teacher appraisal**

Viet Nam is the world's best-performing lower-middle-income country regarding learning poverty—with an impressive teacher workforce at the heart of this achievement. Viet Nam's learning poverty rate is only 15 percent, similar to that of Türkiye with triple the per capita income (in purchasing power parity terms). Scores on recent Programme for International Student Assessment (PISA) rounds are also significantly above what would be expected given Viet Nam's per capita income. Recent research by Glewwe et al. (2021) finds that teachers' superior pedagogical skills are a key reason why Viet Nam's students outperform their peers in other countries.

Viet Nam's success emanates from its long-standing commitment to learning, going back to the role played by agricultural collectives in financing education in the early days after postwar reunification. A focus on mass education and literacy has been a core principle of the country's education strategy. Although the nearly 20-year war and postwar isolation made it difficult for Viet Nam to embark on building a vibrant education system, the country steadfastly pursued this commitment. In contrast to neighboring Cambodia, the Lao People's Democratic Republic, or Indonesia, where nation-building and ideology have historically been important parts of the curriculum, Viet Nam has maintained its focus on learning (Béteille 2022).

Building on its commitment to learning, Viet Nam's teacher policies have a strong focus on performance. First, teacher hiring is meritocratic; teachers are expected to have passed two rounds of tests before they can become teachers. Second, teacher appraisal is regular, free from patronage capture, and fundamental. If teachers get a low grade on a scale of 1 to 4, they have access to training to improve (Viet Nam MOET 2018).

Meritocratic teacher recruitment and credible teacher appraisal, while critical to performance, are also among the most difficult teacher-related interventions across countries. Whereas political forces commonly undermine middle-income countries' efforts to implement effective teacher policies, Viet Nam's political and administrative structures have supported the design and implementation of sound teacher policies (Béteille 2022).

For example, as a one-party state, where elections are not competitive, officials have less need to politicize teacher appointments, facilitating the implementation of strict policies on teacher performance. However, the lack of political competition alone does not guarantee effective teacher-related policies. Whereas Viet Nam has been able to avoid patronage hiring and build a merit-based teaching corps, another one-party state—the neighboring Lao PDR—has not.

In addition, every Vietnamese province has a People's Committee, with a Department of Education and Training. While the central Ministry of Education and Training provides guidance to teachers, the province-level administration controls the budget and has the autonomy to decide on several aspects of policy, including on the share of teacher professional development activities. The Communist Party of Viet Nam also has a grassroots presence, including among teachers and school heads, and through this presence works to ensure that the country's commitment to mass education and learning is realized.

---

bodies have been captured by school principals and local political elites (Rosser and Fahmi 2016). In Cambodia, Indonesia, and the Philippines, complaints against public institutions are not encouraged; hence parents have limited ability to have their voices heard (Bertelsmann Stiftung 2022a, 2022b, 2022c; Hickey and Hossain 2019). More broadly, voice and accountability are low in many middle-income countries in East Asia (figure 7.6), suggesting that parents may have limited scope to contest government decisions or to demand greater quality and accountability within their public education systems.[4]

The widespread presence of private tutoring likely dilutes parental demand for reform of public education. In addition to school fees, many East Asian and Pacific households pay for private, after-school tutoring. The share of households paying for private tutoring is particularly high among wealthy households in the region. Preceding the COVID-19 pandemic,

FIGURE 7.6 **Voice and accountability are low in many middle-income East Asian countries**

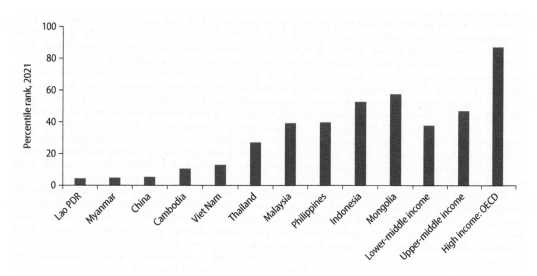

Source: World Bank's 2022 Worldwide Governance Indicators database (http://www.govindicators.org).
Note: Higher percentile rankings are associated with greater voice and accountability—a measure capturing the extent to which a country's citizens can participate in selecting their government, as well as enjoy freedom of expression, freedom of association, and a free media. OECD = Organisation for Economic Co-operation and Development.

roughly two-thirds of the wealthiest 20 percent of households in Myanmar that had education expenditures paid for private tutoring; in Lao PDR and Viet Nam, the share was over 50 percent, and in Indonesia, above 45 percent (figure 7.7, panel a). A substantial proportion of the poorest 20 percent of households also paid for private tutoring: 30 percent or more in Indonesia, Lao PDR, and Myanmar.

This shadow private sector, often focused on test preparation, makes it difficult for parents to accurately ascertain exactly what their children have learned in public school versus through private channels. Moreover, it can create an explicit conflict of interest and a negative accountability cycle where public school teachers are allowed to provide out-of-school tutoring to their students. Under such circumstance, the families of public school students may feel pressured to pay private tuition to public school teachers for additional study sessions, and public school teachers have an incentive to reduce their performance during regular classes to encourage more demand for after-school tutoring from their students (London 2006).

The reliance on private spending to augment what is learned in public school increases inequality—not only because a higher share of wealthy households than poor households can afford private tutoring but also because the amounts wealthy households pay are significantly higher. Wealthy households pay a higher share of their total education spending on tutoring than poorer households do (figure 7.7, panel b). This difference is amplified if one focuses on absolute levels of spending on tutoring and suggests significant quality differentials in private tutoring received by the rich and the poor. In short, that a significant share of households—especially in the upper wealth quintiles—is opting to augment public education with private tutoring suggests that they have weak incentives to pressure public schools to improve, compounding the challenge of increasing education quality and accountability in such schools.[5]

FIGURE 7.7 **Many parents spend their own resources on private tutoring—diluting incentives for quality-enhancing reforms and greater school accountability**

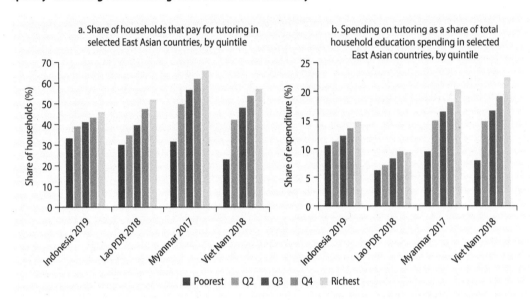

Source: World Bank calculations using nationally representative household survey data from Indonesia, Lao PDR, Myanmar, and Viet Nam (latest available data, pre–COVID-19 pandemic).
Note: The percentages reflect only those households reporting a positive expenditure on education, sorted by wealth quintile (Q).

Defying a history of patronage to enact teacher reform

Although teacher-focused education reforms are difficult everywhere, it is possible to identify cases where constructive change occurred despite political challenges. These cases—from middle-income East Asia and beyond—highlight that challenging political economy situations can be overcome when carefully constructed strategies are initiated by reform-minded politicians or administrators. Moreover, it is possible to identify common elements of these strategies, implemented in a diverse set of circumstances, that can provide lessons for future reforms efforts. (Table 7.1 further summarizes these successful reform efforts.)

Indonesia: Achieving teacher redistribution through incentives and coalitions

In Indonesia, teacher redeployment has proven politically difficult, and consequently many schools have insufficient teachers. A central government decree issued in 2011 (SKB 5 Menteri) threatened regional governments with a range of sanctions, including the withdrawal of central education funding and delays in the granting of new civil service provisions unless they redistributed teachers to meet the shortages. Most regional governments found the threat noncredible and ignored it, but a handful of districts and municipalities successfully introduced programs for teacher redistribution (Rosser and Fahmi 2016).

These districts and municipalities did two things: First, they pitched the redistribution as being in the interest of teachers by linking it with teacher certification and the resulting

TABLE 7.1 **How specific education reforms addressed political economy challenges in selected middle-income countries**

Country	Type of reform	Year initiated	Key political challenges and opportunities	Strategies for managing the political economy
Indonesia: large district with urban, rural, and remote locations	Improving teacher redistribution—initiated by bureaucracy in local education agency	2008	*Challenge* • Teachers did not want to relocate to faraway schools and used political connections to avoid being transferred to such schools. *Opportunities* • In their current postings, some teachers did not have enough work to meet the 24 hours of work per week requirement for certification, which in turn would double their base pay. • Tough auditing from the center (districts and municipalities) made it difficult to fabricate working hours to fit the 24-hour rule.	• Incentives to motivate teachers—but also politicians as more pay for teachers presented them with more rent-seeking opportunities • Coalition building between bureaucrats and politicians in support of reform • Compromise to accommodate unwilling teachers by making participation voluntary
India: Karnataka	Improving teacher redistribution—initiated by bureaucracy with the support of senior political leaders	2008	*Challenge* • Teachers did not want to relocate to faraway schools and used political connections to avoid being transferred to such schools. *Opportunities* • Teachers were in favor of a fair and systematic process that gave them choice. They did not like running around cultivating connections and paying bribes. • Ready-made, home-grown technology helped implement a teacher transfer system.	• Coalition building between bureaucratic and political leadership • Transparency through credible online information • An adaptive approach whereby the government experimented with executive orders for several years and finally sealed the deal with legislation
Ecuador	Changes to the teacher career path, more meritocratic entry, regular performance evaluation, and dismissal if poor performers do not improve—initiated by the president at the time, who made it part of his presidential campaign	2007	*Challenge* • Staunch opposition came from the National Union of Educators (UNE), the main teacher union, with a history of disruptive behavior. *Opportunity* • Strong increase in oil revenues allowed for a massive increase in education spending, including on infrastructure, new teacher hiring, and salary increases.	• Relentless communication strategies to draw attention to poor student results and poor teacher test scores, thereby influencing public opinion • Building a technically strong technical team, with no change in minister in seven years • Building a strong community of parental support through citizens' governing bodies in schools • Initial voluntary participation, followed by quick response to opposition after participation became compulsory • Quick responses to protests, by introducing supplementary policies

(Continued)

TABLE 7.1   How specific education reforms addressed political economy challenges in selected middle-income countries *(Continued)*

Country	Type of reform	Year initiated	Key political challenges and opportunities	Strategies for managing the political economy
India: Delhi	Improvements in classroom teaching practices, requiring dramatic changes in the bureaucracy's functioning and teachers' classroom operation—initiated by the Aam Aadmi Party (AAP) government	2015	*Challenges* • Frontline administrators were demotivated, apathetic, and low in capacity. • Teachers had little focus on performance. *Opportunity* • The AAP-led government leveraged the fact that teachers were not treated as full professionals and built a program that supported that identity and leveraged their intrinsic motivation.	• Improving the professional status of teachers (without teacher pay increases) through media campaigns and school infrastructure improvements • High-quality interactive professional development sessions for teachers, in contrast to the lecture-style trainings of the past • System of parent-teacher meetings to build ownership among parents and create teacher accountability • Regular change management sessions in the bureaucracy
Brazil: Sobral	Meritocratic teacher recruitment, capacity building, and increased incentives for performance—initiated by the mayor of Sobral at the beginning of his term	1997	*Challenges* • Sobral has some of the lowest student test scores in Brazil despite improvements in school infrastructure. • Patronage-based hiring of teachers and principals was pervasive. *Opportunities* • School consolidation freed resources for better infrastructure, school meals, and transportation. • FUNDEF, a federal education program, raised funds from federal, state, and municipal governments and redistributed them according to the number of students, providing funds that could be used to finance reform efforts and incentivize teacher performance.	• Radio addresses to communicate students' low test scores and put the responsibility of improving test scores on everyone, thereby not alienating teachers • Coalition building with parents, with regular meetings to encourage grassroots support for improving student learning • Leadership continuity and a strong design team of technocrats and well-connected political leaders • Financial incentives and professional recognition to motivate teachers • An iterative process whereby lessons from each round of testing were considered and plans made for improvement

Sources: Béteille 2022; Rosser and Fahmi 2016 (Indonesia); Bruns 2022 and Schneider, Estarellas, and Bruns 2018 (Ecuador); Cruz and Loureiro 2020, Loureiro, di Gropello, and Arias 2020, McNaught 2022, and Saavedra 2019 (Brazil).

professional allowance. Second, they undertook a careful change management process, centered on building coalitions at multiple levels. In one large district, for instance, this involved building coalitions between different wings of the district bureaucracy, between the district bureaucracy and district political leadership, and between the bureaucracy and political leadership on the one hand and teachers on the other (Rosser and Fahmi 2016).

Delhi, India: Pushing bureaucracy to prioritize education reforms

In Delhi, India, the Aam Aadmi Party (AAP) made education its priority. It signaled this by giving the education portfolio to one of its top politicians when it came to power in 2015. The AAP wanted to change how teachers taught, and although there was political will at the top, it had to confront a sluggish bureaucratic culture outside and inside the government schools of the Delhi National Capital Territory (NCT) that made reform difficult. Against this backdrop, the AAP-led government did four things (Aiyar et al. 2021):

- *Focused on improving teachers' sense of professionalism* and building coalitions with them. It launched massive media campaigns and held events to celebrate teachers and emphasize the crucial role they play in society. Although teachers' pay did not increase, their working conditions improved.
- *Reformed professional development* to provide teachers with new skills rather than being one-off sessions where teachers were lectured to. The Delhi NCT government also carefully identified change agents in the form of high-quality master trainers to mentor teachers.
- *Instituted regular parent-teacher meetings*, where parental participation and motivation was expected to stimulate teacher motivation and accountability. These meetings were publicized and taken seriously, thereby strengthening teacher-parent coalitions.
- *Focused on motivating management*, especially middle-level management, through motivational training as well as by engaging them in the reform process rather than bypassing them. Delhi NCT government schools have been improving their performance every year in grade 12 exit examinations.

Karnataka, India: Promoting transparency in teacher transfers

In Karnataka, India, the state government passed a new Act on Teacher Transfers in 2007, making it the first and only state in India that has passed such legislation to date (Ramachandran et al. 2017). The noteworthy feature of the act is that it lists a series of objective criteria to determine transfer eligibility and allows teachers to choose schools for which they are eligible through an open and transparent process.

Karnataka relied on respected political leaders, building coalitions with local politicians and union members. When matters came to an impasse with unions, Karnataka's reformers agreed to compromise and allowed union recommendations for teacher transfers to receive weight in the transfer process.

Implementation of the act was facilitated by a home-grown technology to process transfers. Senior politicians and government officials communicated relentlessly with teachers to build trust in the new technology-enabled system, which contrasted with the earlier transfer process whereby teachers sought political or bureaucratic connections and middlemen to get the job done. Finally, the reform was not implemented as shock therapy; rather, elements of the reform were experimented with through government orders, so that teachers, local politicians, and local bureaucrats were gradually socialized into it.

Ecuador: Strengthening a law promoting teacher quality and accountability

In Ecuador, the core teacher law was rewritten in 2009, bringing about fundamental changes in the quality of the teaching cadre by focusing on meritocracy and performance (Bruns 2022; Schneider, Estarellas, and Bruns 2018). Previously, the National Union of Educators (UNE) controlled teacher hiring and Ministry of Education appointments. Under the new law, teacher hiring was based on competency tests and clear standards; all teachers were subject to performance evaluation at regular intervals that included assessment of their classroom practice; promotions were based on performance evaluations rather than years of service; and dismissal was mandatory after two successive poor evaluations. To ensure successful implementation, Ecuador's president at the time

- *Mobilized public opinion* in favor of his reforms through relentless communication on how poorly students were doing as well as through exposure of poor teacher performance in a test of their skills, which only 4 percent passed
- *Built a strong technical team*, with a powerful minister of education who remained in place throughout the president's eight-year tenure
- *Empowered parents and the community* by initiating school-level "citizens governing bodies" tasked with assessing teacher-candidates in demonstration lessons and ensuring school accountability
- *Ensured his government responded quickly to threats of protest* by accommodating those protesting without diluting the reforms

Sobral, Brazil: Making course corrections for reforms to succeed

In Sobral, Brazil—a relatively poor municipality with some of the country's lowest student learning levels—the newly elected mayor began a process of education reform in 1997 (Cruz and Loureiro 2020; Loureiro, di Gropello, and Arias 2020; McNaught 2022; Saavedra 2019). The reforms included making two difficult political decisions: First, the mayor consolidated the school network, closing 40 percent of the schools, which enabled a more efficient use of resources for better infrastructure, school meals, and transportation. Second, his government laid off teachers who failed to meet the basic technical criteria for teaching, amounting to one-third of the teacher workforce.

Despite the reforms, in 2000, a diagnostic assessment revealed that 48 percent of second graders could not read. Instead of hiding the results, the mayor went on radio stations to communicate the results to all citizens. The message was clear: everybody needed to know about the learning crisis, and everybody needed to take responsibility. That year, the mayor was elected to a second term, and he redoubled his efforts to improve education. He formed a new leadership team to define strategies to overcome the learning crisis, headed by his brother as the new secretary of education.

At the center of Sobral's education reform was a set of clear learning targets and a system of regular external student assessments, discussed in regular meetings between teachers, principals, pedagogic coordinators, and the school superintendent team throughout the school year. A Teacher Career Plan was introduced in 2000.

The new leadership team knew that making changes would require the support of teachers, principals, and parents. They routinely met with all parties, explaining the benefits of education. The importance of teachers to the process was repeatedly emphasized, with salaries being increased and well-performing teachers receiving financial incentives as well as recognition for performance. In 15 years, Sobral became the best-performing municipality in Brazil.

Measures to help overcome political constraints to reform

Policy makers in Indonesia, Karnataka, Delhi, Ecuador, and Sobral were able to implement difficult teacher reforms because of reform-minded politicians and bureaucrats, and, in all cases, many willing teachers. These politicians and bureaucrats undertook strategies that addressed some of the key political economy challenges countries face, through their focus on (a) effective communication and dissemination of information, (b) building strong coalitions and teams, (c) buying out vested interests, and (d) adaptive implementation of reforms.

Effective outreach and communication

Information on specific challenges, whether low learning levels or teacher vacancies in schools, should be widely available and presented in a manner that motivates action. Indeed, evaluation studies have shown that providing information to parents and children, including on the quality of local schools, is effective in increasing learning outcomes at low cost per student (World Bank 2020).

In the cases presented in this chapter, communication focused on two levels: the general public and the primary stakeholders (teachers in Karnataka and Indonesia, parents in Delhi and Ecuador, and both teachers and parents in Sobral). The government of Ecuador and the mayor of Sobral drew attention to the low levels of student learning in school, and, in the case of Ecuador, to poor teacher knowledge. Delhi and Sobral also emphasized the important work being done by teachers. Ecuador, Sobral, and Delhi focused on opening the black box of performance and mobilizing public opinion in favor of reforms. In Karnataka, communication efforts focused on ensuring that teachers knew about the new technology-based process that allowed every teacher to see where the job vacancies were and whether they were eligible to apply, eliminating the need to cultivate political connections to identify job opportunities.

Building strong coalitions and teams

Coalition and team building can give reforms greater impetus and help sustain them. Given the long chains of implementation, a crucial strategy employed in each of the reform efforts was to cultivate relationships and build coalitions across the delivery chain. Two types of coalitions proved effective: (a) those between bureaucrats and politicians and (b) those between the education system and parents.

First, coalitions between bureaucrats and politicians were crucial for success. For instance, in Indonesia, successful districts undertook a careful change management process, centered on building coalitions within the bureaucracy and between bureaucrats and politicians. In Karnataka, well-respected senior politicians reached out to their junior-level counterparts seeking their help. In Delhi, senior politicians reached out to local bureaucrats. In Sobral, city councilors and former principals, who previously considered schools as part of their political agenda, were received by the Secretariat of Education and treated equally, irrespective of their political affiliations. The benefits of the process were explained, stressing that good professionals would remain in the system.

Second, coalitions between the education system and parents helped sustain the reforms. In Delhi, Ecuador, and Sobral, parent groups played a vital role in schools, routinely discussing student performance with teachers. The cases also highlight the importance of building competent, motivated, and stable teams to ensure their successful implementation of reforms and hence their political sustainability. Delhi, Ecuador, Karnataka, and Sobral benefited from strong technical teams as well as continuity of leadership over the reform period. This allowed for high-quality inputs as well as consistency and steadiness in the way in which reforms were implemented.

Buying out vested interests

An important mechanism used to neutralize vested interests that oppose reforms may involve buying them out—assuming the gains from reform outweigh the costs, as several cases illustrate:

- *In Indonesia,* the government allowed teachers opposed to the reform to opt out of recertification if they were prepared to lose out on a salary supplement.

- *In Karnataka,* teachers' unions were allowed to nominate teachers for transfers. Although union-nominated teachers were not the first on the priority list for transfers (indeed they were sixth out of a seven-priority list), they nevertheless received priority over the most dominant category (healthy male teachers). This helped bring the union on board with the reform.
- *In Ecuador,* when teachers and school directors opposed the new merit-based policies, the government offered an attractive early retirement package, stemming opposition early.
- *In Sobral,* tough teacher career reforms were initiated, but accompanying salary increases, incentives, and professional recognition muted opposition.

Adaptive implementation

As policy makers undertake difficult teacher reforms, an important question is whether they should roll out the reform in stages or implement it on a national scale all at once. The Ecuador case highlights the advantages of adaptive implementation, with the reforms initially focusing on increasing the selectivity of the teaching profession. In so doing, the reforms did not threaten existing teachers but communicated the importance of quality in the teaching cadre. In the next phase, President Correa introduced performance evaluations for all teachers. Karnataka also experimented with different versions of the teacher transfer policy before finalizing the format. And in Sobral, lessons from the first phase of reforms enabled adjustments that helped make the next phase effective in raising student learning outcomes. Adaptive implementation may help ensure that reforms are politically sustainable because they provide an opportunity to remedy flaws, demonstrate benefits, build ownership, and avoid early confrontation with vested interests that can derail reform efforts.

These examples show what can be done to address political economy challenges across different teacher policies. And bringing these policies all together in major reforms can have direct and sizable impact on learning. As Loureiro, di Gropello, and Arias (2020) found, for example, Sobral—a poor municipality in one of Brazil's poorest states—moved in the 15 years after 2001 from a situation in which 40 percent of its early-grade students could not read to being the best-performing municipality in Brazil, with roughly 84 percent of its third-grade students achieving high proficiency in literacy. This compared with a Brazil-wide average of 55 percent.

Notes

1. "Pancasila" refers to Indonesia's official, foundational philosophy—joining two words derived from Sanskrit: "pañca" ("five") and "śīla" ("precepts")—that was introduced in a June 1945 speech by Indonesia's first president, Sukarno. It was incorporated into the Preamble of the Constitution of Indonesia of 1945 and subsequently strongly supported by Indonesia's second president, Suharto.
2. For information about the Worldwide Bureaucracy Indicators (WWBI)—a unique cross-national dataset on public sector employment and wages developed by the World Bank's "Bureaucracy Lab"—see the WWBI dashboard: https://www.worldbank.org/en/data/interactive/2019/05/21/worldwide-bureaucracy-indicators-dashboard.
3. Since the study was prepared, the ministry has been renamed as Ministry of Education, Culture, Research and Technology (MoECRT).
4. The voice and accountability measure used here (from the World Bank's 2022 Worldwide Governance Indicators, http://www.govindicators.org) captures perceptions of the extent to which a country's citizens can participate in selecting their government, as well as enjoy freedom of expression, freedom of association, and a free media. The higher the score, the greater the voice.
5. Moreover, children from poorer households face inequality within the public sector because they attend lower-quality schools. Private spending from richer households therefore increases this initial inequality, both by enabling richer children to gain more from that private spending and by reducing the incentive of the richer—and more politically powerful—households to push for reform of public education.

References

ACDP Indonesia (Analytical and Capacity Development Partnership Indonesia). 2015. "Development of Quality Assurance for Early Childhood Education Final Report." ACDP Indonesia, Jakarta.

Aiyar, Y., V. Davis, G. Gokulnath, and T. Kapoor. 2021. "Rewriting the Grammar of the Education System: Delhi's Education Reform (A Tale of Creative Resistance and Creative Disruption)." Paper, Research on Improving Systems of Education (RISE), Oxford, UK.

Bertelsmann Stiftung. 2022a. "BTI 2022 Country Report: Cambodia." Bertelsmann Stiftung Transformation Index (BTI) report (for the period February 1, 2019, to January 31, 2021), Bertelsmann Stiftung, Gütersloh, Germany.

Bertelsmann Stiftung. 2022b. "BTI 2022 Country Report: Indonesia." Bertelsmann Stiftung Transformation Index (BTI) report (for the period February 1, 2019, to January 31, 2021), Bertelsmann Stiftung, Gütersloh, Germany.

Bertelsmann Stiftung. 2022c. "BTI 2022 Country Report: Philippines." Bertelsmann Stiftung Transformation Index (BTI) report (for the period February 1, 2019, to January 31, 2021), Bertelsmann Stiftung, Gütersloh, Germany.

Béteille, T. 2009. "Absenteeism, Transfers and Patronage: The Political Economy of Teacher Labor Markets in India." Doctoral dissertation, Stanford University, Stanford, CA.

Béteille, T. 2022. "Vibrant or Stuck?" Background paper for this report, World Bank, Washington, DC.

Béteille, T., and D. K. Evans. 2021. "Successful Teachers, Successful Students: Recruiting and Supporting Society's Most Crucial Profession." Policy Approach (2nd ed.), World Bank, Washington, DC.

Bruns, B. 2022. "Ecuador's 'Pivot to Learning': How One Country Successfully Turned around a Failing System." *Research on Improving Systems of Education (RISE) Blog*, March 27. https://riseprogramme.org/blog/Ecuador_Pivot_to_Learning.

Carnoy, M. 2007. "Improving Quality and Equity in World Education: A Realistic Assessment." Paper presented at the Institute of International Education, Stockholm University. https://jorluiseptor.github.io/EQUIP1/suplemental_docs/PLC/Carnoy,%20M.%20(2007).%20Improving%20Quality%20and%20Equality%20in%20World%20Education..pdf.

Crawfurd, L., S. Hares, A. Minardi, and J. Sandefur. 2021. "Understanding Education Policy Preferences: Survey Experiments with Policymakers in 35 Developing Countries." Working Paper 596, Center for Global Development, Washington, DC.

Cruz, L., and A. Loureiro. 2020. "Achieving World-Class Education in Adverse Socioeconomic Conditions: The Case of Sobral in Brazil." Report No. 150472, World Bank, Washington, DC.

Eberts, R. W., and J. A. Stone. 1987. "Teacher Unions and the Productivity of Public Schools." *ILR Review* 40 (3): 354–63.

Glewwe, P., Z. James, J. Lee, C. Rolleston, and K. Vu. 2021. "What Explains Vietnam's Exceptional Performance in Education Relative to Other Countries? Analysis of the Young Lives Data from Ethiopia, Peru, India and Vietnam." RISE Working Paper 21/078, Research on Improving Systems of Education (RISE), Oxford, UK.

Hickey, S., and N. Hossain, eds. 2019. *The Politics of Education in Developing Countries: From Schooling to Learning.* Oxford, UK: Oxford University Press.

Hoxby, C. 1996. "How Teachers' Unions Affect Education Production." *Quarterly Journal of Economics* 111 (3): 671–718.

Keefer, P. 2012. "Survey of Public Servants, Indonesia 2012." Survey data, World Bank Microdata Library, https://microdata.worldbank.org/index.php/catalog/5226.

London, J. D. 2006. "Vietnam: The Political Economy of Education in a 'Socialist' Periphery." *Asia Pacific Journal of Education* 26 (1): 1–20.

Loureiro, A., E. di Gropello, and O. Arias. 2020. "There is No Magic: The Formula for Brazil's Ceará and Sobral Success to Reduce Learning Poverty." *Education for Global Development* (blog), July 9. https://blogs.worldbank.org/education/there-no-magic-formula-brazils-ceara-and-sobral-success-reduce-learning-poverty.

Mason, A. D., and S. Shetty. 2019. *A Resurgent East Asia: Navigating a Changing World.* Washington, DC: World Bank.

McNaught, T. 2022. "A Problem-Driven Approach to Education Reform: The Story of Sobral in Brazil." RISE Insight 2022/039, Research on Improving Systems of Education, Oxford, UK. https://doi.org /10.35489/BSG-RISE-RI_2022/039.

Moe, T. M. 2001. "Teachers Unions and the Public Schools." In *A Primer on America's Schools,* edited by T. M. Moe, 151–84. Stanford, CA: Hoover Institution Press.

Moe, T., and S. Wiborg, eds. 2017. *The Comparative Politics of Education: Teacher Unions and Education Systems around the World.* Cambridge: Cambridge University Press.

Pierskalla, J. H., and A. Sacks. 2020. "Personnel Politics: Elections, Clientelistic Competition and Teacher Hiring in Indonesia." *British Journal of Political Science* 50 (40): 1283–1305.

Ramachandran, V., T. Béteille, T. Linden, S. Dey, S. Goyal, and P. G. Chatterjee. 2017. *Getting the Right Teachers into the Right Schools: Managing India's Teacher Workforce.* A World Bank Study. Washington, DC: World Bank.

Rosser, A., and M. Fahmi. 2016. "The Political Economy of Teacher Management in Decentralized Indonesia." Policy Research Working Paper 7913, World Bank, Washington, DC.

Rosser, A., and M. Fahmi. 2018. "The Political Economy of Teacher Management Reform in Indonesia." *International Journal of Educational Development* 61: 72–81.

Saavedra, J. 2019. "The Most Important Political Decision: Keep Politics Out of the Classroom. Or Not?" *Education for Global Development* (blog), May 29. https://blogs.worldbank.org/education/most -important-political-decision-keep-politics-out-classroom-or-not.

Schneider, B. R., P. C. Estarellas, and B. Bruns. 2018. "The Politics of Transforming Education in Ecuador: Confrontation and Continuity, 2006–17." RISE Working Paper 18/021, Research on Improving Systems of Education (RISE), Oxford, UK.

Transparency International. 2020. *Global Corruption Monitor, Asia 2020: Citizens' Views and Experiences of Corruption.* 10th ed. Berlin: Transparency International.

Vietnam MOET (Ministry of Education and Training). 2018. "Promulgating the Regulation on Standardized Professionalism for Teachers of General Education Institutions." Circular 20/2018/TT -BGDĐT, August 22, Ministry of Education and Training, Hanoi, Vietnam.

World Bank. 2018. *World Development Report 2018: Learning to Realize Education's Promise.* Washington, DC: World Bank.

World Bank. 2020. "Cost-Effective Approaches to Improve Global Learning: What Does Recent Evidence Tells Us Are 'Smart Buys' for Improving Learning in Low- and Middle-Income Countries?" Recommendations of the Global Education Evidence Advisory Panel, World Bank, Washington, DC.

Yarrow, Noah, Paul Cahu, Mary Breeding, and Rythia Afkar. Forthcoming. "What I Really Want: Policy Maker Views on Education in East Asia and Pacific." Report, World Bank, Washington, DC.

The Way Forward | 8

Introduction

Urgent action is needed to improve foundational learning if the middle-income countries of East Asia and Pacific are to benefit from higher labor productivity and human-capital-induced growth in their next stages of development. Large numbers of students—in some countries, an overwhelming majority—have not learned to read fluently by age 10. Missing this most important foundational skill, these children will struggle with all further education. Consequently, countries will struggle to prepare their workforces for tomorrow's demands.

Simply allocating money to do more of the same is unlikely to improve learning outcomes in the region. As shown in the examples of Indonesia and Thailand, despite increases in public spending on education over time, students' reading skills have not improved (as shown in chapter 5, figure 5.8). Even in countries where progress *is* being made, the status quo is inadequate—as data from the Marshall Islands show (and further discussed in the next section).

This report's main argument is that to dramatically improve children's foundational skills, two things are needed: First, the top political leadership must recognize the current situation as a crisis and make addressing that crisis a high priority. Second, teaching must be improved. Each of these issues is summarized briefly and then, given the diversity of countries in East Asia and Pacific, the chapter then discusses what this heterogeneity implies for establishing county-specific policy priorities.

Recognizing the learning crisis and prioritizing policy action

That so many children in the region are not acquiring basic skills is a problem in the shadows. To make progress, light must be shone on the problem with more and better data showing what students in the early grades can and cannot do when it comes to early-grade reading and mathematics skills. Equipped with better data, countries could prioritize foundational learning, including setting explicit targets for improving outcomes (for example, reducing learning poverty by 10 percentage points by 2025).

FIGURE 8.1   **Faster progress is needed: An example from the Marshall Islands**

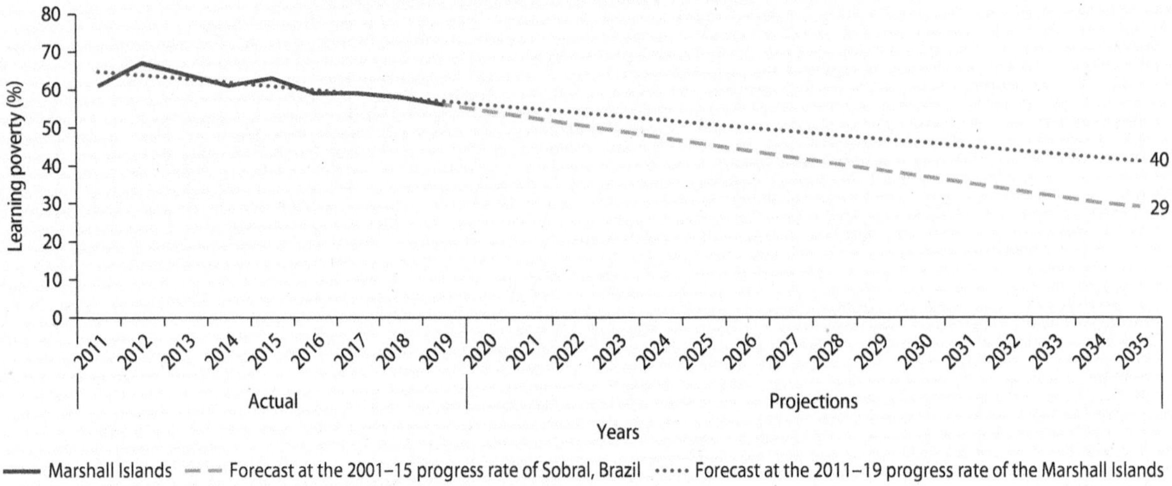

Source: Estimation based on the scores of eighth graders on the Marshall Islands Standards Assessment Test (MISAT) and data from Sobral, Brazil.
Note: The figure shows the 2011–19 learning poverty rates in the Marshall Islands (brown solid line), followed by projections of progress through 2035 at the country's average pace of learning poverty reduction since 2011 (red dotted line). By comparison, faster progress could be attainable (orange dashed line) if, going forward, the Marshall Islands could match the pace of learning poverty reductions achieved in Sobral, Brazil (a relatively poor municipality) in 2001–15 as it implemented ambitious education reforms (as detailed in chapter 7, table 7.1). "Learning poverty" refers to the percentage of 10-year-olds who cannot read and understand a simple, age-appropriate text.

The United Nations Educational, Scientific and Cultural Organization (UNESCO) Institute of Statistics has initiated a process by which countries can report their targets for reducing learning poverty, thereby committing publicly to act and raising awareness of the issue. To date, however, only four countries in East Asia and Pacific have done so: Cambodia, the Lao People's Democratic Republic, Malaysia, and the Solomon Islands. Other countries may not be reporting targets for different reasons. Some may lack current data on learning poverty. This report estimates learning poverty in Pacific Island countries for the first time, and notably, some East Asian countries' reported learning poverty rates rely on student learning data from many years ago (for example, 2007 data from Mongolia and 2011 data from Thailand). Countries may also be hesitating to set public targets because of their uncertainty about how quickly learning poverty can be reduced.

Evidence is now becoming available about the rate at which learning poverty can be reduced if countries are ambitious—and how that rate could differ from historical trends. For example, the Marshall Islands has reduced learning poverty since 2011, albeit by only 5 percentage points (figure 8.1). At that rate, more than 40 percent of primary students will graduate in 2035 without being able to read fluently. However, a projection also shows that, if the Marshall Islands were to duplicate the kind of progress seen in Sobral, Brazil, the country could reduce its learning poverty rate to 29 percent over the same period. We see this report as a contribution to helping countries calculate reasonable, if challenging, targets and designing plans to meet them.

Improving teaching for better learning

To improve teaching, this report argues, reforms are needed on three fronts simultaneously: strengthening teacher selection, enhancing teaching capacity, and encouraging the desired behavior. However, the region's heterogeneity means that countries differ in the extent to which they should focus primarily on either (a) strengthening the inflow of new teachers or (b) improving the quality of their existing teachers. Likely, the countries also vary widely regarding how much focus is needed to improve teacher behavior. Unfortunately, data on teacher absenteeism are only available for a few countries in the region.

Indeed, to effectively improve teaching, there is an urgent need for more and better data on teachers' content knowledge, their pedagogical skills, and their behavior. Such data will be critical for identifying gaps that need addressing, tailoring training content and dosage, and tracking progress over time.

Reflecting country realities in education reforms

Reforms will need to reflect considerable heterogeneity in challenges and outcomes across and within countries. Whereas countries with high learning poverty will need to focus on generating systemwide improvements and supporting all teachers, countries with more moderate learning poverty levels can take more targeted, selective approaches to reform.

All countries in the region, regardless of their national learning poverty rate, must address inequalities in teaching quality and learning outcomes across socioeconomic groups and between major urban centers and remote rural areas. Moreover, to be effective, the region's countries must strengthen their data and information systems—both to ensure that reforms are focused on the most important challenges and that the policy actions are producing the desired results. Finally, successfully implementing measures to raise basic learning outcomes will require policy makers to navigate the political winds associated with undertaking major reforms.

Conclusion

Strengthening teaching for improved foundational learning will be critical for the middle-income countries in East Asia and Pacific to raise productivity and growth in the coming decades. This report highlights important technical remedies, but enacting and successfully implementing reforms will be difficult and will require a long-term effort given the depth of the learning challenge.

Successful reforms require sustained and aligned efforts across a range of stakeholders: heads of government, ministries of education, ministries of finance, teachers, and parents. Heads of government provide vision and political leadership, which will be needed across successive government administrations. Ministries of education must develop credible agendas for reform. Ministries of finance will have to allocate sufficient resources to enable implementation of the reform agenda and get stakeholders on board. Teachers will need new tools, enhanced support, and preparation to step up to the challenge. Parents and caregivers will need to be engaged in, and advocates for, improved learning.

In the aftermath of the COVID-19 pandemic, governments have faced difficult choices about the allocation of scarce resources, and garnering the resources to support successful education reform will be a challenge in many countries. Teachers' salaries are the single largest element in many countries' education budgets and, as such, reforms that strengthen teaching will be key to getting higher returns on public investments in education. To convince officials from the region's finance ministries that additional resources will be used productively, education ministries will need to develop credible, evidence-based programs of reform. To develop such programs, they must improve the data and information underpinning the design, implementation, and evaluation of reform initiatives. Better and more accessible information will also be critical to empowering parents to support teachers—and to hold them to account—in the quest for improved foundational learning for their children.

Such mutually reinforcing, and long-term, relationships between key stakeholders—between ministries of education and finance, between parents and teachers, and between heads of government and the general public—will be critical in countries' efforts to bridge the basic learning gap in middle-income East Asia and Pacific. Those efforts would set the stage for higher productivity and growth and more prosperous societies in the years to come. Since progress takes time in the best of circumstances, action must begin now.

Appendix A: The Long-Term Growth Effects of Raising Education Quality in Middle-Income East Asia and Pacific

It is possible to examine the potential effects of increasing education quality on growth in middle-income East Asia and Pacific using the World Bank's Long-Term Growth Model (LTGM).[1] The standard LTGM adapts the celebrated Solow-Swan growth model to future growth analysis in low- and middle-income countries (Loayza and Pennings 2022; World Bank 2023). The LTGM has a Human Capital Extension that tracks, cohort-by-cohort, how an increase in the quality of education of today's children affects future workforce productivity, which, in turn, affects economic growth.

The change in education quality is modeled in the LTGM as a one-time permanent increase in the education quality of schools to the median of high-income countries. Although stylized, this reform provides a useful benchmark against which other potential reforms can be considered. The increase in education quality fully affects the youngest children but only partially affects older children who spend a smaller share of their total education in higher-quality schools. The reform boosts the human capital of the workforce slowly over time as the younger, better-educated cohorts replace older, less-educated workers. Higher human capital of the workforce has two effects in this model: it *directly* boosts workforce productivity and output in the short term and *indirectly* induces additional accumulation of physical capital in the long term.[2]

The simulations suggest that increasing education quality could be expected to boost gross domestic product (GDP) growth by 0.20–0.75 percentage points by 2050, with the effects varying across countries depending on country circumstances (figure A.1). Simulations were carried out on data from 11 middle-income East Asian and Pacific countries—Cambodia, China, Indonesia, the Lao People's Democratic Republic, Malaysia, Mongolia, Papua New Guinea, the Philippines, Thailand, Timor-Leste, and Viet Nam—using data on education quality based on harmonized test scores generated as part of the World Bank's Human Capital Project.[3]

The boost to growth in each of these countries is calculated as the difference between a scenario with higher education quality and the business-as-usual baseline with constant quality. Under the scenario of higher education quality, three-quarters of the countries would be expected to experience a boost to growth by 2050 of 0.2–0.5 percentage points. Two countries would be expected to experience higher growth effects: the Philippines and Timor-Leste. The analysis suggests that the Philippines stands to experience the largest growth gains from increasing education quality, with GDP growth estimated to accelerate by 0.75 percentage points (relative to the baseline) in the late 2040s. Because Viet Nam has already achieved

FIGURE A.1   **Simulated incremental GDP growth due to higher education quality, selected middle-income East Asian and Pacific countries, 2020–50**

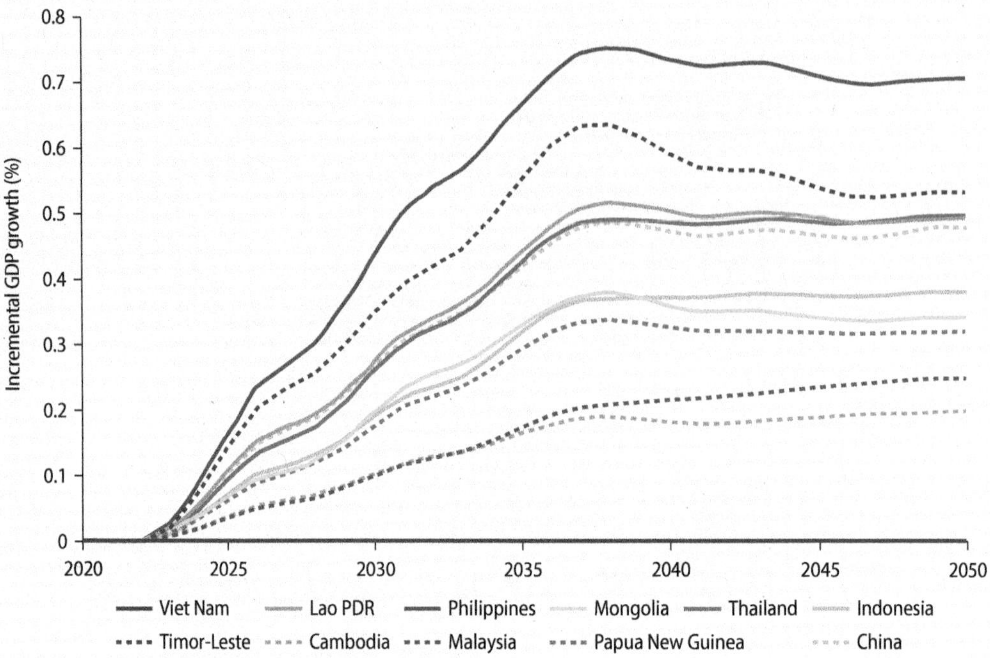

Source: Mendes, Pennings, and Fiuratti 2022.
Note: Each country's boost to GDP growth is calculated as the difference between (a) a scenario of a one-time, permanent education quality increase, and (b) the business-as-usual baseline with constant quality, using the World Bank's Long-Term Growth Model. The benchmark for "higher" education quality is the median of high-income countries, based on harmonized test scores generated as part of the World Bank's Human Capital Project. GDP = gross domestic product.

high-income country levels of education quality (based on harmonized test scores), its growth is not affected in this analysis.

Although the year-by-year effects on growth from higher education quality are modest, the effects are persistent and cumulative, resulting in substantially higher GDP per capita by 2050—typically by around 7 percent (figure A.2). The effects of the reform on economic growth are persistent, lasting for over 50 years (that is, until the youngest cohort *not* affected by the reform retires). These cumulative effects on growth are thus large: by 2050 the effect of education quality improvements on GDP per capita averages 7 percent and reaches 16 percent in the Philippines. The heterogeneity of impacts is mostly driven by country-specific gaps between their current education quality and the reform target as well as by the *quantity* of schooling (because only children attending school will benefit from higher education quality). To a lesser extent, the impact of higher-quality education varies with the labor share in a country's production technology and the country's age structure (because education quality improvements target only the young population).

Increasing educational attainment levels—that is, increasing the *quantity* of education—would also increase growth in the region, especially in countries with relatively low current attainment. To explore this using the LTGM, the model gradually increases the average years of schooling from the currently observed levels in each country to 13.4 years, the median observed in high-income countries. In most of the countries analyzed, increasing education *quality* has greater growth effects than increasing educational *attainment*.

Figure A.3 shows the combined effects on growth of increasing both the quantity *and* quality of education to high-income country levels (with all other model parameters unchanged).

FIGURE A.2   Simulated increases in GDP per capita levels in 2050 due to higher education quality, selected middle-income East Asian and Pacific countries

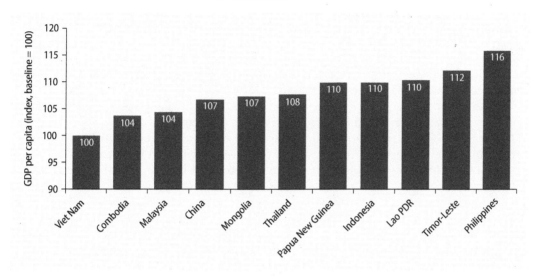

Source: Mendes, Pennings, and Fiuratti 2022.
Note: Each country's boost to GDP per capita is calculated as the difference between (a) a scenario of a one-time, permanent education quality increase, and (b) the business-as-usual baseline (=100) with constant quality, using the World Bank's Long-Term Growth Model. The benchmark for "higher" education quality is the median of high-income countries, based on harmonized test scores generated as part of the World Bank's Human Capital Project. Values shown have been rounded. GDP = gross domestic product.

FIGURE A.3   Simulated incremental GDP growth from increases in both quantity *and* quality of education, selected middle-income East Asian and Pacific countries, 2020–50

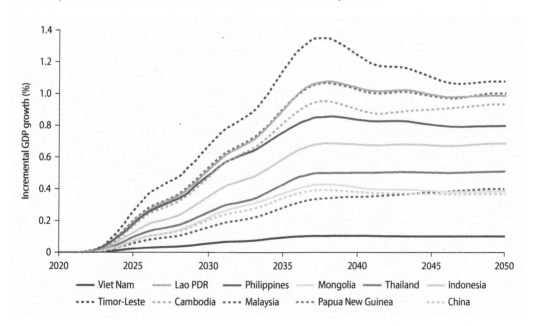

Source: Mendes, Pennings, and Fiuratti 2022.
Note: The figure shows the simulated combined effects on GDP growth of increasing both the quantity *and* quality of education in middle-income East Asian and Pacific countries to high-income country medians. Each country's GDP boost is calculated as the difference between (a) a scenario of a one-time, permanent education quality increase, *plus* a gradual increase in average years of schooling to 13.4 years, and (b) the business-as-usual baseline with constant quality, using the World Bank's Long-Term Growth Model. The benchmarks for increased education quality (proxied by harmonized test scores) and quantity are the medians of high-income countries, generated as part of the World Bank's Human Capital Project. GDP = gross domestic product.

The combined effects are substantial. As a result of these changes, Cambodia, Lao PDR, Papua New Guinea, and Timor-Leste are all projected to grow GDP by an extra 1 percentage point by 2050. The estimated growth effects among relatively higher-income countries in the region (including China, Malaysia, Mongolia, and Thailand) are more modest, with incremental growth estimated at around 0.4 percentage points. Indonesia and the Philippines fall in between, with a boost to growth by 2050 of around 0.7 percentage points. Given its already high education quality, Viet Nam would experience some growth benefits, albeit a relatively small amount under this scenario.

To achieve the same effect on growth as that induced by higher education quality, the countries analyzed here would have to invest an extra 4 percent of GDP in *physical capital*, on average, by 2050. Growth in middle-income East Asia and Pacific to date has been driven largely by capital deepening. One attractive feature of the LTGM is that it enables one to compare the effects on growth of changes in physical and human capital within a consistent framework. Figure A.4 shows the additional investment in physical capital that would be necessary to match the growth path of the scenario with a higher quality of education. Although there is considerable heterogeneity across countries, the figure highlights that it will become increasingly difficult over time to compensate for low education quality with higher investment in physical capital. This is because the higher investment rates required tend to reduce the marginal product of capital, which makes it increasingly hard to boost growth year after year.

FIGURE A.4   **Estimated incremental investment in physical capital to match GDP path generated by higher education quality, selected middle-income East Asian and Pacific countries, 2020–50**

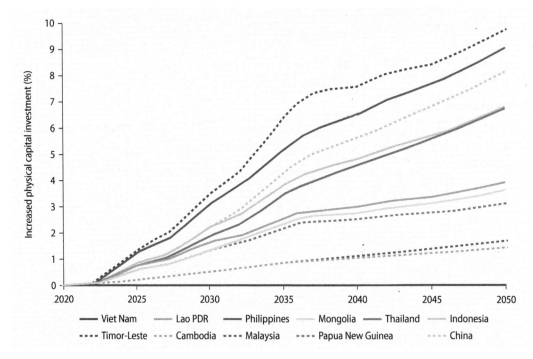

Source: Mendes, Pennings, and Fiuratti 2022.
Note: The figure shows the estimated increase in investment in physical capital that middle-income East Asian and Pacific countries would need to make to achieve the same boost to GDP growth as that induced by higher education quality (as simulated in figure A.1). GDP = gross domestic product.

Notes

1. The LTGM is an Excel-based tool to analyze long-term growth scenarios building on the Solow-Swan growth model. It is not designed for short-term growth forecasting. For more information, see the brief, "The Long-Term Growth Model," on the World Bank website (https://www.worldbank.org/en/research/brief/LTGM) and Loayza and Pennings (2022).
2. The current model does not capture potential increases in total factor productivity (TFP) because of increased technology adoption and innovation and, thus, likely underestimates the growth impacts of raising education quality.
3. Regarding the World Bank's Human Capital Project, see https://www.worldbank.org/en/publication/human-capital.

References

Loayza, N. V., and S. M. Pennings. 2022. *The Long Term Growth Model: Fundamentals, Extensions, and Applications.* Washington, DC: World Bank.

Mendes, A., S. Pennings, and F. Fiuratti. 2022. "The Long-Term Growth Effects of Improved Education Quality in Middle-Income East Asia and Pacific Countries." Background note, World Bank, Washington, DC.

World Bank. 2023. "The Long Term Growth Model." Research and Outlook brief, World Bank, Washington, DC. https://www.worldbank.org/en/research/brief/LTGM.